27

Human Sexuality

Human Sexuality

A Bibliography and Critical Evaluation of Recent Texts

MERVYN L. MASON

GREENWOOD PRESS
Westport, Connecticut • London, England

Library of Congress Cataloging in Publication Data

Mason, Mervyn L.
  Human sexuality.

  Includes indexes.
  1. Sex—Bibliography. I. Title. [DNLM: 1. Sex
behavior—Abstracts. Z 7164.S42 M411h]
Z7164.S42M36 1983 [HQ21] 016.612'6 83-12688
ISBN 0-313-23932-0 (lib. bdg.)

Library of Congress Catalog Card Number: 83-12688
ISBN: 0-313-23932-0

First published in 1983

Greenwood Press
A division of Congressional Information Service, Inc.
88 Post Road West, Westport, Connecticut 06881

Printed in the United States of America

10 9 8 7 6 5 4 3 2 1

Contents

Introduction

A plethora of books published over the past two decades have dealt with the various aspects of human sexuality. This volume summarizes and critically evaluates many of these sexological texts for their appropriateness for professional or student usage. Directed at all persons who must be professionally knowledgeable in some area of human sexuality, this reference text can serve the needs of sexologists, therapists, counselors, educators, research scientists, lawyers, judges, law-enforcement officers, legislators, clergymen, social workers, sociologists, anthropologists, biologists, psychologists, and medical practitioners such as general practice family physicians, psychiatrists, urologists, gynecologists, obstetricians, endocrinologists, proctologists, surgeons, internal medicine specialists, nurses, and the various paramedical professions. Academicians with expertise in philosophy, history, literature, and the fine arts can also benefit from examining pertinent source material.

The books in this volume have been selected using the following criteria: availability (as stated by the publisher); excellence in a specified category; popular usage by professionals in the field; widespread knowledge of a particular book by professionals; and the scientific-sexological approach of a particular book to its subject. The vast majority of the examined books were published in the United States in the English language. A few significant and topical books published in the United Kingdom, the Netherlands, and Canada were also included, as were a few pertinent and important translated works of German and French origin.

The majority of the reviewed books were published since 1970. In a few cases important earlier works of current or historical interest have been included.

Books directed at the lay public are for the most part omitted from this volume unless such a book's message has an overriding secondary importance for the professional or is outstanding enough for the professional to recommend it to suitable lay clients.

All 180 books were personally examined by the author. A very few potentially suitable books, known by reputation, could not be obtained for examination from the publisher or from any other source and had to be omitted for that reason. Also omitted were titles too peripheral to the area of human sexuality such as those whose prime foci concerned sex roles, family issues, or marital counseling, though they may have relevant passages.

The books are listed in nine broad categories, some encompassing several separate subjects. For example, the "Sexual Minorities" chapter notes books dealing with alternative sexual lifestyles, bisexuality, disability and sex, homosexuality, and lesbianism. The Subject Index gives access to these narrower topics. Books fitting more than one category are listed in only one, with additional references made through the Subject Index.

This volume goes beyond the scope of the traditional annotated bibliography. An assessment is provided which critiques each book solely on its objectivity, its factual coverage of the outlined subject-material, the attention it pays to any relevant historical background and cross-cultural comparisons, and the usage it makes of photographs, charts, tables, and other visual aids. Assumptive biases, pejorative phraseology, and sexist prejudice are noted. Unwarranted conclusions based on inadequate or inappropriate references are pointed out. Subjective editorialization is censured when it consists of unsubstantiated generalizations about sociosexual issues. Serious omissions of sexual minority positions, as these pertain to a book's subject, are mentioned as evidencing an indirect form of bias.

The critical opinions here expressed are mine alone. They do not reflect individual or collective viewpoints of persons connected with Greenwood Press, The Association of Sexologists, whose newsletter I have edited, or The Institute for Advanced Study of Human Sexuality, from whom I received my doctorate degree and where I was appointed Assistant Professor of Sexology and Research Methodology.

Mervyn L. Mason
San Francisco, California

Human Sexuality

Female Sexuality

1. Barbach, Lonnie & Levine, Linda. <u>Shared Intimacies: Women's Sexual</u>
<u>Experiences</u>. New York: Anchor Press/Doubleday, 1980. 352 pp.

Brief Summary - The authors, both psychotherapists, state in their
Introduction that this book "is a compilation of helpful hints and
solutions devised by women" (p.xiv). The opening chapter termed
"Qualities of Good Sex" explores these attributes. The next eight
chapters discuss issues involved in "Setting the Scene," the concept
of "Gourmet Lovemaking," hints and alternatives to use in employing
"Solo Eroticism," "Letting Your Partner Know" what is desired by
using verbal and non-verbal communication, "What to Do When You Run
into Trouble," how to enjoy "Being Pregnant and Being Sexual," why
"Parents are Sexual, Too" and how to be open to this, and the fun
and logic of "Being Sexual in Your Later Years." The final chapter
entitled "What to Make of It All" is a summary. The authors
conclude that "the process of making changes in your sex life will
entail taking a risk" (p.312).

Critique - Strengths

a. A 3-page Bibliography (by chapter) plus many anecdotal quota-
    tions are of great value. Limited demographic data about the
    sample are included (p.xx-xxii). The interview technique
    utilized is preferable to a questionnaire.
b. Myths and stereotypes are neutralized (e.g. "A predominant myth
    in our culture is that sex should just happen naturally and
    spontaneously if it's right..." (p.123); also "Some of the women
    felt that their enjoyment of sex had less to do with how they
    felt about their partner than with their feelings about
    themselves as desirable and competent women" (p.13).
c. Positive suggestions are offered (e.g. "A huge step that might
    lead to failure would be to ... attend a group sex party without
    discussing it together first... Your partner might have some
    useful suggestions as well..." (p.311)).
d. Professionals can recommend the book to clients as an adjunct
    to counseling or therapy. The respondent-sample includes

lesbian and bisexually oriented women, and thus covers the
entire female sexual continuum.
e. The book is essentially non-judgmental.

Deficiencies

a. No visual aids, charts, graphs or tables assist the textual
content. No historical or cross-cultural input is included,
even of a peripheral nature. The sample is small (i.e. 120 -
see p.xx), volunteer and atypical (e.g. "They were largely
middle- and upper-income, career-oriented women ... highly
educated and articulate..." (p.xvi)). The study has no
statistics and is not methodologically controlled. It is
idiosyncratic and cannot be extrapolated to represent contemporary behaviors and perspectives.
b. The book has limited direct value to the professional
sexologist, although somewhat more to the student.

2. DeMartino, Manfred F. _Sex and The Intelligent Woman_. New York:
Springer Publishing Company, 1974. 320 pp.

Brief Summary - The author, a psychologist, outlines in his
Introduction how this study was inspired by Maslow. The study was
completed in 1969 "on 327 women members of Mensa, with an average
age of 32" (p.245). This intelligent sample came primarily from the
United States, England and Canada. Chapter 1 details the project's
"Research Design," some demographics of the sample, and the study's
interrelationship to Maslow's two personality inventories dealing
with self-esteem and security levels. The subsequent nineteen
chapters provide data in the areas of frequency, technique,
interests, fantasy, the importance of virginity, and societally
atypical activities. In Chapter 21, "Men as Lovers: A Feminine
Appraisal," DeMartino gives suggestions for improvements (Tables
21.1, 21.2; p.223, 231). The following chapter reports on
"Psychological Dominance and Happiness in Marriage." The final
chapter describes a supplementary study completed in 1972 on fifty
non-Mensa but intelligent women. Dr. Albert Ellis summarizes and
discusses the book's findings in an Epilogue.

Critique - Strengths

a. The extensive uses of cited research, footnotes, and quotations are of immense value. A 13-page References section plus
further references by Ellis are helpful. An Appendix about the
Maslow inventories is a good addition. A profusion of data
includes many tables of statistical information with some
probability figures.
b. The study's concept is unique and includes comparisons to
other, more generalized research on female sexuality such as
that done by Fisher and Kinsey. Relating the research to the
Maslow inventories (refer to Summary above) is innovative.

Deficiencies

a. No visual aids or graphs assist the text. Even minimal
historical and cross-cultural background material is not

provided. The questionnaires (both the regular and the supplemental ones) should have been included in an appendix. As it is, no researcher can replicate the presented study. The inclusion of the supplemental study is a confusing addition which detracts rather than aids the book.

b. While the study has idiosyncratic and comparative value, it contains methodological shortcomings, and biased value-judgments (e.g. "... I can by no means claim that the women ... are representative of Mensa women or of highly intelligent women in general" (p.2); also "In hindsight, the wording and nature of the questionnaire could have been much better" (p.4); also "The relationships ... are particularly important because of their bearing on questions dealing with normal and abnormal sexual behavior" (p.3)).

c. Pejorativity (e.g. "the problem of frigidity" (p.97)) and cloudy terminology (e.g. "The idea of being raped in a forceful but nonviolent manner held a relatively strong appeal ..." (p.137)) detract at times from the textual effectiveness.

3. Fisher, Seymour. <u>The Female Orgasm</u>. New York: Basic Books Inc., 1973. 601 pp.

Brief Summary - Part I is entitled "What is Known About Sexual Behavior and Sex Role in Women?" Five chapters review the existing literature. Part II is termed "Psychological Studies of Sexual Behavior and Attitudes in Women." Nine chapters present the research while the final chapter incorporates the data, both the positive and the negative correlates, into the existing literature of research (as reviewed in Part I). Fisher uses seven sample studies of married women and one study which is exclusively made up of pregnant women. Fisher's major discovery is "that the greater a woman's feeling that love objects are not dependable (that they are easily lost or will disappear) the less likely she is to attain orgasm" (p.446). Important non-reciprocal relations are also deduced by using comparative trait analysis. The author closes his text by suggesting future "priority problems in the study of female sexuality" (p.496).

Critique - Strengths

a. Extensive footnotes, tables of statistics, cited references, case study examples and 47 pages of References are helpful. Eleven appendices detail the actual tests used. Overview summaries complete the various sub-topical sections.

b. Part I furnishes a valuable historical and cross-cultural overview (e.g. p.59).

c. The methodology utilized is impressive. Along with using well-established scales, questionnaires, physiological recording techniques and psychological rating methods, the author has incorporated many innovative ideas of his own (e.g. "Body Distortion Questionnaire" - Appendix A - p.502-503).

d. Significant conclusions emanate from some of the research (e.g. refer to Summary).

e. The tone of the book is objective, easy to follow and non-judgmental.

Deficiencies

a. The lack of photographs, sketches, graphs and charts hinders the book's impact.

b. Much of Fisher's ingenuity and arduous labor has been neutralized by his numerically small samples, his changing of many tests from sample to sample, the narrow-age spectrums of the respondents, and by the limiting of the respondents to married women only.

c. Some answers collated may be the result of respondents giving the researcher answers they feel are the correct political answers to give (e.g. "About 35% of the women indicated that they attain orgasm simultaneously with their spouses..." (p.214)). Adequate cross-checking research is not forthcoming.

d. Fisher is subjectively influenced by neo-freudianism (e.g. the words "ecstatic, happy" (Table 10-1, p.335) are claimed to separate the clitoral-oriented woman from the vaginal-oriented woman, the latter having a more "depersonalized way of experiencing her body" (p.462)). Such conclusions stem from unwarranted postulates.

4. Hite, Shere. *The Hite Report*. New York: MacMillan Publishing Co. Inc., 1976. 511 pp.

Brief Summary - 3,019 women aged 14-78 provided the data input from a series of questionnaires. Nine chapters deal with "Masturbation," "Orgasm," "Intercourse," "Clitoral Stimulation," "Lesbianism," "Sexual Slavery" ("Women are sexual slaves insofar as they are ... forced to satisfy others' needs and ignore their own" (p.297)), "The Sexual Revolution," "Older Women," and lastly, "Toward a New Female Sexuality." Hite's thesis is that historically men have been the sexual instigators and their women-partners have reacted to this defensively and with little expectation of self-pleasure. The so-called sexual revolution leaves women as badly off as ever. "Woman's role has shifted from childbearer to sex object since the decline in importance of childbearing" (p.365). The solution, Hite feels, is for each woman to activate her own sex pleasure whether her partner co-operates or not. "Intercourse ... would become a choice, an option, for each individual woman" (p.401). The author concludes "the truth is that 'sex' is bigger than orgasm, and involves any kind of deep physical intimacy one shares with another person" (p.413).

Critique - Strengths

a. A host of anecdotal personal quotations imparts a dynamic realism to the study. The percentage and numerical data are useful (e.g. Data on "Do you fake orgasms?" (p.164)). The methodology, sampling techniques, respondent-demographics and Questionnaires used are provided for the research-directed reader. A limited statistical breakdown by chapter makes up one of these Appendices. Some Notes including cited references are included.

b. The book is easy to follow and, while geared toward the mass public, is of more than peripheral use to the sexologist.

c. Hite's philosophically derived rationales are thought-evoking (e.g. "The glorification of intercourse (has developed) as the means of ensuring reproduction (with) the crucial role of monogamous intercourse (being) patrilineal inheritance" (p.148)). As a political instrument for heightening women's awareness in sociosexuality, the book is excellent.

Deficiencies

a. The lack of photographs, sketches, charts, graphs, and a bibliography represent serious omissions. Historical and cross-cultural background material is not provided.
b. The research is poorly conceived and executed. Four different questionnaires over 18 months to differing respondents confound any global statistics. Some questions are ambiguously worded and invite potentially erroneous answers (e.g. the distinction between manual clitoral stimulation and masturbation - Q.III, #4, p.432). Furthermore, the sample is of the volunteer, write-in variety. Leading questions invite answers the researcher might have politically wanted (e.g. clitoral stimulation versus intercourse - Q.IV, #23, p.xv).
c. Assumptive conclusions based on hypotheses occur at times (e.g. "... until women see in each other the possibility of a primal commitment which includes sexual love ... (they are) affirming their own second class status" (p.294)).
d. There is a theme of generalized pejorativity against all men. Such over-emphasis might have clouded research objectivity.

5. Kinsey, A., Pomeroy, W., Martin, C. & Gebhard, P. Sexual Behavior in the Human Female. Philadelphia: W.B. Saunders Co., 1953. 872 pp.

Brief Summary - Part I termed "History and Method" describes the scientific objectives, the scope of the study, the methods utilized for sampling and statistical analyses, and the sources of data. Sex histories of 5,940 white females personally taken by the authors are summarized in Part II. Part II deals with evidence about their sexual development and behavior. Statistics and tables are tabulated and discussed on the subjects of masturbation, nocturnal sex dreams, homosexuality, animal contacts, total sexual outlet and in the cases of the married respondents, pre-marital petting, coitus, and extramarital coitus. In Part III, "Comparisons of Female and Male," this study is compared to the earlier male study. Specific references, descriptions and generalizations are outlined about the anatomy of sexual response and orgasm, as well as its physiology, the psychologic factors, the neural mechanisms and the hormonal factors.

Critique - Strengths

a. A vast output of graphs, histograms, diagrams, charts and tables complement the text. A 48-page Bibliography terminates the text.
b. Subsequent studies tended to corroborate this research and subject to its sampling limitations, even today this study is not too out of line with reality.
c. Part III comparing this study to the previous male study is useful and helpful.

    d. An objective scientific approach is utilized (e.g. Concerning
       female masturbation "we ourselves (1948:497-498) were formerly
       inclined to accept the Freudian interpretations. But as we have
       learned more about the basic physiology of sexual response..."
       (p.134)).
    e. Theoretical constructs are uniquely employed to advantage
       (e.g. "The median ... is a useful statistic because it is
       unaffected by the frequencies of activity of the extreme
       individuals in any sample" (p.49); also the 0-6
       Heterosexual-homosexual rating scale combining an individual's
       overt plus psychic components (p.470 including Figure 93)).
    f. Future research possibilities are implied (e.g. "Psychologic
       fatigue must be a prime source of the difficulty in keeping
       married human mates strictly monogamous" (p.411).

Deficiencies

    a. A lack of sketches or photographs detracts from the impact of
       the book. Cross-cultural and historical background material is
       inadequate.
    b. Rigid statistical and sampling techniques are employed (such as
       obtaining a 100% sub-sample among certain groups of women where
       possible), but a bias is evident. The study is only of
       volunteers and its predictive value to other researchers is
       limited to essentially white, under 50 years of age, eastern
       U.S. female groups.
    c. The occasional generalized conclusion is unwarranted (e.g. "The
       data indicate that the factors leading to homosexual behavior
       are ..." (p.497); also "the most striking disparity which exists
       between the sexuality of the human female and male must depend
       on cerebral differences between the sexes" (p.712)).
    d. Certain subjects are not discretely studied (e.g. oral sex is
       only briefly discussed (p.257 and Table 73, p.281)); also group
       sex is only briefly mentioned (i.e. wife swapping - #11,
       p.434-435)).

6. Ladas, Alice Kahn, Whipple, Beverly & Perry, John D. The G Spot and
Other Recent Discoveries About Human Sexuality. New York: Holt,
Rinehart and Winston, Inc., 1982. 255 pp.

    Brief Summary - The authors are all therapists. The opening chapter
    summarizes recent major research and the Ladas-Whipple- Perry
    findings. The latter two persons discovered "a spot inside the
    vagina that is extremely sensitive to deep pressure. It lies in the
    anterior wall of the vagina about two inches from the entrance.
    They named this area the "Grafenberg spot" (p.20). Stimulation of
    this area often leads to orgasms and female ejaculation. The
    following chapter describes The Grafenberg Spot". The subsequent
    chapter talks about the associated phenomenon of "Female
    Ejaculation." Kegel's work on the pubococcygeus muscle is
    documented in Chapter 4. This is followed by the authors
    questioning much of the accepted Masters & Johnson theory and
    instead proposing alternative hypotheses such as the A-Frame effect
    of the uterus pushing on the compressing vagina during ejaculation
    and the postulated "Perry and Whipple Continuum of Orgasmic
    Response" (p.150). The final chapter cautions that the G spot

should not lead women to become "goal-oriented" (p.170).

Critique - Strengths

a. An 11-page Bibliography terminates the text. Anatomical
   sketches, anecdotal and other-expert quotations, and cited
   references with footnotes are provided. Three Appendices detail
   the Kegel work and application, some therapy referral sources,
   and portions of the preliminary Ladas research and inventories
   governing "Women and Bioenergetic Analysis" (p.195). Pertinent
   historical background material is presented (e.g. p.74-77).
b. Disclaimers are offered about the research (e.g. "Much more
   research needs to be done... We do not wish to establish a
   sexual Olympics with new and ever more demanding standards of
   performance" (p.xvi-xvii)).
c. Certain researchers are constructively criticized (e.g.
   "Freud ... made some significant errors..." (p.9)).
d. G spot research is succinctly summarized (e.g. twelve points
   expressed - p.20-21; also "a physician or nurse examine(d) more
   than 400 women who had volunteered to be research subjects. The
   G spot was found in each of the women examined" (p.43)). Future
   research possibilities are suggested (e.g. "Another topic that
   merits study is the relationship between hormones and female
   ejaculation" (p.82)). Hypotheses presented are original,
   provocative and have some basis for further research-probing
   (i.e. refer to Summary above).
e. The authors do not display pejorativity or needless moralizing.

Deficiencies

a. No graphs are included. No research cross-cultural verification has apparently been done. The only statistics (p.210) are
   based on seven specimen samples (four ejaculate, three urine)
   from only one volunteer. Actual methodology used is never
   forthcoming in order to back up factual statements (e.g. "the
   fluids of the other subjects were also analyzed and the results
   were similar to those reported in this article" (p.76)). The
   reported G spot and ejaculation data require replication by
   other researchers (e.g. "prostatic acid phosphatase levels were
   higher in the female ejaculatory fluids than in the urine
   samples" (p.76)).
b. Two research projects are included - that of Perry-Whipple and
   that of Ladas' "Work in Progress" (p.200). Both projects are
   far from complete. The book's title is misleading. Kegel's
   work is not recent nor are the authors' observations as yet
   definitive discoveries.

7. Seaman, Barbara. _Free and Female_. New York: Fawcett Book Group,
1972. 320 pp.

Brief Summary - Nine chapters cover the major gamut of women's
current sociosexual problems and dilemmas in our western culture.
Chapter I gives a biological-anthropological-historical background
and leans heavily on Sherfey's theory of innate female insatiability. The next chapter details the female-orgasmic research of
Masters & Johnson. Chapters III and IV are descriptive sexual

resumes of survey-research conducted by the author on one hundred
women. This is followed by an expose on the attitudes of male
gynecologists in their treatment of females. Chapter VI talks about
marriage, its ideals and current directional-foci while the
subsequent topic is a guide to venereal disease and contraception-
control. Chapter VIII speaks to the issue of "The Children of
Liberated Women" while the final short chapter addresses the
rhetorical question of whether men can be rehumanized.

Critique - Strengths

a. Seaman quotes liberally and shows perspicacity in choosing
    experts and authorities from which to draw her historical,
    cross-cultural and research examples and analogies (e.g. refer
    to Summary).
b. The major contribution of the book is centered in those
    chapters where the author uses irrefutable logic to demonstrate
    how man has socially fettered woman through exercising control
    over her sexuality. These are Chapters I, V (about male gyne-
    cologists), VI and the summing-up Chapter IX.

Deficiencies

a. No visual aids assist the text. References are limited.
b. The author's research study of one hundred women, although
    useful in a descriptive way, was not conducted using proper
    scientific planning. She uses pre-civilization matriarchy
    arguments. These are controversial and have never been substan-
    tiated by direct evidence (i.e. she quotes Sherfey who in turn
    quotes Bachofen (1861) as saying "there are many indications
    from pre-history studies" (p.44) pointing to this matriarchal
    period).
c. It is easy to criticize a system and this Seaman does with
    passion and skill. It is much harder to offer constructive
    solutions and here the author does succeed in some instances
    (e.g. as to how women should handle male-gynecological attitudes
    and practices) but she is not very adept at proposing remedies
    for the deeper issues of how society should seek to re-direct
    itself and its male sexist orientation. She seems content to
    state that "the humanization of men will not come swiftly or
    easily" (p.309).
d. The author shows pejorative sex-negativity at times (e.g.
    "Students of sexual pathology tell us that there are all kinds
    of common perversions which prevent a lover from accepting a
    partner as she really is" (p.217); also "many 'promiscuous'
    persons are idealists in drag ... who are searching - futilely,
    as a rule - for a replay of some transcendent sexual experience
    they once enjoyed" (p.213)).
e. Occasional technical mistakes are evidenced (e.g. "with rare
    exceptions (which are pathological), a sexually mature male must
    have an orgasm to deposit sperm" (p.38-39)).

8. Sherfey, Mary Jane. The Nature & Evolution of Female Sexuality.
New York: Vintage Books, Random House, 1973. 201 pp.

Brief Summary - The author in Chapter 1 reviews the work of Freud,

Benedek and Deutsch. She concludes the traditional clitoral-vaginal
transfer theory of orgasm is outdated and useless. Chapter 2 deals
with "Embryology and the Nature of Bisexuality." Comparing male and
female sexual anatomy, the author contends they are basically
unimorphic. Chapter 3 finds Sherfey documenting the discoveries of
Masters & Johnson. She ties in her cited reference that "90% of the
American women prefer relations during the luteal or premenstrual
phase" (p.96) to the lost female estrus cycle in deciding such a
luteal phase "is homologous to the period of heat of certain higher
primates" (p.98). She goes on to hypothesize "to all intents and
purposes, <u>the human female is sexually insatiable in the presence of
the highest degrees of sexual satiation</u>" (p.112), and could
theoretically go on having orgasms until exhaustion forced cessation
of activity. In Chapter 4 Sherfey postulates "the forceful
suppression of women's inordinate sexual demands was a prerequisite
to the dawn of every modern civilization and almost every living
culture" (p.138). A short "Summary" collates her postulations.

Critique - Strengths

a. An appendix termed "A Primer of Sexual Anatomy" is replete with
    anatomical diagrams. A 17-page Glossary of terms coupled with a
    6-page Sources of References effectively close out the text.
    Further anatomical sketches as well as charts, cited research
    with footnotes complement the text. Historical-anthropological
    arguments are relatively if selectively thorough and are
    essential precursors to the developing of her textual
    hypotheses. Italics and numbered points emphasize key concepts.
b. Sherfey's hypotheses are carefully stated to be just that and
    not predictive theories based on accumulated and definitive
    facts. Nevertheless, enough evidence is mixed with conjecture
    to make them plausible. This produces a thought-evoking book.
    Are her hypotheses (refer to Summary above) major breakthroughs
    of insightful genius? We don't know.
c. The book is an excellent summary on sexual embryology and its
    biological determinants.
d. Pejorativity is not evident.

Deficiencies

a. No index is included nor are any graphs projected. Portions of
    the book are dull and prosaic as well as repetitious (refer to
    Summary) in repeating sexual anatomy in the appendixed Primer.
b. Certain postulates are derived almost completely from conjec-
    ture with little or no germination from previous research (e.g.
    "women with strong sexual guilts ... usually cannot admit the
    possibility of ... 'automatic' sexual arousal; unrelieved sexual
    tension could then be a main component of the premenstrual
    tension syndrome" (p.97); also the extrapolation "if women's
    sexual drive has not abated and they prove incapable of
    controlling it, thereby jeopardizing family life and child care,
    a return to the rigid, enforced suppression will be inevitable
    and mandatory" (p.140)).

9. Tavris, Carol & Sadd, Susan. <u>The Redbook Report on Female
<u>Sexuality</u>. New York: Delacorte Press, 1977. 203 pp.

Brief Summary - The authors have taken the statistics from a Redbook
magazine questionnaire-survey. Chapter 1, "Of Surveys and Sex," is
a background, semi-historical resume of antecedental research and
postulations. Data from 100,000 women who sent in their answers
were compiled "and quantified" (p.17). Chapters 2, 3 and 4 detail
the findings of the survey in connection with premarital sex,
marital sex, and extramarital sex. The final chapter entitled "The
Good News About Men" seeks to correlate male-female orgasmic
response. An Appendix closes the text by outlining the full
questionnaire and its percentage-response statistics.

Critique - Strengths

a. The Appendix collates the research data. A Bibliography,
    humorous quotations from the erotic literature, anecdotal
    stories, charts, and statistical tables aid the textual content.
    Some comparative tables are named Old News - New News and these
    are innovative and historically sound (e.g. #4 on extramarital
    sex - "(Old News): Women anticipate more guilt ... (New News):
    ... than they usually feel" (p.142)).
b. Myths are dissected and exploded (e.g. Four male-female
    relational orgasmic myths - p.147-158).
c. Some comparative historical background is provided (see
    Summary) although more input should have been provided. A
    better job was done in comparing the research data to other
    studies (e.g. concerning premarital sex - the Hunt study (table
    on p.37) versus this Redbook study (table on p.34)).

Deficiencies

a. No visual aids, cross-cultural input or graphs are in evidence.
    The research is of the qualitative variety. The sample is a
    volunteer, write-in type. While such research is useful, it may
    be idiosyncratic. It is heavily weighted in favour of
    college-trained, younger women as compared to the national
    average (Table 1 - p.21-22) and is therefore unlikely to
    represent a definitive cross-section of American women.
b. Conclusions are speculative (e.g. do women with a high religi-
    osity quotient rate themselves sexually happier than the norm
    because it really is so, or because they have given the answers
    they felt they should and must, for loyalty's sake? (Table 11 -
    p.99)).
c. Some pejorativity occurs (e.g. "Promiscuity is not increasing
    among young women" (p.3).

History and Sex

10. Brecher, Edward M. _The Sex Researchers_ (Expanded Edition). San
Francisco: Specific Press, 1979. 433 pp.

Brief Summary - The author points out in his Introduction that the
Kinsey and Masters & Johnson findings of sex research "were the
natural and perhaps inevitable culmination of at least three-
quarters of a century of scientific inquiry by specialists of many
kinds, using diverse techniques applied to diverse populations"
(p.xi). Ten chapters follow as the text. In the first chapter,
Brecher unfolds the saga of Havelock Ellis (1859-1939), the eminent
English physician-researcher. The following chapter chronicles the
biography of Richard von Krafft-Ebing (1840-1902). The subsequent
chapter on Sigmund Freud (1856-1939) implies that Freud would have
deplored his later-following disciples' distortions of his original
psychoanalytic theories. Chapter 4 capsulates the history of T.H.
van de Velde (1873-1937), yet another physician who wrote the
influential "Ideal Marriage" published in 1926. In the next
chapter, Brecher describes Alfred Kinsey's (1894-1956) work.
Chapter 6 tells the story of five famous women and their
contributions, Elizabeth Blackwell (1821-1910), and four
contemporary researchers, Leah Schaefer, Niles Newton, Helena Wright
and Mary Sherfey. Brecher next discusses atypical physical and
psychosocial sexual variations. Here he draws heavily from Dr. John
Money's contemporary endocrinological work. Chapter 8 continues
with Money and adds Lorenz, Gebhard and others in detailing
imprinting in "The Falling-in-Love Experience." A resume in Chapter
9 is on open sociosexual lifestyles as epitomized by the swinging
subculture where Brecher draws on the findings of Bartell and the
Smiths. The final chapter catalogues the contributions of Masters &
Johnson. Two Epilogues, written in 1968 and 1978, update and
comment upon the current state of sex research.

Critique - Strengths

a. Cited references with footnotes and a 14-page "Bibliography and
    References" complement the text. Case studies (e.g. H. Ellis -

    p.41) and actual swingers' ads (e.g. p.248) accord an
    authenticity to the textual content. Some demographic
    statistics are included (e.g. Masters & Johnson - p.305).
  b. Although it utilizes a scholarly approach, the book is easy to
    read and its interspersing of facts with anecdotal information
    imparts an exciting balance to the reader. The author's sex-
    positive advocacy approach is refreshing.
  c. Brecher offers constructive criticism (e.g. concerning Kinsey's
    views on premature ejaculation, the author states in view of
    later research, "it seems to me very clear that on this point
    Kinsey was quite wrong" (p.128)).
  d. Recent and controversial sex research is often covered (e.g.
    the female ejaculation phenomenon - p.362-364).

Deficiencies

  a. The lack of photographs or drawings causes the reader to lose
    some affinity for the text. Charts and graphs, even in
    simplified forms, are never offered. Cross-cultural sex
    research is minimally portrayed.
  b. Some biographical choices are less useful than others. For
    instance, Blackwell's "sweet reasonableness" (p.152) is actually
    a story of a semi-repressed physician of the 19th century and
    may be the author's vehicle by which he contrasts today's female
    sex researchers (i.e. see Summary).
  c. Brecher is sometimes too emotionally subjective about endorsing
    ideas that are as yet unproven and may be fallacious (e.g. the
    terming of poppers (amyl nitrite) as "an anti-frigidity drug"
    (p.330)).
  d. Occasional mistakes occur (e.g. "one female hormone (estrogen)"
    (p.217)).
  e. Pejorative judgmentality at times appears (e.g. "Women were
    much less promiscuous than men in their homosexual contacts"
    (p.134)).
  f. Better coverage on past and present sex-research methodological
    biases in an Epilogue would have rendered an important closing
    perspective on the subject.

11. Bullough, Vern L. Homosexuality: A History. New York: Garland
STPM Press, 1979. 205 pp.

    Brief Summary - Bullough, a historian, presents a 12-chapter socio-
    historical analysis about homosexuality. The opening chapter termed
    "Past Definitions and Explanations" gives a background about the
    lifestyle's historical stigmatization and the various attempts over
    the past one hundred and fifty years to classify homosexuality as a
    sickness to be treated. Chapter 2 discusses its religious
    historical overtones while Chapter 3 attacks the legal sanctions
    imposed throughout the ages. Next comes a chapter titled "Repressed
    Evidence" which speaks about the traditional, careful veneer that
    homosexuals provided for society. The subsequent chapter outlines
    "The Movement in the U.S." and the organizations the lifestyle has
    spawned. Chapter 6 discusses how some famous homosexuals came "Out
    of the Closet." This is followed by enumerating instances of how
    governments such as Nazi Germany have used "Homosexuals as Victims:
    (by intertwining) Scapegoating and Politics." The seeming dilemma

of "Schools and Homosexuals" is analyzed after which a historical
discourse about "Lesbianism" is given. Chapter 10 compares and
historically denotes instances of "Cross-Dressing: Transvestism,
Transsexualism, and Homosexuality." Chapter 11 gives examples of
prominent homoerotic persons who lived down through history. The
final chapter "Homosexuality Today" offers a contemporary view on
the lifestyle and its practitioners as researched by some of today's
scientists. Bullough concludes "there seem to be too many variables
involved to offer any simple answer" (p.162) as to why any
individual is orientated into a homosexual lifestyle.

Critique - Strengths

a. Quotations, cited references and footnotes dot the text. A
    "Guide to Further Reading" completes the text. The book is well
    covered historically and some cross-cultural input is provided
    (e.g. Ford and Beach reference - p.59-60).
b. Much attention is paid to definitions, their nomenclature and
    derivations (e.g. "Westphal ... called the phenomenon 'contrary
    sexual feeling' (kontrare sexualempfindung)" (p.8)).
    Historically cross-comparing the phenomena of transvestism and
    transsexualism to homosexuality is also useful (refer to Summary
    above).
c. A good critique of the differing research probes is usually
    given (e.g. Weinberg and Williams - p.14, also Ford and Beach -
    p.62).
d. Discerning philosophical insights are proffered (e.g. "perhaps
    American adult society is concerned not so much specifically
    with homoerotic play among children and adolescents as with sex
    itself" (p.116)). The final chapter is an excellent resume of
    hypothetical possibilities interspersed with warnings and
    admonitions (e.g. "One of the difficulties with labeling,
    however, is that the people so labeled often tend to react
    according to labels, and this has presented complications in
    studying homosexuality" (p.152)).

Deficiencies

a. No photographs, drawings, charts or graphs assist the text.
    Also, there are not enough bibliography references provided.
    Many statements require citations when none is given (e.g. "As
    far as current research indicates, most homosexuals do not
    become homosexuals through recruitment" (p.114)).
b. Occasional mistakes can be noted (e.g. "Kinsey put sexual
    behavior on a continuum from 0 to 6 ..." (p.73) leaves out the
    other Kinsey component of stimuli fantasy arousal).
c. Minor pejorativity can be seen (e.g. "Just how much more
    promiscuous the male homosexuals are than ..." (p.157); also
    "... and 'frigidity' is as common among female homosexuals
    as..." (p.157)).

12. Bullough, Vern L. Sex, Society & History. New York: Science
History Publications, 1976. 192 pp.

    Brief Summary - This book is a collection of fourteen reprints of
various journal articles. In a brief Introduction, Bullough advises

that concerning human sexuality, "I know of no development in
science ... which has been so threatening to past traditions and
assumptions" (p.vii). "Sex in History: A Virgin Field" details the
erroneous assumptions which hinder the objectivity of many
historians, social and political scientists. The next topic
discussed is "Attitudes Toward Deviant Sex in Ancient Mesopotamia."
Subsequently, "Homosexuality as Submissive Behavior: Example From
Mythology" postulates a dominance-submission model for the ancient
Egyptian culture's male homosexuals. In "Medieval Medical and
Scientific Views of Women," Bullough attributes that era's view of
female inferiority having a scientific basis as providing its
medical writers a "justification for their 'scientific' hostility to
women" (p.55) in order "to bolster ... (their) prejudices" (p.59).
Next follows a compilation of "Transvestites in the Middle Ages"
after which "Heresy, Witchcraft and Sexuality" are explored. "An
Early American Sex Manual, or, Aristotle Who?" alludes to the sex
manuals falsely attributed to Aristotle and by which Colonial
America titillated itself in the 18th and 19th centuries. In
"Problems and Methods for Research in Prostitution and the
Behavioral Sciences," the author describes the historical misinformation of prostitute census-results published over the past one
hundred and fifty years. The topic "Homosexuality and Its Confusion
with the 'Secret Sin' in Pre-Freudian America" examines how
masturbation and homosexuality were often equated. After a brief
treatise entitled "Polygamy: An Issue in the Election of 1860?"
about Lincoln's anti-polygamy-Mormon stand, "Women, Menstruation,
and Nineteenth-Century Medicine" come under critical scrutiny as
regards the promulgation of dangerous misinformation. After
detailing "Transsexualism in History," Bullough next dissects the
"continued classification of homosexuality as a pathology" (p.161)
in "Homosexuality and the Medical Model." In the final paper "Sex
and the Medical Model," Bullough feels "a social and behavior
science model is still far more valid for dealing with sexual
behavior than the medical model" (p.183).

Critique - Strengths

a. The articles are well researched utilizing many original
    sources. Some minimal statistics and tables are employed where
    required.
b. Little-known information is often made available (e.g. From
    cuneiform "incantations it seems clear that self or mutual
    masturbation was a technique utilized to give potency" (p.24)).
c. Not only are historical figures critically examined as to their
    sexual beliefs and pronouncements (e.g. refer to Summary above),
    but in Chapter I, contemporary historians themselves are
    constructively attacked (e.g. "... generalizations such as those
    of Toynbee ... are used as historical truth..." (p.5); also
    Taylor's "study is motivated by a Freudian concept and he
    arranges his history to fit his concept" (p.13)).
d. Subjective moralizing is minimal. Pejorative phraseology is
    basically absent.

Deficiencies

a. Visual aids are distinctly lacking. More graphs and charts

would have been helpful. Cross-cultural input is heavily
weighted in favor of the ancient mid-East, medieval Europe and
recent America.

b. Some papers seem either irrelevant (i.e. Chapter 8 on prostitution) or confusing with regard to another (i.e. Chapter 5 on
   transvestites and Chapter 12 on transsexuals leave one wondering
   if the transvestites were not in fact transsexuals).

c. Neofreudian assumptions occasionally enter the text (e.g.
   "transvestites themselves suffer from castration anxiety, for
   which they compensate by making themselves into phallic women"
   (p.60)).

13. Bullough, Vern L. Sexual Variance in Society and History. New
York: John Wiley & Sons Inc., 1976. 732 pp.

   Brief Summary - Bullough, a historian, divides his book into six
   parts as it traces the convolutions of human sexual attitudes and
   behavior from the earliest recorded times up until the 1970's. In
   his Preface, Bullough explains that he has "not adopted any theory
   about sexuality" (p.xi). Part I entitled "The Background" in four
   chapters examines historical mythology, recent-past and contemporary
   cross-cultural comparisons, and early sexuality with its
   reproductive biases. Part II, termed "The European Inheritance" in
   four chapters, describes the early Greco-Roman-Christian sociosexual
   facets and their influences on today's culture. Bullough suggests
   that the Greeks even more than Judaism influenced "traditional
   Western sexual attitudes" (p.93). After an early sex-positive
   phase, this influence came from an "ascetic, asexual trend, which
   the later Christians emphasized" (p.119). In Part III, "Attitudes
   Toward Sex in the Non-Western World," the author contrasts the
   sex-positive Islamic, Indian and ancient Chinese cultures. Part IV
   called "The Christian world" has four chapters stressing the
   reinforcement of sex-negative beliefs and practices that surfaced in
   the Middle Ages. Part V, "New Horizons and the New World,"
   encompasses five chapters and delineates the sexually uptight epoch
   of our Western heritage which culminated in the so-called Victorian
   Era. Science began to slowly displace religion as the dominant
   sex-negative force. In Part VI, "The Twentieth Century: Trends and
   Assumptions," two small chapters outline how sex researchers such as
   Krafft-Ebing, Havelock Ellis, Freud, and later Kinsey, Masters &
   Johnson and others commenced a breakthrough toward understanding
   human sexuality. Bullough sums up his book by noting a contemporary
   acceptance of sexual variety, and how women are beginning to see
   themselves as sexual persons. Indeed there is "organized propaganda
   for new forms of sexuality" (p.682) such as nudity.

   Critique - Strengths

   a. Copious footnotes and quotations plus four pages of Suggestions
      for Further Reading assist the textual interpretation.

   b. The book is scholarly and avoids the trap of most other books
      of its type by utilizing original-source references wherever
      possible. Consequently, novel shadings of interpretation often
      surface (e.g. refer to the Greek reference in the Summary
      above).

   c. Insightful phrases and research diligence into word-

originations are bonuses (e.g. "antinatal philosophy" (p.680);
also the origin of che word "buggery" (p.390), about which even
the Oxford English Dictionary was mistaken).
d. Cross-cultural information is extensively provided (e.g. refer
to Summary above).

Deficiencies

a. The lack of photographs, drawings, tables and charts is a
drawback.
b. At times, conclusions are implied which may not follow from the
hypotheses or facts presented (e.g. Stekel "implied there is no
cruelty not tinged with sexual pleasures, and the Roman
experience might well support Stekel's hypothesis" (p.133)).
c. There is a lack of average-person sexual practices portrayed in
the book. More factual and anecdotal information on lower-class
and peasant sexual proclivities would have added more balance to
the text.
d. Some pejorativity occurs (e.g. "pudenda" (p.100); also
"encouraged them in their vices" (p.302)).

14. Dover, K. J. Greek Homosexuality. Cambridge: Harvard University
Press, 1978. 254 pp. (Also New York: Random House, 1980. 254 pp.)

Brief Summary - In his Preface, Dover describes his book as covering
"those phenomena of homosexual behavior and sentiment which are to
be found between the 8th and 2nd centuries B.C., and so to provide a
basis for more detailed and specialised exploration (which I leave
to others) of the sexual aspects of Greek art, society and morality"
(p.vii). This he does in four parts. Part I, "Problems, Sources
and Methods," explores the visual arts of that period. On the topic
of vase-paintings, there is a "predominance of male over female
nudes" (p.9), many of which are homosexually oriented in both scene-
depiction and in language-engraving. The literature period which
followed similarly had much material on homosexuality. Dover closes
this section with a discussion on this era's Greek vocabulary. For
example, the erastes, an active older male, acts as social,
scholastic and sexual tutor for the eromenos, a passive, pubertal
young male recipient. In Part II, "The Prosecution of Timarkhos,"
Dover uses the vehicle of this obscure trial to illustrate many
points about Greek male sociosexual behavior. "Special Aspects and
Developments" comprise Part III, into which one hundred and five
photographs of erotic art are included. A small chapter of Part III
explores "Women and Homosexuality" and includes references from
Sappho of Lesbos. Part IV entitled "Changes" in two brief chapters
delineates myth from fact in the emergence of the erastes-erominos
phenomenon. Most eromenoi eventually married because "on growing
up, in any Greek community, the eromenos graduated from pupil to
friend, and the continuance of an erotic relationship was
disapproved, as was such a relationship between coevals" (p.203).

Critique - Strengths

a. A proliferation of photographs, footnotes and cited references
add immeasurable vigor to the text. The cross-tribe and
historical material is exactingly presented.

b. Clear and perceptive observations dominate the text (e.g. The
    Greeks "did not expect the passive partner in a homosexual
    relationship to derive physical pleasure from it" (footnote,
    p.36); also "What the erastes hopes to engender in the erominos
    is not eros but love" (p.53)).
c. Precisely defined philosophical assumptions are presented (e.g.
    "The long-standing, Western European assumption that homosexual
    eros is essentially diabolical may be responsible for a certain
    reluctance, even on the part of those who would immediately
    reject moral condemnation of homosexuality per se, to recognise
    that homosexual eros can inspire as much unselfish devotion as
    heterosexual" (p.50-51)).
d. Subjective moralizing utilizing value-judgments is negligible.
e. Language analyses and interpretations (e.g. refer to Summary
    above) are succinctly evaluated. This book is required reading
    for all sexological scholars and researchers interested in homo-
    sexuality, relationships or sociosexual issues from an
    evolutionary historical perspective.

Deficiencies

a. As clearly admitted by the author (refer to Summary above),
    this book is only a stylized beginning to answering its subject.
    More historical research by others will hopefully supplement its
    contributions.
b. Occasionally, Dover seems to overly idealize certain writings
    of the early Greek intellectuals and to deemphasize unduly any
    importance they might have attached to sexuality for its own
    sake. He may or may not be right in doing so, but insufficient
    proofs are presented to justify such a weighting of his
    arguments (e.g. "We may well feel that 'erastes' is so freely
    used in the Socratic circle ... that (possibly) eros is not a
    desire for bodily contact but a love of moral and intellectual
    excellence" (p.157)).

15. Lewinsohn, Richard. (A. Mayce (1956), translator). A History of
Sexual Customs. New York: Harper & Row, 1971. 384 pp.

  Brief Summary - In its twenty chapters, this book views sexuality
  and its impact on history from 20,000 years ago up to the mid-20th
  century. Chapter 1 contains speculative sociosexual prehistory, the
  projections of which are extrapolated from the examinations of early
  paintings and carvings in southern France, Spain and along the
  Danube River. The author feels that early civilization was
  originally not matriarchal, and "monogamy thus went hand in hand
  with the evolution of private property" (p.13). The next chapter
  traces the development of societal sexual value-systems in early
  Babylon, Egypt and India. Lewinsohn then recounts the liberal-to-
  ascetic sexual transition of the early Greeks, the Roman era, and
  Christianity's emergence as a social force influencing sexual
  conduct. In Chapter 6, the author discusses Islam which encouraged
  polygamy. He then returns to Europe in the Middle Ages as the
  church succeeded in instituting sexual control over its followers.
  But there was always a sex-permissiveness tacitly accepted amongst
  the nobility and the higher clergy in contrast to the peasant class
  and this was a major reason which caused the Reformation. In the

17th century came the first significant physiological discoveries
pertaining to fertilization and reproduction. The onset of the
French Revolution in 1789 allowed Frenchwomen of higher social
levels some improvement in sexual expression. Soon such feminists
as Annie Besant of England and Susan Anthony of the U.S. aligned
themselves with the causes of birth control and/or anti-
prostitution. Aided by sexologist-theoreticians such as
Krafft-Ebing and Freud and scientists such as Kinsey, recent society
has acknowledged the dilemma of "the sex-instinct and the
reproductive instinct" (p.408) as being a complex and mutual
interaction which could be separated.

Critique - Strengths

a. The many reproductions of old paintings, wood-cut engravings,
    and photographs reinforce the authenticity of the text. A
    9-page References section closes out the book. Many quotations
    are employed.
b. Some major cross-cultural data are given (refer to Summary
    above). The first chapter on prehistory with its visual aids
    speculates on an oft-neglected area.
c. Startling anecdotal stories at times occur which imply
    incredible sex-power struggles (e.g. Lucrezia Borgia allegedly
    gave a "public confirmation of twofold incest" (p.166) with
    Cesare her brother and Pope Alexander VI, her father.
d. The book is easy to follow and sexological students especially
    should follow its train of thought.

Deficiencies

a. Too many secondary reference sources are utilized. Tables and
    graphs are not used.
b. Assumptive phrases occur (e.g. "Rousseau laboured under ... an
    Oedipus complex" (p.236); also "he remained an onanist all his
    life" (p.236)).
c. Subjective bias including homophobia often invades the text
    along with some serious pejorativity (e.g. "it remains
    remarkable that youths of the age ... were able to endure
    without disgust the embraces of much older persons of the same
    sex" (p.58); also "as over-sexed as her mother" (p.77); also
    "Verlaine ... was sexually a monstrosity" (p.337)).
d. A few errors of serious degree are present (e.g. "It is only
    between Lesbians or where hygienic conditions are exceptionally
    bad, that occasional non-heterosexual infection is possible"
    (p.352); also a vasectomy turns men into" ... eunuchs..."
    (p.385)).

16. Marcus, Steven. The Other Victorians (2nd edition). New York:
Basic Books, 1974. 294 pp.

Brief Summary - In two Introductions, Marcus outlines the textual
content and his reasons for including the material he chose. Seven
chapters comprise the book. The book's title refers to the
characters representing the mirror images of the very sexually rigid
citizens associated with England of the 19th century. In the first
chapter, Marcus highlights the biography of the physician William

Acton. Although he viewed prostitution as "an inevitable, almost an organic, part of society" (p.4), his writing on masturbation is very ill-informed. Chapter 2 details how the three-volumed reference indexes of Librorum were compiled by the "pornographer royal" (p.34), the so-called Pisanus Fraxi who in reality was Henry Ashbee. These volumes are important resources for the sexual fantasies and attitudes of that era. The next two chapters probe the vast anonymous works of the 11-volume "My Secret Life." The "authenticity" (p.118) of the myriad details, Marcus surmises, is obvious. As well as the sexual patterns to be studied "as simple social history ... (it can) thicken our sense of the Victorian reality" (p.103). Chapters 5 and 6 get into examples of pornographic stories of the time. The final chapter is termed "Conclusion: Pornotopia." Earlier the author defines pornotopia as "the imagination of the entire universe beneath the sign of sexuality" (p.242). Marcus sees pornography developing because of the rising complex privatization of our culture. He projects that as society legalizes pornography, its impact on our culture will be minimized.

Critique - Strengths

a. Copious appropriate quotations, cited references and footnotes aid the text. The book is an erudite rendition of Victorian sexuality set in abstract prose suitable to an advanced historical-sociological researcher.
b. Precise analyses of components of Victorian sexuality are offered and logical themes are developed (e.g. That era's sexual repression was a result of "an immense effort of self-discipline and self-denial" (p.148); also "money and class operate in relation to sex in similar ways" (p.159); also "pornography characteristically envisages a world in which conscience and real conflict do not exist... It adapts by subtraction and ... the whole is smaller than the sum of its parts" (p.209-210)).

Deficiencies

a. Surprisingly, no bibliography, visual aids, charts or tables enhance the text. A brief earlier-history and cross-cultural overview on the antecedents leading to the Victorian sociosexual attitudes and behavior would have been helpful.
b. Marcus is a professor of English and not a sexologist. He is, however, a student of Freud and relies too much on neo-freudian phraseology and theory (e.g. "his early Oedipal terrors" (p.168); also "the castration fears, anxieties and fantasies that every boy must suffer" (p.170)). Factual conclusions are sometimes based on such hypotheses (e.g. "the Oedipal components in this homosexual impulse are self-evident" (p.174)).
c. Marcus is both a good and a bad choice to write this book. Although competent in handling literary-sociological analyses, he is phobic in personally handling sexuality (e.g. "I would indeed be troubled if I came across my small son studiously conning Justine" (p.285); as well, his bias that "we know ... that pornography is not literature" (p.278)).
d. The author patronizes and is morally judgmental toward some of the people about whose works he writes (e.g. Concerning Ashbee,

"ideals, it seems, can find expression even in such a morass as
this" (p.39); also about "My Secret Life," he intones "it is all
rather like 'The Solitary Reaper' written in a sewer" (p.102)).

17. Murstein, Bernard I. Love, Sex, and Marriage Through the Ages.
New York: Springer Publishing Company, 1974. 652 pp.

Brief Summary - Twenty-five chapters trace the evolution of these
intertwined subjects starting from the dawn of recorded civilization
up to contemporary times. A brief introductory chapter abstracts
the goals of the book. Chapter 2 is a "review of theories on the
origin of marriage" (p.4) and their various forms. The concepts of
matriarchy, monogamy, patriarchy, group marriage, polygamy, nuclear
and extended families, the incest taboo, and mate selection methods
are defined and described. The next three chapters deal with these
topics as they relate to the Old Testament Hebrews, the ancient
Greeks and the early Romans. Chapters 6 and 7 discuss the early
Christian and medieval church's influences as sex-negative forces.
The following five chapters accord an insight into love, sex, and
marriage from the evolving perspectives of the medieval laity, the
Renaissance, the Reformation, the so-called "age of reason and
licentiousness: 1615-1789" (p.204), the Romantic and the Victorian
eras. Chapter 13 is devoted to biographies of Havelock Ellis and
Sigmund Freud. The subsequent five chapters trace American marital
and sex customs from the colonial period to contemporary times.
Chapters 19 through 22 accord past and present cross-cultural views
and practices as they have evolved in Russia, China, Japan and
"Black Africa" (p.502). The final three chapters give "some
literary and theoretical approaches" (p.520) to the future of
marriage, the "current marital innovations" (p.532) and an overview
summarizing the book's major conclusions as well as offering some
predictions. It "seems likely that a somewhat more open kind of
monogamous marriage than exists at present will predominate"
(p.567).

Critique - Strengths

a. Over a 1,000 cited references and footnotes plus a profuse
    number of apt quotations (e.g. Chaucer - p.134) make the text
    invaluable to the scholar. A 43-page Bibliography ties in the
    references. Many sketches and drawing-reproductions enhance the
    text as do numerous charts, tables, and graphs. Key phrases are
    in italics. A summary ends the major chapters.
b. Cross-cultural data are plentiful and broad in scope (e.g.
    refer to Summary above).
c. The reporting is mainly objective and the literary style is
    easy to follow.
d. Interesting seldom-found information is recounted frequently
    (e.g. "... brother-sister marriage was not a rarity among
    Egyptian commoners during the Roman rule of Egypt" (p.19 - cited
    reference given); also the 18th century French club "the
    Aphrodites" (p.211 - cited reference given)).
e. Valid, positive criticism of other research studies is given
    (e.g. Winch's "methodology, however, has been severely criti-
    cized..." (p.388 - three cited references given); also a
    critique on Kinsey's studies - p.421-426).

f. Hypotheses add an extra dimension to the historical reporting
    (e.g. Chapters 2 and 23 - refer to Summary above).

Deficiencies

a. Some editorializing clouds portions of the final three chapters
    (e.g. "From the point of view of society ... a 'committed'
    marriage is much more desirable than an 'exchange' one"
    (p.565)).
b. More than half of the cited references are not from the
    original sources. Such a high ratio tends to produce
    distortions of interpretations and facts.
c. Occasional assumptions mar the text (e.g. "... he suffered
    more from an overly suppressive super-ego..." (p.89); also
    "good sex is rare in the absence of a genuine interpersonal
    relationship" (p.442)).
d. More data about the customs of the common people should have
    been provided.
e. Pejorativity surfaces at times (e.g. "sexual excesses of the
    clergy" (p.117); also "promiscuous homosexuality..." (p.542)).

18. Pomeroy, Wardell B. Dr. Kinsey and the Institute for Sex Research.
New York: Harper & Row Publishers Inc., 1972. 491 pp.

Brief Summary - After a short Preface, Pomeroy embarks in Part I on
his story about Kinsey's early life and how Kinsey eventually
transferred his gall-wasp biological research to that of human
sexuality. Part II, "The Making of the Books," and Part III, "Male
and Female," elucidate the evolution of the research culminating in
the publishing of "Sexual Behavior in the Human Male" in 1948 and
"Sexual Behavior in the Human Female" in 1953 under a staff headed
by Kinsey and with co-researchers Pomeroy, Martin and eventually
Gebhard. Kinsey's hectic relationships with the press and with his
scientific critics are documented. Part IV is entitled "The Last
Years" and covers the eventual withdrawal of Rockefeller Foundation
support. This blow is claimed by Pomeroy as a major reason for
Kinsey's death in 1956. Part V recounts the later evolution of the
Institute up to the time of the book's writing and how it came to be
recognized as a foremost pacesetter in sex research and education.

Critique - Strengths

a. Historically important photographic plates plus numerous
    anecdotal quotations from Kinsey and others accord a real
    historical impact to the reader. The book gives a unique
    viewpoint to any professional with regard to the immediate-past
    evolution sex research has taken.
b. The final chapter "What it all Meant" is especially valuable to
    the researcher and the student in that it summarizes the eight
    key contributions of Kinsey's work (p.465-470).
c. Chapter 25, "Kinsey Abroad," is historically useful in the way
    it correlates 1950's European sex attitudes and behavior cross-
    culturally with those of North Americans (p.401-430).
d. The book is free from pejorative bias and judgmentality of
    sexual minorities.
e. Criticism of the weaknesses inherent in Kinsey's methodology is

proffered (e.g. "The truth was that Kinsey did not have all the
mathematical advice he required at the beginning, and as the
research went on the resulting defects were built in and could
not be changed" (p.464).

Deficiencies

a. The book is less useful for the scholar. No bibliography, or
    properly cited references, footnotes, or suggested additional
    reading lists are given. Furthermore, not even the most
    elementary tables or graphs are included.
b. Intra-staff policy differences and goals are tantalizingly
    mentioned, but not properly dealt with. (e.g. "Martin quietly
    carried out some projects of his own without staff permission or
    approval. They gave him great satisfaction, and in the end he
    turned out to be correct in what he had planned" (p.463).

19. Stone, Lawrence. The Family, Sex and Marriage in England
1500-1800. New York: Harper & Row, 1977. 831 pp.

Brief Summary - Utilizing some comparisons to contemporary-period
New England and continental Western Europe, Stone develops his
presentation in five Parts. His sixth and final Part interprets his
findings and cross-compares them to the post-1800 era which has
followed. Three types of family operated over this period. "The
Open Lineage Family" existed from 1450-1630 followed by "The
Restricted Patriarchal Nuclear Family" (1550-1700) and lastly "The
Closed Domesticated Nuclear Family" from 1640-1800 and in fact up to
the present day. Part I defines and puts boundaries on these
concepts, along with the criteria, methodology and demography used
in studying these eras. The next three Parts analyze in depth the
aforementioned era-types of Family. In his Part V on "Sex," Stone
acknowledges that during the entire 300-year period, sex play was
much less in quantity than is prevalent today. Lack of personal
hygiene, malnutrition, illnesses, rotting teeth, religious guilt,
early deaths, lack of privacy and the dangers of venereal diseases
were all significant factors in inhibiting interpersonal sexual
outlet. Myths were commonplace. For example, "The great Swiss
mid-18th century Dr. Tissot ... stated that the loss of one ounce of
semen is the equivalent of the loss of forty ounces of blood"
(p.495). Premarital sexuality declined from 30% in the 1500's to 17%
during the 1600-1750 repressive period and then skyrocketed to over
40% from 1750 to 1800. After 1800, sexual repression arrived.
Stone concludes in Part VI that family-type variations should be
thought of as "gains and losses, not moral progress or decay"
(p.683).

Critique - Strengths

a. Forty-three illustrations along with plentiful footnotes,
    quotations, demographic tables and sixteen graphs (e.g.
    Prenuptial Conception Ratio - p.610) are of great assistance.
    An informative Bibliography in twenty-three pages of
    sub-sections terminates the text. Original-source references
    are assiduously pursued.
b. Historical-era myths are recounted in detail (e.g. refer to Dr.

Tissot in Summary).

c. The author is objective and non-judgmental (e.g. refer to Part
VI in Summary above).

d. The author at times notes sexual variations seldom reported
elsewhere and does so with detachment bereft of moralizing (e.g.
"In Elizabethan Essex, court records quite incidentally turn up
evidence of a man having intercourse with a girl while her
sister was in the same bed and of a case in which the girl's
mother was in the same bed" (p.256)).

e. Chapter 11 portrays the sexual biographic resumes of Forman,
Pepys, Boswell and others. This accords a perception into the
sexual tenor of the times described.

f. Constructive criticisms are sometimes offered about sexual
theories (e.g. "The Freudian assumption ... has ... no basis in
reality, so deeply is it overlaid by cultural norms" (p.484)).

Deficiencies

a. Although some cross-cultural comparisons are provided (refer to
Summary), somewhat more material on other then-present cultures
such as the Near East or India, would have been an additional
asset.

b. A few cases of assumptive bias surface in the text (e.g. About
Louis XIII of France, Stone claims "it certainly seems possible
that his childhood of overstimulated sexual expression..."
(p.509); also about Boswell's father, "a more obvious attempt at
the sexual castration of his son could hardly be imagined"
(p.583)). Additionally, the words "promiscuous" and "frigidity"
are often used (refer to Index) pejoratively.

20. Talese, Gay. Thy Neighbor's Wife. New York: Doubleday & Co.
Inc., 1980. 568 pp.

Brief Summary - The author weaves a tapestry about the obsessive
involvement of the Unites States with sex over the past one hundred
and fifty years. He writes about real persons, some famous, some
not; some notorious, others less so. The book opens during the
repressive era of the 1950's and slides back and forth along the
span of its time scale. In a context of the sociopolitical and
legal arena, Talese describes the motivational background and
philosophical rationale for our cultural preoccupation with
sexuality, using as examples the fortunes and misfortunes of
personages such as Hugh Hefner of Playboy, Al Goldstein of Screw
magazine, and John Williamson of Sandstone. Interspersed with these
contemporary individuals are historical figures such as Anthony
Comstock, and John Noyes of the Oneida Community.

Critique - Strengths

a. The author, a journalist by training, writes in a very free-
flowing style which is easy to follow.

b. The intimate descriptions of the real people discussed add
impact to the book. Talese, although pro-sex and liberal, still
keeps an objective balance and is not afraid to elucidate the
frailties and blemishes of the persons depicted as well as their
dreams, philosophies and achievements.

Deficiencies

a. No visual aids, charts, tables, graphs, cited references or
    bibliography reinforce the text.
b. The book imparts an air of discontinuity by its flipping to a
    new personality before finishing with the original one, and then
    at a later part of the book, again returning to the original
    person.
c. The book relies too much on a few personalities, ignoring many
    others just as important. Furthermore, the author cannot seem
    to decide whether to approach his subject from the perspective
    of history, or contemporary emerging lifestyles, or from an
    anthropological viewpoint of American sexual philosophy.
d. Talese could have avoided uncorroborated generalizations (e.g.
    "There were numerous swing clubs, of course, but these tended to
    be surreptitious gatherings in overcrowded suburban houses ...
    frequently raided by the police following complaints by prying
    neighbors" (p.513)).
e. Although the author's research is meticulous and generally
    accurate, he makes one serious mistake when he says "Roth did
    telephone Dr. Alfred Kinsey to ask if he would serve as a
    defense witness, but Kinsey firmly refused, saying that he could
    not support obscenity" (p.106). Kinsey was not against
    obscenity per se, but instead never agreed to testify for or
    against anyone because he did not want to prejudice his position
    which he felt was that of a dispassionate research scientist.

21. Taylor, G. Rattray. Sex in History. New York: Ballantine Books,
1954. 320 pp.

Brief Summary - In his Foreword, Taylor states this book "offers a
working theory to account for the changes in sexual attitudes which
it records" (p.14). The main text is composed of four Books, after
an opening chapter in which he compares Eros (love) and Thanatos
(hate). In Book I, "The Pattern is Made," Taylor explores the
medieval age. After the frank positive sexuality of the earlier
Middle Ages, the imposition of church-inspired negative sexual
strictures slowly led to changes in the populace bringing "a
mounting toll of perversion and neurosis" (p.22). Taylor next
introduces his theoretical construct of patrism and matrism where
the former societal structure represents a father-figure
authoritarian model and the latter the mother-figure love
role-model. The author theorizes that these concepts alternated in
epochal sequence while occasionally coinciding to some degree. In
Book II, "The Pattern Developed," Taylor recounts sociosexual mores
through the "matrist-individualist" (p.130) Renaissance, the
patrist-inspired Reformation, the later Restoration with its "signs
of matrism" (p.180), the admixture of both isms in the so-termed
Romantic era, and the firmly superimposed patrism of the Victorian
times. Book III, "Origins of the Pattern," explores the
pre-Christian beginnings of these later sex attitudes. Not only
Jewish religious sanctions and Graeco-Roman civil ones were of
influence, but also the early multiracial prevalent view of "the
sacramental view of sex" (p.214) was a major contribution. The
final Book IV, in two small chapters, finds Taylor ridiculing the

20th century arbitrary modes of censorship in the matrist society of
today and which he attributes to the patrists being attracted to the
police and legal positions where power is located.

Critique - Strengths

a. Footnotes plus a 13-page Sources referral section are included.
   Two Appendixes dealing with English law of the 1950's and
   "Theories of Matriarchy and Patriarchy" (p.295) are somewhat
   useful. Quotations proliferate throughout the text, are
   appropriate and in context from the original sources.
b. A chart listing comparable patrist-matrist attitudes is most
   useful (e.g. Patrist - "3. Women seen as inferior, sinful...
   (Matrist -) Women accorded high status" (p.81)).
c. Book III is the best one. Here Taylor narrates sex-custom
   history.
d. Conjectural hypotheses challenge the reader. (e.g. "in matrist
   periods, incest is a common preoccupation and seems invested
   with a peculiar horror; while in patrist periods homosexuality
   seems to dominate men's thoughts and appears to them as the
   unspeakable sin" (p.78); also "the Church was more concerned to
   struggle with sex than to eliminate it, and always avoided a
   resolution of the battle, since this removed its raison d'etre"
   (p.241)).
e. The book is mainly non-judgmental.

Deficiencies

a. No photographs or sketches give dimension to the text.
   Historical and cross-cultural sex-customs are plentifully
   supplied for the pre-Christian era, but are limited to mainly
   European and North American cultures after that period.
b. Taylor is highly influenced by Freud but is without Freud's
   gift of flexibility. His patrist-matrist theory, while
   interesting, is much too simplistic to explain what he
   endeavours to do with it. (e.g. "the patrists' new anal
   preoccupations..." (p.161)). Unwarranted generalizations are
   reported from each era. Furthermore, hypothesis is treated as
   fact (e.g. "The second ... strain in the sexuality of the period
   seems to have been a fear of impotence" (p.175); also "it was an
   age of failure to sublimate sexual libido" (p.184)).
c. Books I and II are clearly inferior to Book III. The book in
   its present form is disjointed and unwieldy.
d. In Appendix B, the author states "the present theory provides
   a tool with which the social evolution of prehistoric periods
   may be explored more readily than at present" (p.299). This
   statement is unrealistically optimistic.

Male Sexuality

22. Hite, Shere. <u>The Hite Report on Male Sexuality</u>. New York: Alfred A. Knopf, 1981. 1164 pp.

<u>Brief Summary</u> - Hite's Preface states "this book, begun in 1974, had many purposes: To find out what American men are feeling, thinking, and doing" (p.xiii) about their sexuality. Chapter 1, "Being Male," speaks to the early male bonding experiences as well as "what does it mean to be a man?" (p.54). Relationships with women in Chapter 2 refer to the involved factors, how men define love, the concept of monogamy and the alternate lifestyles available. In Chapter 3, the subject of "Intercourse and the Definition of Sex" is discussed. The subsequent chapter, "Other Forms of Male Sexuality," dissects findings on masturbation, fellatio, foreplay, touching, and anal stimulation. Chapter 5 gives "Men's Views of Women and Sex." The issues of "Rape," "Paying Women for Sex," and "Pornography" comprise Chapter 6 and this is followed by the homosexual variables in "Sex and Love Between Men." A short Chapter 8 delineates the data concerning "The Sexuality of Older Men." A final Chapter 9 details "Thirty Men (who) Speak About Their Lives" and is segmented into chronological decades.

<u>Critique - Strengths</u>

a. A giant number of anecdotal quotations as well as footnoted citations aptly fortify the text. The Questionnaire IV is presented (p.xxi-xxxiii). Six Appendices accord some feedback to the questionnaire along with percentage-type demographic and regular statistics. The respondent sample is demographically well represented by age, geographic and occupational variation (i.e. p.1061-1076). Some anatomical diagrams are presented.
b. Myths are effectively destroyed by the accummulated data (e.g. "stereotypes about intercourse" (p.430)).
c. Some questions elicit information not usually found in most such studies (e.g. "161. Do you find kissing feet sexual? Golden showers?" (p.xxxiii)).
d. Italicized conclusions are generally valid (e.g. "it is the man

with the lowest self-esteem who is most likely to rape women..."
(p.719)).
e. The text is basically free from editorial pejorativity and
reasonably objective in its value-judgment.

Deficiencies

a. No graphs complement the text. No index or bibliography is
included nor is even a brief introductory historical and cross-
cultural input supplied. Because of the various methodological
design-weaknesses (e.g. a volunteer, write-in sample),
statistics are only superficial in nature and result in an
inherent bias (e.g. "119,000 questionnaires were distributed,
and 7,239 received in return" (p.1057)). Sampling techniques
are inadequate, with validity and reliability verification of
the results not being forthcoming.
b. An article from the AASECT journal is reprinted in an Appendix
(p.1057÷1060) to justify Hite's assertion that this study is
scientific in nature. This selective citation is not a proper
defense of the study's methodological shortcomings.
c. The study is incomplete. Many sub-topics are omitted and not
addressed (e.g. males who fake orgasm when with partners; cross-
dressing activities; group sex practices). Insufficient
information is asked in the occasional anecdotal story. (e.g.
" 'I exposed myself to my daughters...' " (p.722)).

23. Kelly, Gary F. <u>Good Sex: The Healthy Man's Guide to Sexual</u>
<u>Fulfillment</u>. New York: The New American Library, Inc., 1981. 216 pp.

Brief Summary - An educator, the author in his Introduction states
"my clientele in counseling and therapy is predominantly male"
(p.1). Thus this book speaks to issues surrounding the healthy
sexual functioning of males. Chapter 1 discusses male societal
sexual scripts while the following chapter details sexual partner-
communication. This leads to self-knowledge and "Getting in Touch
with Your Body" (p.51). Chapter 4 delves into problems and
solutions to ejaculatory problems of prematurity after which the
topic of erectile dysfunction is explained. Chapter 6's "Other Sex
Problems" talks about retarded ejaculation; "gamesmanship sex"
(p.127); sexual-desire difficulties; some various physical-
physiological problems; and some health-related causative factors
such as sexually transmitted diseases and drugs. The subsequent
chapter explores the subjects of jealousy, relationship variables,
female issues of physiology, sex-desire and potential dysfunctions,
criteria for seeking a sex therapist, and "sexual gadgetry" (p.172)
helpful in improving sex between partners. The final Chapter 8
imparts information about social brotherhood with other males,
issues involving fatherhood and understanding how to reduce "sexual
self-alienation" (p.197).

Critique - Strengths

a. A 5-page "Books on Human Sexuality" concludes the text.
Numerous apt anecdotal examples and anatomical sketches
complement the book while key concepts are stressed either in
italics or in bold type. Some resource organizations are listed

(p.171). Continual reader-questionnaires and exercises add a useful practical dimension (e.g. p.13-18); also "Getting in Touch with Your Body" (p.51 - extending to p.67)). One exercise dealing with orgasm-achievement has four levels of exercises (p.123-127).

b. Myths are often clarified and dispelled (e.g. "Trap 2: sex proves we love each other" (p.130); also "Men are not always more interested in sex than women, nor are they always ready for action..." (p.12)).

c. Thoughtful and incisive insights are given (e.g. "For every sexual problem, there are usually one or two people who have trouble communicating thoughts and feelings to each other" (p.23)). Advice is often extended (e.g. "Avoiding penis watching..." (p.109)) and catchy phrases are explained in logical, sensible terms (e.g. "Don't Let Your Penis Do the Talking..." (p.28)). Controversial topics are objectively treated (e.g. "There are no black-and-white answers here. Some couples get along very nicely with sexually open relationships... Other couples are happier agreeing not to share sex outside the relationship..." (p.151)). A page on "Sexual selfhood" (p.200) lists eight essential qualities.

d. The book is not morally judgmental or given to pejorativity and explains culturally denigrating expressions (e.g. "... stop calling it impotence, because that word magnifies the difficulty all out of proportion..." (p.89)).

e. The book can be recommended to clients of professionals, not only for their own problems, but also for its suggestions concerning parental sex education of children (p.191-192).

Deficiencies

a. The major flaw in the book is its almost complete lack of historical and cross-cultural background material. Such input would have greatly aided the reader in understanding and evaluating contemporary western sociosexual belief-systems with their attendant emotional biases. A total absence of photographs, charts, tables and graphs as well as cited references is a detraction.

b. Certain topics are inadequately covered (e.g. the section on venereal diseases mentions little about herpes 2 virus and ignores the fungal infection of trichomoniasis; also the section "Alcohol, drugs, and your sex life" (p.146) leaves out the negative effects on sexual performance of certain prescription drugs. Only the illicit drugs are described in this context.) Some subjects such as sadomasochism and transvestism are not mentioned at all.

24. Kinsey, A., Pomeroy, W. & Martin, C. Sexual Behavior in the Human Male. Philadelphia: W.B. Saunders Co., 1948. 819 pp.

Brief Summary - The authors in their Acknowledgments salute the 5,300 males who voluntarily contributed their sex histories to this study. Part I entitled "History and Method" deals with a historical background, developed interview techniques, statistical problems and the establishing of data validity. Nine chapters comprise Part II, "Factors Affecting Sexual Outlet." After detailing "Early Sexual

Growth and Activity," the comprehensive topic of "Total Sexual
Outlet" is explored. Eleven major factors determine "the frequency
and sources of human sexual outlet. They are sex, race, age, age at
onset of adolescence, marital status, educational level, the
subject's occupational class, rural-urban backgrounds, religious
affiliations, and the extent of the subject's devotion to religious
affairs" (p.218). Part III, "Sources of Sexual Outlet," offers
descriptive and numerical statistics on the outlets of masturbation,
nocturnal emissions, heterosexual petting, premarital intercourse,
marital intercourse, extramarital intercourse, intercourse with
prostitutes, homosexual outlet and animal contacts. In conclusion,
the authors decide "the scientific data which are accumulating make
it appear that, if circumstances had been propitious, most
individuals might have become conditioned in any direction, even
into activities which they now consider quite unacceptable" (p.678).

Critique - Strengths

a. Data in the forms of tables, graphs, diagrams, histograms and
   charts flesh out the written text. The final chapter lists
   Clinical Tables for professional use when one is desirous of
   comparing any patient with the norm established by this
   research. Additionally, an Appendix lists the proper
   statistical sample sizes for various sub-populations. A 22-page
   Bibliography terminates the book.
b. Later less extensive studies seem to corroborate this research.
   The research data are still worthy of close scrutiny.
c. The text is scientific, objective, and almost always free from
   subjective value-judgments (e.g. "such designations as ...
   over-sexed ... refer to nothing more than a position on a curve
   which is continuous. Normal and abnormal, one sometimes
   suspects, are terms which a particular author employs with
   reference to his own position on that curve" (p.199).
d. Innovative theoretical constructs are useful (e.g. "means
   measure average frequencies, medians describe the average
   individuals" (p.113); also the 0-6 Hetero-homosexual orientation
   scale combines an individual's overt plus psychic components
   (several references - see index)).
e. This book anticipates later discoveries (e.g. "the most common
   error ... is the assumption that stimulation of the interior of
   the vagina is necessary to bring maximum satisfaction to the
   female" (p.576)). New research questions are often posed (e.g.
   "It is evident that nocturnal dreams are not the product of
   education in itself ... is this a measure of some difference in
   the psychologic or physiologic capacities of the two groups?"
   (p.345)).
f. Incisive deductions are prevalent (e.g. "These data ... provide
   an important substantiation of the Freudian view of sexuality as
   a component that is present in the human animal from earliest
   infancy, although it gives no support to the Freudian concept of
   a pre-genital stage of generalized erotic response..." (p.180)).

Deficiencies

a. More visual aids in the forms of photographs and sketches would
   have helped. Cross-cultural background-material is inadequate;

the historical background is better, but also could have been
improved.

b. Although scrupulous precautions were implemented by the
researchers (such as effecting a 100% sub-sample in certain sets
of persons wherever possible), the sampling techniques were
still volunteer in nature. Furthermore, the study is weighted
into predictions being possible only for other essentially
white, under fifty years of age, eastern U.S. male groups.

c. The authors display bias toward the word 'promiscuous' (e.g. "a
girl who is merely promiscuous" (p.51) or "persons with more
promiscuous histories" (p.135)).

d. The study only minimally alludes to the sexual variations of
oral sex (fellatio and cunnilingus) in the section on
heterosexual petting (i.e. refer to Index). Likewise, group sex
is only peripherally mentioned (p.552).

25. Nowinski, Joseph. Becoming Satisfied: A Man's Guide to Sexual
Fulfillment. Englewood Cliffs: Prentice-Hall, Inc., 1980. 368 pp.

Brief Summary - Nowinski, a clinical psychologist and sex therapist,
opines in his Preface that "the goal of this book is to provide
tools and guidelines that men can use to help improve the quality of
their relationships, especially their sexual lives" (p.ix). The
11-chapter book sequentially discusses the following subjects:
"Reassessing Male and Female Sexuality" by understanding sociosexual
scripts and myths; "Self-Discovery" through knowledge of sexual
scripts and schemas plus developing one's male sensuality;
"Enhancing Your Sexual Relationship" through sexual communication,
an expanded sexual repertoire and using the correct sexual situation
through foresight; "Developing Your Sexuality Further" using the
tools of appearance, fantasy, shared expression and sex-histories;
"Learning to Relax" through exercises; "Overcoming Sexual Tension"
by choosing appropriate settings and times for relaxation, massage
and intimacy; "Overcoming Fears of Women" caused by shyness and
phobias; "Understanding Erection Problems," their causes and complications; "Dealing with Erection Problems" through desensitization
techniques; "Learning to Delay Orgasms" through planned programs;
and "Learning to Accelerate Orgasm" through effective programming.

Critique - Strengths

a. Anecdotal stories, references, quotations and a few charts
(e.g. "Sexual Dysfunction Process" (p.271) dot the text. A
Summary concludes each chapter. Many apt exercises (e.g.
"Exercise 7.6: Exploring Bodies..." (p.224)), questionnaires
(e.g. "Erection Dysfunction Questionnaire..." (p.236)) and
exercise charts (e.g. "Character Schema Chart" (p.55)) are
included.

b. Unrealistic and erroneous sociosexual assumptions are positively analyzed (e.g. 6 points - p.20). Sexual myths are
properly countered (e.g. "Sexual Myth 1: Simultaneous Orgasm
means True Love..." (p.26)).

c. Useful insights are proffered (e.g. "If you can learn one
sexual script, you can learn others" (p.4)). Constructive conclusions are given (e.g. "The idea that men are constantly
sexual implies that they are not sensitive, at least not

sexually sensitive" (p.7)). Good therapeutic suggestions (e.g.
"guided fantasy..." (p.209)) are offered and philosophically
logical statements (e.g. "premature ejaculation ... is not
something abnormal, but rather is a normal tendency that some
men would like to change" (p.307)) made. Controversial topics
are dispassionately examined (e.g. "For those people who are not
personally attracted to it, however, monogamy can have negative
effects on their sexuality. Today, there are more alternatives
available... Persons who are considering open marriage should
first think about whether they may want to open the marriage as
a way of saving it... This approach often backfires..."
(p.64-65)).

d. The book is non-judgmental, even by inference (e.g. "You may
    experience homosexual fantasies... Such reactions indicate that
    you are opening the doors of your sexuality ... not ... that you
    are losing all control over yourself" (p.111)).
e. The professional can learn some innovative techniques (e.g.
    refer to Summary above) and can also recommend the book to
    clients.

Deficiencies

a. No cited references, no visual aids and no bibliography for
    additional reading are found. The total lack of historical and
    cross-cultural background material useful in explaining and
    dealing with sexual contemporary mythologies is also a drawback.
b. Unreferenced statements at times detract from the book's use-
    fulness (e.g. "The experiences of sex therapy centers that have
    used paid 'surrogates' have not, by and large, been good..."
    (p.301)).
c. Certain relevant topics are not discussed (e.g. sexually trans-
    mitted diseases) while the atypical sexual variations are not
    examined at any depth in the contextually appropriate areas
    (e.g. homosexuality, consensual sadomasochism, transvestism).

26. Pietropinto, Anthony & Simenauer, Jacqueline. Beyond the Male
Myth. New York: New American Library, 1978. 479 pp.

Brief Summary - The authors, a physician and writer team, surveyed
4,066 men across the United States "encompassing all age groups,
geographical areas, and social strata" (p.2). As their Introduction
states, "We do not feel that sex can be separated from the concepts
of love, dependency, marriage, self-image, and life goals" (p.2).
The balance of this chapter lists the parameters of the study, its
questionnaire and the format utilized in obtaining the sample. The
next seven chapters state certain questions asked, give background
material about each issue and percentage statistics and respondent-
quotations about each particular question. Chapters 8 through 10
examine love and marriage factors. The following chapter termed
"The Other Woman" delves into extramarital feelings and behavior.
Question 39 asks "What would be most likely to tempt you to cheat?"
(p.314) and discovers that the highest percent of 26.7 listed "poor
sex at home" (p.314). The final chapter provides information on the
males' fantasies and dreams. The authors conclude that many men
dichotomize female images and symbols because "at the foot of the
cross ... we find a madonna and a prostitute" (p.367).

Critique - Strengths

a. A proliferation of literary and respondent quotations add
    authenticity to the text. In addition, historical (e.g. p.112),
    cross-cultural (e.g. p.129) and cross-species (e.g. p.110)
    background-related information is provided.
b. The survey is suitably large in sampling numbers, and achieves
    a pseudo-randomicity through utilizing Crossley Surveys Inc.
    Simple statistics are prevalent while forty detailed Tables
    summarize the research. An Appendix also provides the
    demographic breakdown data. Listing the actual questionnaire
    (p.10-15) is also done.
c. Incisive criticism of other experts is often forthcoming (e.g.
    "Dr. Theodore Rubin ... falls into a basic error when he
    says..." (p.50 - after analyzing respondent feedback); also
    "Hite's problem seems to be her sample..." (p.197)). Comparison
    of other research to this research is also often provided (e.g.
    Married-female orgasm-reported frequency - Kinsey, Hunt and this
    study - p.193).
d. Some useful findings are made (e.g. the reasons given for
    delaying male orgasm - p.176; also the educational class-
    breakdown of "Users of Cunniligus" (p.223) with this study's
    differences from the Kinsey and Hunt studies).

Deficiencies

a. No visual aids or graphs are utilized. The lack of cited
    references and a bibliography is a serious omission.
b. There are methodological shortcomings. The sample is volunteer
    in nature. The data are very simplistic in nature. Validity of
    the questions was extracted from a limited non-random female
    input and no reliability studies have been done. Probability
    statistics are totally ignored. Some biased phraseology in
    certain questions tends to invite answers the respondents feel
    they should give (e.g. "37. Have you ever cheated on your wife
    or steady girl friend?" (p.12)).
c. There are many unreferenced assumptions (e.g. " 'Bisexuals' are
    usually men who prefer homosexual relationships, but believe
    that heterosexuality is healthier..." (p.67)).
d. Pejorativity and judgmentality mar certain questions and
    phrases (e.g. "Do men feel the new woman is promiscuous?"
    (p.123); also "When S-M fantasies and bedroom games enter the
    darker areas of..." (p.352)).

27. Zilbergeld, Bernie. Male Sexuality. New York: Bantam Books,
1978. 424 pp.

Brief Summary - "A common myth in our culture deals with the
supposed sexual differences between men and women" (p.1). This
first sentence of the book sets up the route that Zilbergeld takes
in discussing male sexuality. The first five chapters differentiate
between the traditional cultural sexual expectations and aspirations
of men and women. The author especially details the implicit
fantasy model men have of sexual interaction. Chapter 3's "It's Two
Feet Long, Hard as Steel, and Can Go All Night: The Fantasy Model

of Sex" depicts present-day male sexual mythology. Beginning with Chapter 5, exercises are prescribed. After delineating "Your Conditions for Good Sex and How to Get Them," Chapters 7 through 13 educate the reader and clarify his sexual knowledge while deemphasizing the traditional mythology. Non-sexual partner-touching and individual self-relaxation methods are stressed. The content of Chapters 14 through 21 deals with correcting the mental attitudes that help cause and maintain sexual dysfunctions. Programs for reversing these malfunctions are advocated. Chapter 22 entitled "The Uses of Sex and Sex Problems" outlines the various wrong reasons why men often engage in sex. The concluding chapter states "You (as a male) will have to exercise your own judgment and be responsible for it" (p.384).

Critique - Strengths

a. Eleven pages of explanatory chapter-references conclude the text. Various explicit exercises (e.g. #15-5, p.275) graphs and diagrams augment the text. Apt quotations, anecdotal histories and catchy slogans proliferate (see Summary above). The author evinces a relaxed, positive style in discussing his subject. Easily-understood case studies are appropriately employed.
b. Useful criticisms of other sexologists are often offered (e.g. "Even Masters & Johnson show little understanding in their three books that real sex can be anything but intercourse" (p.50)).
c. Although the book is primarily written for laypersons, insights can also benefit the professional (e.g. In Chapter 22, Zilbergeld concludes that a sex problem can often hide a more serious difficulty).
d. Future research possibilities are inherently proposed (e.g. in discussing the Masters & Johnson 4-phase response cycle model, the author states "we strongly believe that future research in this area will confirm that there are many different ejaculatory patterns in men" (p.126)).

Deficiencies

a. More visual aids could have accompanied the text. There is a dearth of historical and cross-cultural background material.
b. Some errors of omission occur (e.g. in discussing penis sizes, nowhere does Zilbergeld note that although they vary greatly in the flaccid state, upon achieving erection they are generally much closer to a uniform size).
c. Bias and negative judgmentality surface on occasion (e.g. "S-M: The Last Taboo" (G & C Greene, 1974) is inaccurately interpreted as supporting "violence and brutality... Apparently the authors ... feel that there shouldn't be any prohibitions on behavior" (p.64); also "bizarre experimentation tends to cheapen almost everything... The bodies make contact but the people do not. There is little curiosity, warmth, caring, closeness, or feeling of any kind" (p.367-368)).

Philosophy and Sex

28. Ard, Ben N. Jr. Rational Sex Ethics. Washington: University
Press of America, 1978. 153 pp.

Brief Summary - The author, a psychotherapist, in his Preface states
"this book is offered as an introduction to rational or humanistic
sex ethics which are based on the latest scientific knowledge from
pertinent disciplines" (p.ix). A Forward is given by Dr. Albert
Ellis upon whose earlier work this philosophy is largely derived.
An opening chapter deals with backgrounds, both historical and
cross-cultural, which have caused our contemporary negatively biased
"Conventional Sex Morality." The subsequent chapter lays down the
author's "basic principles of rational sex ethics" (p.27) which are:
the legitimacy of sex; the right of sexual freedom; the equality of
all in sexual matters; the necessity of force or coercion being
absent from sexual activity; the consideration that the frequency
and character of sexual acts is a private matter of personal
hygiene; and no sexual act be banned unless its consequences are
harmful to another. The following chapters incorporate these
philosophical ethics as they apply to the areas of: children and
sex; adolescents and sex; premarital sex; birth control and
abortion; sex and marriage; divorce; sex and the unmarried adult;
sex and guilt; and the sexual behavior of variations such as
homosexuality, transvestism, fetishism, and transsexualism. A final
chapter termed "Science and Ethics" offers value analysis plus four
standards for effecting rational value judgments dealing with sexual
ethics.

Critique - Strengths

a. A host of apt quotations supports textual arguments and is in
   italics. References concerning citations end each chapter and
   an 8-page Bibliography closes out the text. Considerable
   historical (e.g. p.8-9) and cross-cultural (e.g. p.43-44)
   appropriate background material is presented.
b. Misconceptions are attacked (e.g. "The concept of ... 'latent
   homosexuality' ... has little scientific eveidence to support

it... The myth that every individual has both heterosexual and
homosexual traits dies very slowly..." (p.52)). Neofreudian
assumptions are challenged (e.g. Chapter 10 - "Sex and Guilt" -
p.93-99)).

c. Insights are usefully proffered (e.g. "Human beings are multi-
sexual or plurisexual animals" (p.52 - cited reference given)).
Recommendations are offered (e.g. "Anthropologists can
contribute to rational sex ethics by revealing ... how various
cultures have handled sex in a variety of settings" (p.62); also
concerning extramarital sex "... see what sort of an arrangement
one can work out in a sane, reasonable and realistic fashion"
(p.79)). Research is cited (e.g. concerning premarital sex
leading to later "adulterous affairs... Emperical research
evidence (Ard, 1974a) does not support such a point of view..."
(p.64)).

d. Pejorativity is denigrated (e.g. "... it is logically false to
say that a promiscuous person is necessarily indiscriminate..."
(p.65)). Emotional value-judgments are assailed (e.g. twenty
societally recognized rules for sexual conduct are critiqued -
p.5-7).

Deficiencies

a. No visual aids, charts, graphs or tables assist the text.
Cited research contains minimal statistical support.

b. Unreferenced and unwarranted conclusions are at times presented (e.g. "As a result of this overemphasis on preventing any
premarital sex ..., we get increasing homosexuality..." (p.56);
also "homosexuality cannot rationally be touted as simply an
acceptable variation of the norm, an alternative life-style
equal to heterosexuality" (p.105)). Atypical sexual variations
often produce the very value-judgments the author purports to
wish to avoid (e.g. "we can agree with Nagel that 'intercourse
with animals, infants, and inanimate objects seem to be stuck at
some primitive version of the first stage' " (p.107 - cited
reference given)). Other variations are not discussed (e.g.
consensual sadomasochism and pedophilia).

29. Baker, Robert & Elliston, Frederick, ed. Philosophy & Sex.
Buffalo: Prometheus Books, 1975. 407 pp.

Brief Summary - The editors in their Preface and Introduction wish
"to aid, abet, document and describe a background for the recent
philosophical interest in the subject" (p.ix) and begin by
presenting their historical sociosexual perspective. Five Parts
follow entitled "The Semantics of Sex" (four contributors), "Sex and
Morality" (three contributors), "The Morality of Marriage" (two
contributors under "The Tradition," three under "Monogamy" and two
under "Adultery and Promiscuity"), "The Logic of Deviation" (four
contributors), and "Feminism and Abortion" (four contributors).
Differing polarities around each position are examined, both
subjectively and objectively, by the varous philosophical scholars
who author their respective chapters.

Critique - Strengths

a. A 16-page Bibliography as well as Footnotes included after most
    essays are important additions. Historical-anthropological
    references are included (e.g. Verene - footnotes, p.114-115).
b. Careful interpretations of such word-concepts as "promiscuity"
    (e.g. Elliston, p.222) and "perversion" (e.g. Solomon, p.269) by
    many authors are of immense benefit toward an understanding of
    the stigmata placed on these words.
c. Many contributors offer insights not usually found in most
    textbooks on sexuality (e.g. "one welcomes a painful thrust or
    bite not because of masochism but because of the meaning, in
    context, that it conveys" (Solomon, p.281); also "as a language,
    sex has at least one possible perversion: the nonverbal
    equivalent of lying, or insincerity" (Solomon, p.286).
    Interpretive sexual ethics are well presented (e.g. "human
    sexual interaction is essentially manipulative - physically,
    psychologically, emotionally and even intellectually" (Baumrin,
    p.116)). Ideological comparisons and analogies are often
    skillfully portrayed (e.g. Lawrence's "Four-Letter Words Can
    Hurt You" incisively compares ethnic pejoratives (deplored by
    liberals) to sexual pejoratives (often less questioned by the
    same persons)).
d. Positive suggestions are sometimes offered (e.g. "there is a
    big difference between pointing out a conceptual confusion and
    its remedy and actually changing the behavior that the confusion
    helps maintain. To do the latter it is necessary to change the
    concept of the standard sexual activity to one that involves the
    arousal and satisfaction of all participants" (Moulton, p.42)).

Deficiencies

a. No visual aids, charts or graphs complement the text. No index
    is included.
b. The text is occasionally indecisive (e.g. "it is difficult to
    know what to say about this objection because it is difficult to
    know what to say about the case of..." (Brody, p.343); also "I
    am not a fervent abortionist nor a fervent antiabortionist..."
    (Hare, p.361)).
c. Judgmental bias is textually present in a few places (e.g.
    "promiscuity might undercut the tendency of complete sex acts to
    promote emotions that magnify their object" (Ruddick, p.102)).
    Subjective absolutism is displayed in the treatise on "Male
    Chauvinism" (e.g. "It should be noted that such theories are
    sexist only if they are false..." (Frye, p.79)).

30. Brain, James Lewton. The Last Taboo: Sex and the Fear of Death.
New York: Anchor Press/Doubleday, 1979. 262 pp.

Brief Summary - The author, an anthropologist, in fifteen chapters
develops his thesis that humans subconsciously equate sex with
incest and ultimately death. Various examples of fact are cited
such as the cultural influence of speech through "liminal" (p.7)
categorization (i.e. "things, places, persons, words that don't fit"
(p.7). Numerous anthropological examples are also offered to
support the position that we equate sex with dirt because "humans

standing erect must cleanse themselves... They have to be taught to
do these things. There is little doubt that this is where humans
universally acquire the idea that sex is 'dirty' " (p.58).
Furthermore the human fear of sex and death is interrelated because
"we find sex threatening because it reminds us of defecation, which
reminds us of decomposition and death" (p.87). The author states
"if I am correct and we make an unconscious equation between sex and
death, then avoidance of sex equals a conquest of death - precisely
what is claimed as the reward for nuns and priests. As St. Paul
puts it (Romans 8:6), 'For to be carnally minded is death; but to be
spiritually minded is life and peace' " (p.170). Other theories are
advanced. For example "in the West, millenia of misplaced medical
practice in the custom of phlebotomy, leeching, and cupping was
almost certainly based on the wholly mistaken idea that the physical
reason for menstruation was to rid the body of impurities" (p.153).
The final chapter concludes that liminal constructs, male initiation
rites, male womb envy, cultural authoritarianism, incest taboos,
ritual pollution-avoidance, stereotyped sex roles and the equating
of witches as females all superimposed on our various cultures the
obsession equaling the fear of death with sexual interaction.

Critique - Strengths

a. Well-constructed theories (see Summary) allow the reader to
    continually challenge her/his belief-systems. From this per-
    spective, the book has merit in its innovate conceptualizations.
b. Referenced notes on each chapter appear at the end of the book.
    Appropriate quotations are utilized.
c. Numerous examples illustrate the textual points. Especially
    comprehensive are the anthropological examples (e.g. the sex
    initiation rites of the East African Luguru - p.146-147).
    Useful historical references are also given (e.g. refer to
    Summary).

Deficiencies

a. No visual aids assist the text. At times the author wanders
    from his topic. For instance, the chapter entitled "Witches and
    Mothers" adds little to his arguments.
b. Brain introduces some concepts of dubious value. (e.g.
    "Oedipal conflict" (p.125)).
c. Pejorativity creeps into the text occasionally (e.g. "extreme
    promiscuity" (p.32)). A few unwarranted value-judgments take
    place (e.g. "the really awful aspects of the 'sexual revolution'
    - the mass of pornography encouraging child abuse, rape, and
    other forms of sexual violence" (p.29)).

31. Calderone, Mary S. ed. Sexuality and Human Values. New York:
Association Press, 1974. 158 pp.

    Brief Summary - In her Introduction, the editor explains that this
    book is an outgrowth of a 1971 Siecus Conference on Religion and
    Sexuality and which brought together "primary researchers in the
    fields of sexuality and of values" (p.7). Eleven contributors offer
    essays in six segmented sections of the text. The first section
    termed "Gender Identification" consists of material on the possible

antecedents of "Heterosexuality" (Broderick) and "Homosexuality" (Marmor). Pomeroy next discusses some salient points in "The Sex Interview in Counseling" in the section "Talking about Sex." "Sexual Knowledge, Attitudes and Values in Three Subcultures" consists of "Adolescence" (Broderick), "Black Sexuality" (Staples) and "The College Subculture" (L. and P. Sarrel). Masters & Johnson dictate "The Role of Religion in Sexual Dysfunction" in a section called "Sexual Responsiveness." The final Conference topics under "Moral Reasoning and Value Formation" are entitled "Sexual Dilemmas at the High-School Level" (Gilligan) and "Moral Stages and Sex Education" (Kohlberg). In the final section, "Evaluation and Prospect," some prominent theologians dialogue with the Editor. Rev. John Thomas decides that new societal forces such as a longer life-expectancy and educational time-span require "the arduous task of clarifying our conceptions of human sexuality, of reappraising our cherish sexual values ... and of devising feasible social structures for implementing these..." (p.151).

Critique - Strengths

a. Some contributors utilize footnotes and cited references. Two pages termed "For Further Reading" at the book's end comprise a limited bibliography. An Appendix detailing a 1968 Interfaith Statement on Sex Education is of peripheral value. A few case studies appear (e.g. p.91).
b. Occasionally, myths are exposed (e.g. "There is the image of the black male as being sexually superior..." (Staples, p.68)) and insights proffered (e.g. "... and so everyone is always protecting the next younger age group (Broderick, p.52); also "there really is nothing in the act of sex, per se, which is right or wrong" (Kohlberg, p.121)).
c. Thomas in the final chapter gives a thoughtful and incisive discourse on some contemporary issues (i.e. refer to Summary above).

Deficiencies

a. Visual aids, charts and graphs are lacking. Research alluded to is descriptive without tables and statistics. Some cited research has since been disproven or uncorroborated (e.g. Kolodny, Masters et al. (1972) and Dorner (1967) - by Marmor, p.28).
b. Although Staples gives some descriptive cross-cultural and historical material, the book on a whole is lacking such background information.
c. Kohlberg's contribution never gets down to sexual specifics.
d. Value-judgments sometimes occur (e.g. "It should teach that sexual intercourse within marriage offers the greatest possibility for personal fulfillment and social growth" (Appendix - p.156).
e. A few meaningless phrases (e.g. "hedonistic relativism" (Gilligan, p.107)) and pejorative statements cloud the text (e.g. "homosexuals tend to be more promiscuous than heterosexuals" (Marmor, p.31)).

32. Foucault, Michel. (Robert Hurley, translator). The History of
Sexuality - Volume 1: An Introduction. New York: Vintage Books,
Random House, 1980, 173 pp.

Brief Summary - In five Parts, the author philosophically develops
the causal factors historically influencing societal sexuality.
From these precursors, he structures his theoretical model
applicable during the past 380 years. This causality, Foucault
feels, has been an amalgam resulting from a major religious-
economic-political influx of sub-components tied into the
individual-collective social psyches of Western European power-
manifestations. In Part I, "We 'Other Victorians'," he sets up his
debate. Is the answer to be one of cyclic or linear sexual
repression? Or is it to be found in "the regime of power-knowledge-
pleasure that sustains the discourse on human sexuality in our part
of the world"? (p.11). Foucault endorses the latter theory. In
Part II, "The Repressive Hypothesis" is compared in depth to his new
preferential alternative. Especially over the past 200 years,
rather than a repression of enunciation of sex, "a discursive
ferment that gathered momentum" (p.18) has ensued. "One had to
speak of sex... Sex was not something one simply judged; it was a
thing administered" (p.23-24), studied, policed. Thus any attempt
to quantify repression in history is unimportant and useless.
Termed "Scienta Sexualis," Part III adduces that knowledge of sex
has been an " 'interplay of truth and sex' " (p.57), "even if this
truth was to be masked at the last moment" (p.56). The medicine of
sex, rooted in the confessional box, has not kept pace with advances
in "scientific normativity" (p.54). Thus Foucault rejects "the
hypothesis of a power of repression exerted by our society for
economic reasons" (p.72). Part IV is entitled "The Deployment of
Sexuality" and analyzes the arena of sociosexual power causality.
"Four great strategic unities ... beginning in the 18th century,
formed specific mechanisms of knowledge and power centering on
sex... (1) A hysterization of women's bodies... (2) A
pedagogization of children's sex... (3) A socialization of
procreative behavior... (4) A psychiatrization of perverse
pleasure" (p.103-105). Part V, "Right of Death and Power Over Life"
is a discussion of these three dynamics. The author concludes "it
is the agency of sex that we must break away from... The rallying
point ... ought not to be sex-desire, but bodies and pleasure"
(p.157).

Critique - Strengths

a. The book is compelling in its logic of presentation, and in its
    innovative creativity. Hypotheses and historical facts are
    offered in a specific manner and lead inexorably to his overview
    theory (refer to Summary above). The arguments are
    thought-provoking and worthy of study by any scholar.
b. Rich, selective language, effective catchy phrases and novel
    imagery of ideas are not lost in translation (e.g. "A great
    sexual sermon ... has swept through our societies" (p.7); also
    "... a kind of interior androgyny, a hermaphrodism of the soul"
    (p.43)).
c. Subjective, negative and specific moralizations are never
    utilized.

d. Some footnotes and cited references are given as aids to the scholar.

Deficiencies

a. Except for an imaginative cover, no visual aids are included. Also, surprisingly, no bibliography is provided.
b. By definition, the book is intended as an opening volume of several by the author on the subject. As such, it is slim in source-material required to support in-depth arguments.
c. Part V is the weakest section and at times wanders off the main track of its subject into brief, unproductive by-paths of comment and speculation.

33. Gordon, Sol & Libby, Roger W. ed. Sexuality Today and Tomorrow. Belmont: Duxbury Press, 1976. 447 pp.

Brief Summary - The Editors Preface their selective offerings from forty-one contributors in thirty-seven Chapters and five Parts by stating "the purpose of this book is to acquaint readers with the major social, political and personal issues related to sexuality and sex roles" (p.ix). Part I's "The Visibility of Changing Sex Roles and Sexual Behavior" speak to the issues of "masculinity and femininity, the women's liberation movement, and changing male roles, and the political implications of shifting sex roles and more liberal sexual attitudes and behavior" (p.xi). Part II, "The Politics of Socio-Sexual Issues," concerns itself with the political legal-moral aspects of abortion, rape, prostitution, obscenity, sexually transmitted diseases as well as the various major religious groups' view about sexuality and its management. Part III deals with "Variations in Sexual Expression." Social scripting as it influences adolescent behavior, cohabitation, open relationships, masturbation, gay lifestyles, transsexualism, "Sexual Adventuring and Personality Growth" (A. Ellis) and orgasmic fulfillment is explored. Part IV's "Social Ethics and Personal Morals" discusses the societal impact stemming from humanistic and female-liberation influence. The topics of sex education, the medical-model approach to sex and the sexist double-standard about aging are likewise covered. The final Part V, "The Future of Sexuality," is devoted to present-day trends and possible future scenarios of sociosexuality.

Critique - Strengths

a. Many contributors utilize footnotes, cited references and quotations while a few use graphs and charts to bolster their arguments. A 3-page Selected Bibliography terminates the text. Each Part has at least one apt article called "Signs of Our Times." A short preamble by the Editors precedes each Part. Many chapters are original with this book (e.g. #'s 1, 10).
b. Rhetorical questions pose interesting philosophical points (e.g. "Does society care that homosexuals, nonmonogamous hetero-sexuals, and other so-called deviants are socially, politically, and economically coerced in ways that endanger their very livelihood and happiness?" (p.x)).
c. Thought-evoking statements often occur (e.g. "The trivializa-tion of woman's sexuality is reflected in the not uncommon male

response to woman's serious demands: 'All she needs...' "
(Coyner - p.61)).
d. Demythologizing research with philosophical implications is
    cited (e.g. "Women taught that they shouldn't react to erotica
    apparently have difficulty in recognizing their own reactions or
    admitting them. In fact, women react as strongly to erotica as
    men do" (Coyner - p.69 - reference cited)). Also the sacred
    myths of the physician are well covered in Chapter 30's "The
    High Cost of M. Deity's Prudery" (Myers).
e. The text is essentially non-pejorative.

Deficiencies

a. No photographs or sketches complement the text. Many articles
    are written in a popularized reworking of subject and have been
    extracted from mass magazines (e.g. "Psychological Frontiers for
    Men" (Pleck); also "Bisexuality What's It All About?" (Mead)).
    No index is included. Insufficient historical and cross-
    cultural input is provided (i.e. only in Chapter 2 (Bernard)).
b. In their selection of topics, the editors show an ambivalence
    as to what to emphasize (e.g. "We present a range of ideas
    related to lifestyles and value systems that can be used by
    people who wish to explore important areas of communication and
    behavior" (p.x)). The result is confusion with most topics
    one-sidedly being offered in a single brief chapter. Effective
    contrasting philosophical viewpoints are insufficiently
    discussed.

34. Kirkendall, Lester A. & Whitehurst, Robert N. ed. The New Sexual
Revolution. New York: Donald W. Brown Inc., 1971. 251 pp.

Brief Summary - In a Preface, Kurtz explains the rationale for this
collection of essays in book form; namely to explore "the
possibility of both sexual freedom and sexual responsibility for
contemporary man" (p.xi). Whitehurst in an Introduction
acknowledges that "man is now emerging into a new age" (p.xiii) and
the book is therefore "an effort to place sex in the context of the
total gestalt of man in his total lifespan" (p.xiv). Sixteen
articles by eighteen contributors are included in seven book parts.
These are titled respectively: "Background," "Sex and Morality,"
"Understand Human Sexuality," "Cultural Influences," "The Marital
Ideal," "Sex Education," and "Putting the Lid on Population Growth."
Kirkendall in an Epilogue comments on the ongoing struggle by our
culture to come to grips in a sensible humanistic way with these
sexual issues.

Critique - Strengths

a. A 5-page Bibliography, footnoted references and quotations
    assist the text. Historical (e.g. "American Sexophobia"
    (Whitehurst)) and cross-cultural (e.g. "Cross-Cultural Sexual
    Practices" (Seal)) information is included.
b. In general the articles are thoughtful, positive contributions
    to the subject by eminent social scientiests. Interesting
    philosophical issues are competently examined from many
    perspectives (e.g. Sagarin's article "On Obscenity and

Pornography" (p.105)).

Deficiencies

a. No visual aids or index are included.
b. Occasionally a concept is judgmentally expressed (e.g. "the
    child should not be left at the mercy of what he can glean from
    the world about him: a world saturated with pornography,
    obscenity, sadomasochism, and the empty, false, romantic glamour
    versions of sex" (Stokes, p.80-81)).
c. Sometimes assumptions are presented as facts (e.g. "sexual
    expression should be proportional to the depth of a
    relationship" (R. & D. Roy, p.143)).
d. The worst article is Salzman's "Sex Research." He claims about
    Kinsey's work that "some of the unfortunate myths about female
    orgasms, masturbation, homosexuality, and female sexuality
    tended to be perpetuated" (p.67). Such a statement is based on
    interpretations which satisfy his psychoanalytic model.
    Conversely, Salzman praises the Masters & Johnson research
    without critically analyzing their research-design assumptions.
    Finally his concept of "promiscuity in girls" (p.71) is
    contextually pejorative.

35. Masters, William, Johnson, Virginia & Kolodny, Robert ed. Ethical
Issues in Sex Therapy and Research. Boston: Little Brown & Co., 1977.
249 pp.

Brief Summary - Seven chapters explore various dimensions of the
problems as follows: "The Historical Background of Ethical
Considerations in Sex Research and Sex Therapy," "Theological
Perspectives on the Ethics of Scientific Investigation and Treatment
of Human Sexuality," "Ethical Requirements for Sex Research in
Humans: Informed Consent and General Principles," "Ethical
Requirements ... Confidentiality," "Issues and Attitudes in Research
and Treatment of Variant Forms of Human Sexual Behavior," "The
Ethics of Sex Therapy," "Training of Sex Therapists." A final
chapter finds Dr. William Masters summarizing the presentations and
briefly dealing with "Future Considerations."

Critique - Strengths

a. Cited references and quotations are amply provided. Historical
    input is included (e.g. Mudd, chapter 1). After each lecture, a
    "Designated Discussion" sets a guideline for the "General
    Discussion" which follows. In this way, healthy verbal
    exchanges ensue with disagreements and differences of
    perspective serving to clarify issues for the reader.
b. Subject-content is usually well-explored (e.g. "Ethical
    Requirements for Sex Research in Humans" (Kolodny, p.52)).
c. Perceptive insights often surface (e.g. "If any lesson can be
    learned from the reception of the Kinsey materials, it would
    seem to be: Take care about the content in which findings are
    presented" (Hiltner, p.28); also "I am impressed that current
    methodologies for maintaining confidentiality of collected data
    are far more sophisticated than methodologies for collecting the
    data" (Green, p.106)).

d. The panelists come from a varied and well-credentialed back-
    ground of medicine, social science, religion and the law and as
    such, impart a multi-disciplinary tone to the conference.

Deficiencies

a. No visual aids and minimal cross-cultural background material
    are included.
b. The conference is biased in content-structure and has guide-
    lines which reflect editorial priorities and perspectives.
    Ethical criticism of the host Foundation is circumspect in tone.
    Therefore complete objectivity is not always forthcoming (e.g.
    concerning the since-disbanded surrogate program, "the intent
    was admirable, but I gather from verbal reports ... that the
    attendant problems have been considerable" (Redlich, p.154)).
c. Patronizing assumptions at times occur (e.g. "the homosexual as
    a suffering fellow human being, deserves compassion and under-
    standing" (Gordis, p.37-38)).

36. Millett, Kate. _Sexual Politics_. New York: Avon Books, 1969. 405
pp.

Brief Summary - There are three Parts to this book; "Sexual
Politics," "Historical Background," and "The Literary Reflection."
In her Preface, Millett remarks that "the first part of this essay
is devoted to the proposition that sex has a frequently neglected
political aspect" (p.xi). Exploitive patriarchy throughout the
millenia has evoked male power-control over women through (1)
ideology ("through pervasive assent" (p.26)), (2) biology, (3)
sociology (the male-dominated family), (4) class ("the caste of
virility" (p.36)), (5) economics and education, (6) force
(intimidation and legal codes), (7) anthropological input (myth as
well as religion), (8) and psychology ("the interiorization of
patriarchal ideology" (p.54)). Part II portrays a first-phase
1830-1930 sexual revolution in its progression of political,
polemical, and literary contributions. The second phase constructs
a 1930-1960 conservative backlash which stultified and even negated
earlier sociosexual female gains. Freud was "beyond question the
strongest individual counterrevolutionary force..." (p.178). Part
III dissects the works of D.H. Lawrence, Henry Miller, Norman Mailer
and Jean Genet in the context of sexual politics. Only Genet
attracts Millett's admiration since "he appears to be the only
living male writer of first-class literary gifts to have transcended
the sexual myths of our era" (p.22).

Critique - Strengths

a. Copious footnotes and appropriate quotations abound in the
    text. A 13-page Bibliography also aids the serious scholar.
    The historical section is well presented and cross-cultural
    references are included (e.g. p.223).
b. Insightful analyses furnish pervasive arguments (e.g. In Nazi
    Germany, "the mystical idealization of chaste motherhood
    (became) ... a particularly efficient means ... of utterly
    equating sexuality with procreation ... and converting it into a
    state-directed process of human reproduction for what were often

lethal state ends" (p.164)).

c. Catchy phrases sometimes stand out (e.g. "revolution is always heresy, perhaps sexual revolution most of all" (p.127); also "a vaginal trap" (p.132, 148); also "imperious clitoral command" (p.153)).

d. The core of the book and its best chapter is the second one entitled "The Theory of Sexual Politics" (refer to Summary above).

e. Table 1 (p.230) termed "Traits Assignable to Male (Instrumental) or Female (Expressive) Roles" is an excellent reinforcement for the author's argument of how social scientists often show subjective bias in assuming inherency of traits.

Deficiencies

a. A lack of visual aids and graphs plus a paucity of charts detracts from the book's effectiveness.

b. Unsubstantiated axioms are unwarranted and may not always be appropriate (e.g. "Prostitution, when unmotivated by economic need, might well be defined as a species of psychological addiction, built on self-hatred through repetitions of the act of sale by which a whore is defined" (p.123)).

c. Unspecified judgmentality occasionally occurs (e.g. "sexually perverse" (p.129); also "unfortunate sexual peculiarities" (p.151)).

37. Petras, John W. The Social Meaning of Human Sexuality (2nd Ed.). Boston: Allyn and Bacon Inc., 1978. 250 pp.

Brief Summary - The author asserts in his Preface "this book concerns sexuality - not sex - in society" (p.xi). After his initial chapter interweaves the personal, social, and interaction perspectives, Petras expands this theme in Chapter 2 by historically recounting "the sexualization of society" (p.27) in our contemporary times from inputs by Freud, Havelock Ellis, and Krafft-Ebing. Chapter 3 is termed "Sexuality and Ideology: From Sacred to Scientific, to Secular," and traces this evolutionary path. "Sex and Gender" plus the "Ideological Bases for Sexual Images" comprise Chapter 4. Petras decides "gender refers to the clusters of socially learned behaviors that provide meaning for the sexual" (p.97). Chapter 5's "Sexuality and Interpersonal Relationships" proceeds from infancy to adolescence to adulthood to old age. Chapter 6 in "Unapproved Sexuality and Society" shows how changes have affected the societal views on masturbation, noncoital relations, homosexuality, rape, and sex crimes with children. Indeed "interpersonally, affection, consent, and individual rights have emerged as the new indicators of appropriateness in a mass depersonalized society" (p.203). The final Chapter 7 entitled "The Sexual Revolution" asks if such an event has actually taken place. The author decides if so, "it is part of a larger revolution" (p.218).

Critique - Strengths

a. Copious referenced notes, appropriate quotations, graphs and compared-research data (e.g. Kinsey and Hunt on oral-genital

foreplay - p.185) are scattered throughout the text. "Notes"
and a "Selected Bibliography" conclude each chapter.
b. Good historical overviews are offered (e.g. refer to Summary
above).
c. Myths are frequently dispelled (e.g. "Myth 4: A person is
either a homosexual or a heterosexual because these are separate
categories..." (p.192)).
d. The text is basically non-judgmental (e.g. For so-termed
"sexual abnormalities and perversions ... or sexual deviance
..., rather than refer to such behavior in pejorative terms, I
have chosen the term <u>unapproved sexuality</u>" (p.173)).
e. The material is scholarly presented and dispassionate in tone
(e.g. "Gender roles ... can be defined as polar opposites <u>only</u>
<u>by accident of their historical definitions</u>" (p.115).
Philosophical insights are often presented (e.g. "If ...
extramarital sexuality is not defined as disruptive to marriage
by the participants, then it will not be destructive" (p.161)).
Research is often dissected as to its value, implication, and
soundness (e.g. "Some of the oldest forms of stereotypic
thinking have become institutionalized in scientific studies on
sexuality" (p.101 with many cited references following).
f. A good critique of biased positions is often available (e.g.
concerning David Reuben on homosexuality - p.40); also the
dichotomous current sexual-position dilemma of the Roman
Catholic Church - p.71).

<u>Deficiencies</u>

a. No photographs or sketches are included. Cross-cultural data
are minimal.
b. The writing, while often brilliant in ideological construction,
is abstract and lacks vigor. Furthermore, in Chapter 6, more
controversial examples of societally unapproved sexuality might
have been chosen (e.g. consensual sadomasochistic play). Also,
some topics are scarcely mentioned (e.g. transvestism is only
briefly named on p.96).

38. Szasz, Thomas. <u>Sex by Prescription</u>. New York: Anchor
Press/Doubleday, 1980. 214 pp.

<u>Brief Summary</u> - The author, a psychiatrist, in his Preface comments
that a "reversal of values as blind as it is stubborn, epitomizes
the basic change in the Western perspective on sex - from the days
of the Church Fathers to those of the sex therapists" (p.xi).
Indeed he feels " 'scientific' sexology is a veritable Trojan horse:
appearing to be modernity's gift to mankind in its struggle for
freedom and dignity, it is in fact, just another strategy for its
pacification and enslavement" (p.xvi). Two sections termed "Sexual
Medicine" and "Sex Education" are employed to attack the
past-negative and present-positive recommendations that the
religious-legal-medical-establishments have used. Szasz draws a
parallel between food and sex. Food we casually accept but we label
sex acts by cataloguing these sexual patterns we see. So-called
sexual dysfunctions are not "ipso facto medical diseases or
problems" (p.7) and "cannot be diagnosed objectively" (p.13).
Modern-day sex therapy and education are subjectively beneficial to

their practitioners. Cultivated sex attitudes, whether supportive
or denunciatory, always serve the concerned state-government in the
way that it wishes. Labelling succeeds in achieving a popular
belief-system. The analogy of prostitutes to sex surrogates with
sex therapists acting as panderers in place of the formers' pimps
(p.49) is one example upon which Szasz elucidates. A closing
chapter proposes that "individuals (be) free to choose the source of
their sexual enlightenment and 'training' " (p.163).

Critique - Strengths

a. Footnotes, references and apt quotations are included.
b. Szasz is good at picking out the weaknesses of both the sex-
    negative and the sex-positive attitudinal approaches to sexual
    counseling and therapy. Using historical and cross-cultural
    arguments, he cleverly attacks the religious model (e.g. Luther
    - p.108); the medical model (e.g. Masters & Johnson - p.27); and
    the educational model (e.g. Siecus - P.117).
c. The cynical nihilistic approach on the subject of merchan-
    dising sexual cultural belief-systems is thought-evoking and
    stimulating. His generalized hypotheses are sometimes useful
    (e.g. "in general, our position ... will depend on whether we
    favor an authoritarian/paternalistic type of society or a
    libertarian/individualistic one" (p.94)).

Deficiencies

a. No visual aids or generalized bibliography are present.
b. The author often jumps to conclusions after starting from
    illogical analogies and untenable axiomatic postulates (e.g. he
    assumes that today's sexologists are basically medical in
    training and always utilize the medical model. The cross-
    disciplinarian as sexologist is not acknowledged. The statement
    "when people want to enjoy ... masturbation ... they turn to
    doctors" (p.xiv) is only partially correct). He compares
    behavior that is destructive to that which is constructive (e.g.
    "if what the new sex therapists teach is self-pleasuring, why
    don't they teach people how to drink and smoke and take drugs?"
    (p.68). He condemns Siecus for supporting masturbation as
    natural behavior when "... theft and murder are all natural.
    Does that make them desirable or therapeutic?" (p.68)). Szasz
    pronounces generalizations which by inference he extrapolates to
    anyone he can (e.g. concerning psychiatrists' involvement
    sexually with patients, he asserts "this is intellectual
    bankruptcy compounded by moral paralysis" (p.150) in a way that
    seems to label all psychiatrists).
c. Positive cultural remedial suggestions are couched in generali-
    zations and are not specific (refer to the end of the Summary
    above).
d. Unreferenced and subjectively biased judgmentality occurs (e.g.
    "the methods include procedures intended to 'shock' and
    'reprogram' the students..." (p.129))

39. Vannoy, Russell. Sex Without Love: A Philosophical Exploration.
Buffalo: Prometheus Books, 1980. 234 pp.

 Brief Summary- Vannoy in two Parts reveals his "The Philosophy of
Sex" and "The Philosophy of Love." Such chapters as "Sex With Love
vs. Sex Without Love," "Sexual Perversion - Is There Such a Thing?"
and "What is 'Good Sex'?" highlight Part I. Two major chapters in
Part II are entitled "Erotic Love - Is It a Viable Concept?" and
"Can One Define 'Love'?" In it Vannoy compares such philosophers of
love as Irving Singer, Schopenhauer, Freud and Sartre. The final
chapter termed "Erotic Love: A Final Appraisal" summarizes Part II.
Vannoy's final comment becomes "I now leave it to the reader to
judge if I have proved the central thesis about the superiority of
sex with a humanistic non-lover" (p.219).

Critique - Strengths

a. Extensive references (e.g. historical and cross-cultural -
    refer to Summary) and copious appropriate quotations are
    presented in the text. A 4-page "Suggestions for Further
    Reading" closes the book.
b. All sides, arguments and counter-arguments are assiduously
    examined in a dispassionate manner (e.g. "In summary, it seems
    clear that many of the traditional arguments against rape are
    not going to prove that rape is evil in all cases. Yet this
    goes against all our intuitions that rape is an absolute
    evil..." (p.56)).
c. Clear conceptualizations proliferate (e.g. "... human dignity
    is not a theoretical concept for which one can offer a
    philosophical proof. It is, rather, a practical concept in
    which we must all believe not only for our own self-preservation
    but also for our sense of self-worth as free beings" (p.60)).
d. Personal opinions are qualified and appropriate disclaimers are
    noted (e.g. "My own view, then, is that the liberal position is
    the best of the three, although I leave it to the reader to
    decide for himself whether I have proved my case or whether I
    have merely revealed my own life-style" (p.127)).

Deficiencies

a. No visual aids are included.
b. In the section "Sex and Privacy," Vannoy's abstract rationale
    should have included referenced feedback from experiential
    experts (e.g. "In summary..." (p.111). Here the author fails to
    distinguish between public sex, and group sex in private or in a
    consensually public area.
c. A lapse of logic occurs in which Vannoy presupposes all
    sadistic acts including consensual ones with a masochist are
    inappropriate (i.e. "Even the sadist believes he has some kind
    of human dignity and rights to protection derived therefrom;
    otherwise he would be unable to survive and engage in his
    criminal deeds" (p.60)). Also in his critique of the
    instrumentalist reasons for sex, Vannoy gives a poor analogy
    (i.e. "sex (can be) used like a tranquilizer pill to relieve
    tensions and frustrations, including sexual ones. Such persons
    rush to the orgasm the way one rushes to the toilet for a bowel
    movement" (p.97)).
d. Subjective judgmentality is sometimes displayed (e.g. "a
    promiscuous person ... is more likely an overindulgent eater

than a sinner, and he might be encouraged to go on a sexual diet
out of a simple self-interest" (p.102)).

40. Wilson, John. Love, Sex, & Feminism: A Philosophical Essay. New
York: Praeger Publishers, 1980. 132 pp.

Brief Summary - Part I termed "Sexuality and Eroticism" analyzes the
arguments surrounding "Sex, Perversion, and Morality"; "Love" which
he sees as "a pathos and not a praxis, something one finds oneself
feeling rather than deciding to do" (p.18); "Love-Objects and the
Body"; sexual "Aggression" with its components of forcefulness,
hostility, and power; "Integrity" with its personal "self-images"
(p.45); and "Obscenity and Pornography" where "we want, if we are
interested in purity, to get the person to make a marriage between
his enjoyment ... and the truly good" (p.55). Part II entitled
"Feminism and Sexual Politics" discusses the liberal-conservative
arguments of "Sexual Insults" through language, male-female sex
roles and "Sex Differences," the "Equality, Wants, and Interests"
dichotomozing males and women (especially between feminists and
non-feminists of both sexes), "Power, Influence and Justice" issues,
constructive and destructive "Feminist Strategies," and the topic of
"Abortion" in which Wilson decides "that embryos should be regarded
as a kind of property" (p.117). A Postscript is called "Sex and
Education." "Only an effective tradition within the school can
overcome these difficulties" (p.124).

Critique - Strengths

a. Footnoted references, apt quotations and some cross-cultural
    with historical background are provided (e.g. p.53). Italics
    emphasize key phrases.
b. Wilson provides criticism of contrasting viewpoints (e.g. of
    the feminist Frye - p.80).
c. Concepts are logically demonstrated (e.g. "we tend to imagine
    either that sexual matters can be dealt with by some general
    moral theory ... or that they are beyond the scope of reason and
    morality" (p.14)). Belief-systems are challenged (e.g. "sexual
    activity is not an activity with standards or rules, and sex has
    no proper or 'given' object" (p.11)).

Deficiencies

a. No visual aids, charts or graphs complement the text. The lack
    of a comprehensive bibliography and index is a drawback.
b. Pejorative overtones occur on occasion (e.g. "Promiscuity ...
    is like having many friends but no close friends" (p.30); also
    "... what we might call 'trashy' literature" (p.55)).
    Value-judgments cloud the text (e.g. "We need to prevent
    (censor) such things only where it can be shown..." (p.54)).

Physiology and Sex

41. Barlow, David. <u>Sexually Transmitted Diseases: The Facts</u>. Oxford: Oxford University Press, 1979. 144 pp.

> <u>Brief Summary</u> - The author, a physician specializing in genito-urinary medicine, in his Introduction warns that "many more infections can be considered as sexually transmitted than was the case even fifteen or twenty years ago" (p.2). Twelve chapters discuss the following topics: male-female sexual anatomy and its functioning; some historical and cross-cultural considerations and background; contemporary world-wide descriptive comparisons on various governmental approaches to these diseases; gonorrhoea; non-specific genital infection including causation, complications and treatment; infections causing vaginal discharge, these being candida albicans, trichomonas vaginalis, foreign-body causes, and types of cystitis; virus infections of herpes simplex, molluscum contagiosum, hepatitis, genital warts, and cytomegalovirus; syphilis in its various manifestations; the infestations of phthirus pubis, sarcoptes scabiei; the tropical diseases of chancroid, lymphogranuloma venereum, granuloma inguinale, and the various tropical treponematoses related to syphilis; the procedural and logistical information required to set up and maintain a clinic devoted to these diseases; and a final chapter termed "Control" which analyzes social and educational factors, plus high-risk groups and gives the roles which health treatment must play in the future.

<u>Critique - Strengths</u>

a. An 8-page Glossary of appropriate technical terms plus a list of British clinics along with their addresses and telephone numbers are of value. Excellent photographs including definitive color plates, plus anatomical sketches, myth-disproving cartoons, and balanced case studies are of immense value. Treatment modes are effectively covered. Chapters 2 and 3 furnish an excellent historical and cross-cultural resume (i.e. refer to Summary above).

b. Good definitional statements are given (e.g. "<u>Pathogenicity</u> is

the capacity of certain organisms to produce disease" (p.53)).
The final chapter is very useful with its recommendations (e.g.
"... it is better to concentrate on prophylaxis rather than
scaremongering" (p.112)).

Deficiencies

a.   The lack of a general bibliography, cited references, graphs,
     charts and tables is a serious omission. Conclusions, while
     useful, should have been reference-cited (e.g. "... trichomonal
     infection ... is found significantly more often in the coloured
     races" (p.59 - no citation given)).
b.   At times, pejorative phraseology is in evidence (e.g. "The same
     groups of women are at risk; those of a promiscuous nature..."
     (p.68)).

42.   Butler, Robert N. & Lewis, Myrna I.   Sex After Sixty: A Guide for
Men and Women for Their Later Years.   New York: Harper & Row, 1976.
175 pp.

Brief Summary - Butler, a physician, and Lewis, a social worker,
combine their talents in this book of ten chapters. The opening
chapter details the myths and stereotypes our society has engendered
concerning the sexuality of the aging. Unfortunately for many older
people, such a belief-system is very negative in its impact upon
them, and otherwise avoidable sex problems, habits and self-images
become self-fulfilling. The next eight chapters detail at length
the subjects captioned in their titles. These are "Normal Physical
Changes in Sex and Sexuality with Age," "Common Medical Problems and
Sex," "Common Emotional Problems with Sex," "Do Yourself a Favor"
(as to exercise, nutrition, rest, hearing problems and personal
aesthetics), "Learning New Patterns of Love-Making," "People Without
Partners," "Dating, Remarriage and Your Children," and "Where to Go
for Help" (concerning knowledgeable physicians and/or therapists).
The final chapter, "The Second Language of Sex," refers to the
development of the "emotional and communicative as well as the
physical" (p.140) aspects of sexual interrelationships. Ten
positive attributes accruing to older persons who practice an active
personal sexuality are listed (p.136-139). The authors conclude
that "love and sex are twin arts requiring effort and knowledge.
Only in fairy tales do people live happily ever after without
working at it" (p.139).

Critique - Strengths

a.   Four excellent anatomical diagrams (p.146-149), a 6-page
     Glossary, many footnotes and a 3-page "Recommended Reading"
     section are useful adjuncts to the text. Support groups for
     single older people are listed (e.g. p.100).
b.   Although designed as a lay text, the book has significant
     peripheral value to professionals. In addition, it can be
     recommended by them to older persons, or institutional staff and
     younger people in contact with older individuals and groups.
c.   The exploding of the sexual myths and stereotypes is done with
     clarity and completeness (e.g. "there is no foundation to the
     common folklore that prostate trouble is related to 'excessive'

sexual activity" (p.44)).
d. The text is non-judgmental (e.g. "It is possible for sincere
    and caring relationships to exist without marriage if the older
    man and woman elect to live this way" (p.111)) and is bereft of
    patronizing moralizations.
e. Innovative phrases are often employed (e.g. "aesthetic narrow-
    ness" (p.6); also "the process of enshrinement" (p.117)).
f. Proper cautions about research unknowns are included (e.g. "The
    true range of risks and benefits for estrogen therapy is not yet
    established" (p.15)).

Deficiencies

a. There is a total lack of citations of research and comparative
    studies necessary to the authors' claims. Simple charts, tables
    and statistics would have helped the situation. Few case
    studies except the occasional anecdotal one (e.g. p.54) are
    included. Also, an appendix of resource materials such as films
    and tapes available for rent or purchase would have made a
    valuable addition.
b. A brief chapter giving some historical and cross-cultural back-
    ground information would have been useful. Only occasional
    fleeting historical references occur.
c. The word "impotence" (p.37) and the subsequent talk about it
    tend to accentuate biases and insecurities in readers. A safer
    phrase such as "erectile difficulties" should have been
    employed.
d. A mistake of emphasis occurs concerning sexual female
    functioning after a hysterectomy. The statement "there is no
    medical evidence that careful removal of the uterus, with or
    without removal of the ovaries, produces any change in sexual
    desire or performance in women" (p.41) is only partially
    correct. Subsequent less androgen produced might cause
    diminishing sexual desire.

43. Corsaro, Maria & Korzeniowsky, Carole. STD: A Commonsense Guide to
Sexually Transmitted Diseases. New York: Holt, Rinehart and Winston,
Inc., 1980. 143 pp.

   Brief Summary - In a short Foreword, Dr. Joseph A. Sonnabend
   evaluates the importance of the book and acknowledges "sexually
   transmitted diseases are a reality for every person who is sexually
   active" (p.1). The authors follow with an "Introduction: How to
   Use This Book." Thirteen chapters discuss the modes of trans-
   mission, the symptoms, the valid tests, treatments and safeguards
   for the various diseases in the following order: "Crabs" (pubic
   lice), "Cystitis," "Enteric STD's" (shigellosis, amebiasis,
   giardiasis), the different sub-types of "Gonorrhea," "Hepatitis"
   (types A, B, and nonA nonB), "Herpes" (types 1 and 11 simplex
   virus), "Nongonococcal Urethritis" (mainly chlamydia trachomatis and
   ureaplasma urealyticum), "Nonspecific Proctitis," "Pelvic
   Inflammatory Disease," "Scabies," "Syphilis," "Vaginitis"
   (candidiasis, trichomoniasis and nonspecific vaginitis which usually
   is gardnerella vaginalis, and anogenital "Warts" (condylomata
   acuminata).

Critique - Strengths

a. Various anatomical diagrams, sketches and italicized key
    phrases highlight the text. A 7-page Glossary of terms is
    useful. Three Appendixes termed "How to Use a Speculum," "How
    to Find Proper Testing and Treatment," and "How Not to Use This
    Book: Prevention" are important adjuncts to the presented
    textual material.
b. The book's title and content impart an objective and non-
    judgmental attitude (e.g. "We aren't advocating any particular
    sexual practices; the length of an encounter doesn't necessarily
    say anything about its quality" (p.123)).
c. The chart called "The STD Key" to treatment (p.11-12) is
    innovative, concise and a most important reference-tool.
d. Current medical and research uncertainties are factually
    acknowledged (e.g. concerning Pharyngeal Gonorrhea, "too little
    research has been done to reach definite conclusions" (p.41)).

Deficiencies

a. The book is insufficiently detailed in many areas. Case
    studies, pertinent clinical photographs, cited contemporary
    ongoing research, cited references, a general bibliography and
    anthropological-historical information are all totally missing
    in the book (e.g. "... some researchers think..." (p.46)). The
    book is, however, suitable for a clinician or therapist to
    recommend to a lay client.
b. Some unusual but important omissions from the text include such
    diseases as chancroid, Granuloma Inguinale, and Lymphogranuloma
    Venereum. Furthermore, a degree in error is reflected by the
    statement concerning trichomoniasis that "men are almost always
    asymptomatic" (p.96).

44. DeMartino, Manfred F. Human Autoerotic Practices. New York:
Human Sciences Press, 1979. 378 pp.

Brief Summary - Albert Ellis provides a lengthy Foreword describing
fifty advantages to masturbation. The author in a Preface comments
"perhaps the most dramatic and striking change ... has been in
regard to the attitudes by eminent sexologists toward the practice
of autoeroticism" (p.21). Six Parts make up the text. In Part I,
"Autoeroticism Viewed Psychologically," chapters are offered by
Dearborn, Albert Ellis (on myths), Brooks, Gordon, Comfort and
Brashear, all of whom view masturbation in a positive light. Part
II, "Autoeroticism During Adolescence," details a boy-girl study
(Sorensen) and a college male-female study (Arafat and Cotton).
Next follows Part III, "Autoeroticism in Women," with technical
contributions by Masters & Johnson, Fisher, the author concerning a
sample of intelligent women, and a manual by Dodson on the best
settings and ways for a woman to masturbate. In Part IV,
"Autoeroticism in Women and Men," historical and cross-cultural
prespectives are offered by Havelock Ellis and Ford and Beach. Two
more technical articles follow by Masters & Johnson (on the penile
aspects) and by McCary (on techniques). Hunt discusses recent
"Changes in Masturbatory Attitudes and Behavior" and Albert Ellis
closes with a review. Part V is termed "Use of Autoeroticism in the

Treatment of Sexual Dysfunction." Abridged articles by LoPiccolo
and Lobitz, Kaplan, and Barbach outline the successes of these
therapists. The final Part VI by DeMartino sums up and extends the
discussion and is titled "Research on Autoeroticism: An Overall
View." He closes by listing twenty-three "General Conclusions"
(p.354) pertinent to various physical, psychological and
sociological societal issues.

<u>Critique - Strengths</u>

a. Footnotes and cited references are summarized after each
    chapter. An author's "Introduction" abstracts each Part of the
    book. A 6-page general Bibliography terminates the text.
    Anecdotal and other-expert quotations abound while some
    contributors review their research and offer various tables and
    statistics (e.g. refer to Part II in the Summary above). A
    comprehensive coverage of historical and cross-cultural material
    is presented (e.g. refer to Summary).
b. In many places, destructive myths are neutralized (e.g. "...
    masturbation mitigates against sex adjustment in marriage...
    The available facts do not support this conclusion..." (A.
    Ellis, p.57)).
c. Both Albert Ellis and DeMartino provide excellent, point-
    summarized reviews (e.g. refer to Summary). Recommendations are
    often useful (e.g. "... since it produces the most intense
    orgasm, it logically seems to be the preferred treatment for
    enhancing orgasmic potential in inorgasmic women" (LoPiccolo and
    Lobitz, p.283)).
d. Some contributors express positive behavioral sex biases (e.g.
    "in addition to heterosexuality, homosexuality, bisexuality, and
    group sexuality, ... self sexuality as a total sex life is
    absolutely valid" (Dodson, p.174)).

<u>Deficiencies</u>

a. No photographs, sketches or graphs enhance the text.
b. Unproductive and subjective value-judgments often occur (e.g.
    "masturbation can be a psychologically unhealthy practice ...
    <u>when other sex outlets are easily available</u>" (A. Ellis, p.55);
    also similarly expressed - McCary - p.220). As well,
    unsubstantiated assumptions not backed up by referenced research
    sometimes show up (e.g. "a vibrator ... is inclined to damp down
    sensitivity with prolonged use" (Comfort, p.81); also
    "Masturbation ... would be considered pathologic..." (Brooks,
    p.63); also "the clitorally oriented ... (and) vaginally
    oriented woman" (Fisher, p.134-135)).
c. The report research studies have methodological weaknesses
    which are not acknowledged. Also, some research is
    insufficiently expanded (e.g. "our survey did not tell us..."
    (Sorenson, p.97)).
d. Pejorativity exists in places (e.g. "latent homosexuals"
    (Gordon, p.73); also "compulsive masturbators" (Hunt, p.241)).

45. Dickinson, Peter A. <u>The Fires of Autumn: Sexual Activity in</u>
<u>the Middle and Later Years</u>. New York: Drake Publishers Inc., 1977.
192 pp.

Brief Summary - In his Preface, Dickinson states "sex is living - not statistics and clinical studies. I've tried to translate factual data into realistic drama" (p.11-12). The opening chapter discusses sexual myths in terms of our cultural historical backdrop. This is followed in Chapter 2 by a discourse on alleged sexual enhancers, both physical and chemical. Next comes gerontological information, both fact and fiction, as this relates to sexuality. Chapter 4 is devoted to sexual myths still current in our culture. The subsequent two chapters delve into key health and sex problems that aging women and men are apt to encounter. In Chapter 7, the author explores the various female and male sexual dysfunctions from the aging perspective. The traumas of illness and surgery as they complicate sexuality next follow after which the importance of sexual innovations is stressed. To complement this, the Kegel exercises are recommended. Chapter 10 finds the topic of pornography being considered as an aid. Sexual variety such as homosexuality and bisexuality is next commented upon after which the final chapter gets into lifestyle alternatives and their possible trends. The author concludes that in addition to its physical component, "sexuality in the middle and later years ... may express itself in the need for continued closeness, affection, and intimacy" (p.190).

Critique - Strengths

a. Footnotes, italics emphasizing key points, and many studies are described. Many anecdotal and other-expert quotations bolster the text. There is considerable historical input (e.g. Chapter 1 - p.15; also p.147).
b. Many societal myths are dispelled (e.g. nine listed and discussed - p.63-64) and cultural assumptions are attacked (e.g. "A nurse ... told me that in her medical ward they didn't take sexual history after age fifty" (p.40)). Positive suggestions occur (e.g. the "don'ts" and "do's" - p.103). Good insights are revealed (e.g. "When people lose their sense of identity, they often choose one of the stereotypes that society casts for them" (p.26)).
c. The book is a useful backup text for sexological and health-care professionals and as such, can be recommended to their clients who directly or indirectly require the knowledge.

Deficiencies

a. The total lack of an index, a bibliography, visual aids, graphs and charts is a drawback. Uncited statements and research are given (e.g. "Some sociologists assert..." (p.19)) Additionally, cross-cultural information is basically ignored.
b. Value-judgments (e.g. "masturbation can be considered excessive only in the same light that too much reading or TV-watching might be considered excessive" (p.69) at times could be better phrased.) Conclusions are not referenced (e.g. "Other causes of lesbianism may include..." (p.164)). Some subjects are approached from the wrong perspective (e.g. "Can Mate-Swapping Save a Marriage?" (p.178)). The statement "some psychiatrists believe that a 'new' form of homosexuality may be emerging that

is more 'bisexual' in nature" (p.167) is not only unreferenced,
but is contradictory.
c. There are occasional mistakes (e.g. "... produce hormones-
    androgen in the male, estrogen in the female" (p.44) require the
    two hormone family-names to be pluralized).
d. Some pejorativity is in evidence (e.g. "... through sadism,
    perversions, and sexual excesses" (p.153)). Biased belief-
    systems are counter-productive to other presented arguments
    (e.g. "Unfortunately, some studies confirm the effects of new
    and varied sex partners in stimulating activity" (p.88)).

46. Gordon, Sol, Scales, Peter & Everly, Kathleen. The Sexual
Adolescent: Communication With Teenagers About Sex (2nd Ed.). Belmont:
Duxbury Press, 1979. 427 pp.

Brief Summary - The authors, all educators, stress in their Preface
"this is an action-oriented book. We have not tried to discuss
adolescence within a particular developmental scheme or theory"
(p.xiii). An Introduction outlines the book's goals. Twelve
chapters and six Appendixes follow. Chapter 1 discusses "Facing
Facts - An Adult Responsibility" after which "What Adolescents Need
to Know" is stressed. Further topics covered are "Sexual
Communication and the Persisting Double Standard," "Problems of
Adolescent Pregnancy," "The Abortion Controversy," "Sexually
Transmitted Diseases," "The Religious Perspective - An Overview,"
"Sex Education for Handicapped Youth," "The Effects of Sex Education
- A Review and Critique of the Literature," and "Current Innovations
and Suggestions for Creative Action." In Chapter 11, "Toward a
Politics of Humanistic Sexuality," the authors propose acceptance
through knowledge, of the homosexual subculture and suggest "if we
want young people to believe ... that 'any prejudice is morally
wrong,' then we need to stop our own selective truth telling in the
form of censorship and our own selective obedience to the law"
(p.239). The final chapter is termed "Rights and Responsibilities
in the Egalitarian Era." Appendix I by Bauman, a physician, offers
information about "Contraception, Conception, Pregnancy and Birth
Facts for Everyone." Research by Zelnik and Kantner is summarized
in Appendix II's "Contraceptive Patterns and Premarital Pregnancy
Among Women Aged Fifteen to Nineteen in 1976." The subsequent three
appendixes deal with abortion and are contributed by Prescott (with
collaboration by Wallace in Appendix V).

Critique - Strengths

a. Tables, charts, graphs, photographs and educational cartoons
    complement the text. Cited references, quotations, research
    studies, anecdotal stories and footnotes are included. An
    extensive "Selected Resources" comprise Appendix VI.
b. Succinct questions with direct answers demythologize the
    reader from any "mistaken assumptions" (p.9) (e.g. "Questions
    and Answers" - p.24-30).
c. Critical evaluation of other researchers' work is often forth-
    coming (e.g. "... Goldsmith's explanation for their findings is
    compelling..." (p.168); also "Spanier did not distinguish the
    kinds of knowledge that are necessary antecedents... The low
    gamma coefficients ... and the poor reliability of the perceived

knowledge scale suggest caution in drawing any conclusions from the data" (p.175)).
d. Constructive plans of action are suggested (e.g. "The legality of abortion creates an opportunity to perform some greatly needed research in the field" (p.101-102)).
e. Biases are backed up by research data (e.g. "We believe that it is best for teenagers not to impregnate, become pregnant, or have children" (p.xiii); also "Every young adult has the right to decide sexual morality for themselves, free from patronizing or condescending attitudes on the part of adults and free from conformist pressures from friends" (p.257)).

Deficiencies

a. Although Prescott gives cross-cultural data on abortion (p.316-317; 328-332), historical and cross-cultural background material is otherwise basically omitted.
b. Occasional assumptions and subjective value-judgments surface (e.g. "Increasingly, young people are fed up with sex as an avoidance of intimacy" (p.257 - no cited references); also the statement "... my taking a moral position about promiscuity" (p.47)).

47. Green, Richard, ed. Human Sexuality: A Health Practitioner's Text. Baltimore: The Williams & Wilkins Company, 1975. 265 pp.

Brief Summary - Eighteen topics by nineteen contributors including two by the Editor comprise the book. Green in the Preface describes the rationale for the book's existence. At that time there were "ninety-five medical schools teaching human sexuality and no appropriate book!" (p.vi). The opening chapter relates why sex education is essential for medical students. The timing and the effective modes of "Taking a Sex History" (Green) make up Chapter 2 after which Diamond discusses some clinical aspects of sexual anatomy and physiology. The various heterosexual liaisons of patients are sociologically examined by Reiss after which Bell and Messer respectively address the topics of "The Homosexual as Patient" and as physician. Transvestitic and transsexual patients' phenomena follow after which the concepts of birth control and child-rearing are detailed. Chapter 9 finds Money analyzing "Sex Assignment in Anatomically Intersexed Infants" after which the procedures and psychological problems inherent with female pelvic examinations are explored. The next four chapters deal with "Sexuality During Pregnancy and Postpartum" (Butler and Wagner), with the spinal cord injured (Cole), the cardiac patient (Wagner), and the mentally retarded (Hall). Chapters 15 to 17 contrast three approaches to clinically dealing with sexual dysfunction. The final chapter by Vandervoort and McIlvenna discusses the usage of "Sexually Explicit Media in Medical School Curricula." Green provides a brief Epilogue.

Critique - Strengths

a. Each chapter displays a useful preface and often cited research (e.g. Butler & Wagner, p.137). Anatomical sketches (e.g. Money, p.114), innovative charts (e.g. Cole, p.152), tables (e.g. Diamond, p.32), case studies (e.g. Diamond, p.29) and the use of anecdotal dialogue (e.g. Vincent, p.200) are of great benefit. The listing of resource agencies (e.g. Vandervoort & McIlvenna, p.237) available at the time of the book's release is also an asset.

b. Many authors throughout the book take pains to dispel sexual myths (e.g. Bell, p.56; Cole, p.148; Hall, p.185).

c. Certain authors bring into the discussion historically (e.g. Reiss, p.37) and cross-culturally relevant material (e.g. Money, p.109).

Deficiencies

a. No photographs and not enough sketches and diagrams are found (e.g. Chapter 3 by Diamond lacks graphic illustrations. No general bibliography is present. Only the citations are given at the ends of the chapters.

b. No discernible evidence is offered by which to justify the book's implicit and exclusive medical-model approach to human sexuality. Contentious issues are not dealt with (e.g. consensual sadomasochistic practices, consensual and non-consensual incest).

c. Recent valid criticisms and improvements on original research are not and cannot be included (e.g. Masters & Johnson's statements on dysfunction - Biggs & Spitz, p.226). Some myths are not attacked (e.g. Diamond misses one pertaining to erect penis sizes being similar to flaccid sizes - p.22).

d. Minor pejorativity is noted (e.g. "... young man with impotency" (Green - p.10)). Poor phraseology occurs in a leading question suggested by Green (i.e. "Some say homosexuality is a mental disorder... What is your attitude...?" (p.14)).

48. Hatcher, R., Stewart, G., Stewart, F., Guest, F., Josephs, N., & Dale, J. Contraceptive Technology 1982-1983 (11th Revised Edition). New York: Irvington Publishers Inc., 1982. 280 pp.

Brief Summary - In their "Preface and Dedication," the senior four authors who are health-care professionals state that this book "meets the needs of a number of providers of health services including physicians, medical students, nursing students, nurse practitioners, nurse midwives, educators and family planning clinic personnel" (p.iii). Twenty-four subject-chapters make up the text. The first three chapters give a background into the efficacy, safety, and life-style choice of the various contraceptive methods, a review of "The Menstrual Cycle," and a "Hormonal Overview" of the estrogens and the progestins. The subsequent six chapters describe the mechanisms of action, efficacies, contraindications, side effects, and non-contraceptive benefits of the combination-type oral contraceptives, the progestin-only pills, the various intrauterine devices, diaphragms and cervical caps, the condom, and certain vaginal spermicides. The next six chapters explore less reliable procedures such as the natural methods, abstinence, sex without intercourse, coitus interruptus, the lactation process after child-birth, and the various post-coital contraceptive methods. Further topics covered concern "Pregnancy Testing," "Abortion,"

"Sterilization" techniques of both men and women, some possible
"Future Methods of Birth Control," the causal factors and some tests
for "Infertility," "Informed Consent and Legal Considerations,"
"Family Planning and Family Health," "Sexually Transmissible
Infections," and "Nutritional and Drug Interactions" with certain of
the contraceptive agents.

Critique - Strengths

a. The many graphs, charts, tables and anatomical diagrams (e.g.
    Figure 2.2, "The Menstrual Cycle," p.21) are very helpful.
    Footnotes and cited References at the end of each chapter are
    further assets. Warnings and boxed messages in bold capital
    letters or italics make important information stand out.
    Textual arrows point to new material added to this edition.
    Limited historical and cross-cultural topical information is
    often found, especially early in most chapters (e.g. concerning
    the condom - p.110-111). An unusual Appendix lists laboratory-
    range values of essential chemicals found in the human body.
b. The book is useful for health-care professionals as well as for
    sexologists and their students.
c. Innovative sections can often be found (e.g. the 1-page
    Introduction featuring "Principles of Family Planning" (p.xiii);
    also patient-questions concerning "Development of a Reproductive
    Life Plan" (p.11)).
d. Research results are often cited and listed (e.g. "References
    on Contraceptive Failure Rates, Table 1:1" (p.16-17)), while
    recent problems are covered (e.g. "Toxic Shock Syndrome"
    (p.25)), various alternative hypotheses offered (e.g. Seven
    "mechanisms of action of IUDs have been suggested:..." (p.73)),
    and future research speculated upon (e.g. refer to Summary
    above).
e. The text is non-judgmental (e.g. "others choose to ... engage
    in other forms of noncoital sexual pleasuring" (p.127); also
    "the authors feel that it should be the right or prerogative of
    each woman to make decisions regarding her own pregnancy"
    (p.166)).

Deficiencies

a. A glossary of defined terms would have been helpful. Certain
    terms are never properly explained (e.g. "androgenic potency"
    (p.41)).
b. The text is medically oriented. Further input on sociological
    and anthropological issues would have been beneficial (e.g.
    "Population concerns should not be the major focus..."(p.xiii)).

49. Kaufman, Sherwin A. Sexual Sabotage. New York: Macmillan
Publishing Co. Inc., 1981. 349 pp.

Brief Summary - The author, a gynecologist, opens with an
Introduction which states "sexual sabotage can take many forms, and
is often involuntary" (p.xiv). Another preliminary section termed
"The Doctor and Patient" mentions that "each section of the book
therefore devotes itself to a separate field of practice, with sex
the common denominator" (p.xxi). Ten health-care-oriented Parts

follow. Part I called "Sexual Impediments in Reproduction"
discusses potential difficulties arising from "Pregnancy,"
"Infertility," "Contraception," "Abortion," and "Sterilization."
Part II's "Sexual Frustration and the Female Body" devotes itself to
"Breasts," "Weight," "Menstruation," "Painful Periods,"
"Premenstrual Tension," and "Vaginal Discharge and Discomforts -
Sexual Hygiene." Part III termed "Sexual Consequences of Emotional
Problems" describes "Depression," "Insomnia," "Fatigue," "Headache,"
Neuroses," "Psychoses," and "Mental Retardation." In Part IV,
"Sexual Impairment from Medical Disorders," sexual concerns are
discussed as they apply to "Eye, Ear, Nose, and Throat Problems,"
"Dermatologic Disorders," "Venereal Disease," "Cardiovascular
Disorders," "Diabetes," "Gastrointestinal Diseases" including
ileitis, "Orthopedic Problems," "Respiratory Ailments," "Urological
Diseases," certain "Neurological Afflictions," "Glandular
Disorders," "Menopause," and "Drugs, Medications, and Aphrodisiacs."
Part V, "Male and Female Sexual Behavior and Conflict" analyzes
female-male sexual behavior and marital sexual conflict.
"Variations in Sexual Behavior" comprises Part VI. Part VII
recounts "Sexual Effects of Surgery and Cancer." The final chapters
are in three Parts termed "Sexual Separation" due to "Divorce and
Widowhood," "Sex and the Elderly," and a 7-page discussion
illustrating "Sexual Sabotage Throughout History."

Critique - Strengths

a. The textual formula of questions and answers hones directly in
    on specifics. Italicized statements and quotations plus
    anecdotal, often humorous stories (e.g. p.13) give further
    impact to the book. The final chapter imparts some pertinent
    historical and cross-cultural background material.
b. Misinformation and popular myths are often assailed in an
    effective manner (e.g. "Mental Retardation" as this applies to a
    person's sexuality; also "Are the elderly sexually inactive?
    This is a myth..." (p.305)).
c. Some resource materials and persons are given (e.g. concerning
    quadriplegics, "a film called Possibilities, which was produced
    by ..." (p.172); also p.220-221).

Deficiencies

a. No bibliography and cited references back up the many claims,
    statements and conclusions offered. Furthermore, no visual
    aids, charts, or graphs are included.
b. The book holds completely to the medical-model approach to
    sexuality. Unreferenced, controversial statements abound (e.g.
    concerning group sex activity in a marriage, "objective
    observers have commented ... that such sexual activities tend to
    undermine a relationship that really needs strengthening"
    (p.219)). Fallacious advice is sometimes proffered (e.g. "... a
    third of homosexuals in psychiatric therapy become exclusively
    heterosexual" (p.233)). Incorrect sweeping statements do not
    reflect a continuum approach to certain behaviors (e.g. "If
    there is adultery, marital sex is already undermined" (p.241);
    also "incest is really child abuse" (p.259)). Some variations
    are inadequately discussed (e.g. transvestism, consensual

    sadomasochism - p.266).

  c. Some topics are incomplete (e.g. the reversal chances of undoing sterilization are not discussed - p.30-33; also the cortisone treatment necessary for women who have the adreno-genital syndrome is not mentioned - p.176-177).

  d. Pejorativity occurs (e.g. "... compulsively promiscuous female" (p.251)).

50. Kelly, Gary F. Learning About Sex: The Contemporary Guide For Young Adults. Woodbury: Barron's Educational Series, Inc., 1977. 205 pp.

    Brief Summary - Kelly is an educator who acknowledges in his Preface that this book helps "readers - particularly teenagers - clarify their needs and values relating to sex" (p.xiii). The Introduction is furnished by Mary Calderone, President of the Sex Information and Education Council of the U.S. The ten chapters cover various topics as follows: the author's sexual value-systems and book outline, male-female sexual physiology coupled with "Emerging Sexual Feelings" (p.30), sex-role stereotypes plus the Masters & Johnson human sexual-response model, variations of sexuality, sexual sharing, "Communicating About Sex," problematic and exploitive sexual issues, "Loving and Being Together as Sexual People," bonded relationships, and issues surrounding whether or not to be a parent. A closing section termed "More Nitty-Gritty" poses questions and answers not covered earlier in the text.

Critique - Strengths

  a. Two appendixes cover a glossary of "Four-Letter and Other Words" plus "Organizations That Can Provide Information and Help." "For Further Reading" sections can be found after most chapters. Many sketches and anatomical diagrams abound while some apt graphs (e.g. p.42), histograms (e.g. p.100), and charts (e.g. "Spectrum of possible sexual values" (p.79)) are included. Numerous anecdotal stories as well as appropriate questionnaires (e.g. p.62-63) and exercises (e.g. p.47-49) are also to be found.

  b. Innovative and useful concepts are included (e.g. "Table 1 The Old Stereotypes of Women and Men" (p.35)). Empathy and rapport are effected with sexual-minority readers (e.g. "... I have often been confused, afraid, guilty, or worried about my sexual feelings and sexual behaviors" (p.1)).

  c. Myths are exposed and explained (e.g. "Many myths still exist about homosexuality..." (p.57)). Objective pros and cons are sometimes listed (e.g. "Deciding About (premarital) Sex..." (p.73)).

  d. The author is objective toward atypical sexualities (e.g. "... I cannot judge the 'rightness' or 'wrongness' of any of these behaviors" (p.4); also "... There are no indications that such animal contacts are harmful..." (p.61)).

Deficiencies

  a. Except for the Masters & Johnson study (i.e. p.41), little research is outlined and no references are ever cited. Almost

no historical and cross-cultural background information is
imparted as to how our society acquired its cultural sexual
misconceptions and inconsistencies.
b. Some topics are inadequately explored (e.g. consensual sibling
   incest - p.98; also sexually transmitted diseases such as herpes
   2, venereal warts and trichomoniasis).
c. Better phraseology could have been used on occasion (e.g. "As
   with oral sex, some people find anal sex to be immoral and
   disgusting..." (p.71)). Unreferenced assumptions are in
   evidence (e.g. "... there is also evidence that many people do
   not adjust well to group sex experiences..." (p.77)).
d. Implied pejorativity surfaces on one occasion (i.e. "Casual,
   promiscuous sex..." (p.105)).

51. Kolodny, Robert, Masters, William & Johnson, Virginia. Textbook
of Sexual Medicine. Boston: Little, Brown & Co., 1979. 649 pp.

Brief Summary - The three authors, directors of The Masters &
Johnson Institute in St. Louis, preface their text by stating the
book "is not written for physicians alone ... (but also for)
psychologists, social workers, nurses, counselors and other health-
care professionals." (p.v). Twenty-four chapters follow with the
first five dealing with sexual physiology, genetics and endocrine
factors, and the spectrum from childhood to geriatric sexuality.
Chapters 6 through 14 concern themselves with illness and sexuality
in the areas of endocrinology, cardiovascular disease, gynecology,
urology, chronic illness, the oncology patient, psychiatric illness,
drugs, and the handicapped. Chapter 15 delineates "Sex and Family
Planning." The rationales for helping rape victims and the
etiologies of homosexual and transsexual patients are next examined.
"Sex Therapy" occupies Chapters 19-21. The final three chapters
cover "Sexual Aversion and Inhibited Sexual Desire," "The
Paraphilias," and "Practical Management of Sexual Problems." The
authors close the book by stating "with routine attention to sexual
health concerns, ... health-care professionals can have a decided
impact on the quality of their patients' lives. This is the
essential message of this book" (p.599).

Critique - Strengths

a. Good textual support-systems include graphs, tables, photographs and sketches. These are often rarely covered items of
   interest (e.g. karotypes of 46XX female and 46XY male chromosome
   patterns - Figure 2.1, p.30)). Additionally, extensive
   references are listed after each chapter. Historical background
   is in a proper context of objectivity (e.g. "Valid objections
   have been raised to the universality of the oedipal complex, the
   importance of penis envy, the true nature of 'latency'... For
   example, Marmor (13) writes..." (p.61)). The text is well
   constructed, easy to follow and comprehensive in detail.
b. Unanswered research questions are often acknowledged (e.g. "The
   precise hormonal explanation of the so-called 'witch's milk'
   phenomenon ... has not been determined (12)" (p.60)).
c. Some clinical suggestions are well presented (e.g. Nine points
   to consider in "the assessment of the effects of chronic illness
   on sexual function" (p.234)).

Deficiencies

a. Cross-cultural data are lacking. Research is often not updated
    (e.g. "The evidence for an increased incidence of criminality in
    47, XYY men has been substantiated in numerous studies (29, 31,
    39-41), although the cause of this is not clear" (p.43); also
    Table 1-1 - Typical ranges of serum of plasma testosterone
    concentration (p.21) are unreferenced and controversial as to
    accuracy and predictability.)
b. Cited personal research by the authors is often based on faulty
    methodology. Replication of results by other researchers has
    not followed (e.g. Homosexual to heterosexual conversion-
    reversion statistics and rationales - Table 17-3, p.457).
    Alternatives in therapy-treatment to the original Masters &
    Johnson techniques are not offered (e.g. the dual-sex therapy
    team approach only is discussed (p.483)).
c. Some topics are sparsely covered and should have been presented
    in greater detail (e.g. non-specific Chlamydia trachomatis -
    briefly only on p.213, 453). Occasional errors are present
    (e.g. "amyl nitrate" (p.342) should read "amyl nitrite").
d. Judgmentality is at times evident (e.g. "Sexual promiscuity is
    often a prominent feature of sociopathy" (p.309)).

52. Llewellyn-Jones, Derek. Sex & V.D. London: Faber and Faber,
1974. 112 pp.

Brief Summary - The author, an Australian gynecologist-professor, in
his opening chapter relates the global parameters of this problem
and how the problem has grown in scope, in part due to more inter
and intra-continental travel and population drift toward the major
cities. The subsequent chapter gives female and male anatomical
information. This is followed by a chapter "About Gonorrhoea" and
one "About Syphilis." Chapter 5 furnishes a historical resume of
these two major diseases and begins with the biblical time of Moses,
includes the alleged introduction of syphilis into Europe by the
sailors of Columbus, and continues into today's world with pertinent
cross-cultural demographic data. In Chapter 6 entitled "Other
Sexually Transmitted Diseases," non-specific urethritis, trichomoniasis, candidiasis, genital warts, and chancroid are described.
In Chapter 7 the author concludes that "education in human sexuality
... should start in primary schools and continue throughout the
school years. It should also continue, through the mass media..."
(p.108).

Critique - Strengths

a. A reference page of Further Readings along with graphs, case
    studies, anatomical sketches and historical drawings add
    required impetus and value to the text. The book has good
    historical and cross-cultural contemporary coverage (e.g. refer
    to Summary above). In addition, research references are given
    (e.g. "In the year 1891, Professor Brock of Oslo, Norway..."
    (p.62)).
b. Myths are often exposed (e.g. "most people who have gonorrhoea
    or syphilis cease to be infectious within twenty-four hours of

starting treatment..." (p.13)).

c. Positive recommendations are put forth (e.g. refer to Summary above).

Deficiencies

a. Research conclusions, while interesting, are uncited and often even unreferenced as to names and times and places (e.g. "In two large series of patients, investigated by two eminent physicians specializing in venereal diseases, between fifty and eighty per cent of women diagnosed as having gonorrhoea were completely symptomless..." (p.14-15)).
b. Actual photographs of a variety of case studies would have been a great asset.
c. Certain sexually transmitted diseases are not even mentioned (e.g. herpes simplex 2).
d. Unproductive and judgmental phraseology crops up on occasion (e.g. "What is not clear is whether homosexuals are sexually promiscuous because of an emotional defect, or whether their promiscuity is due to society's reaction to homosexuality..." (p.18); also "If he is a good considerate lover, he will also seek to bring his female partner to orgasm" (p.34) implies that women are not responsible for their own sexual pleasuring).

53. Mims, Fern H. & Swenson, Melinda. **Sexuality: A Nursing Perspective**. New York: McGraw-Hill Book Co., 1980. 378 pp.

Brief Summary - The authors, both nursing professionals, indicate in the Preface they wish to achieve "the promotion of sexual health in primary or secondary health care nursing" (p.x). Five Parts comprise the text. The Introduction displays a sexual-health "Model for Nursing Education and Nursing Practice" coupled with a "Historical Background" and an overview on "Sexual Responses and Dysfunctions." Part II termed "Typical and Atypical Psychosexual Development" includes a legal analysis of various lifestyles (chapter 6), "Taking a Sexual History," and "Physical Examination with Sexual Health Teaching." Part III is entitled "Reproductive Decision Making" (i.e. "Contraception," "Pregnancy," "Abortion"). In Part IV, "Sexuality and Health Disruptions," eight chapters cover the topics of "Psychosexual Effects of Changes in Health," "Pharmacologic Modification of Human Sexuality," "Sexually Transmitted Disease," "Postcoronary," "Diabetes Mellitus," "Spinal Chord Injury," "Surgical Interventions," and "Sexuality and Dying." The final Part V discusses "Education Programs" and "Sex Therapy and Research." The authors conclude "there is a lack of descriptive and controlled research in this area... Nurses ... may be surprised to find opportunities to study etiology, preventive measures, and treatment approaches in sexual health care with many different populations" (p.346).

Critique - Strengths

a. Textual aids include Learning Activities, References and a Bibliography (in subsets of topic) after most chapters. Also included are quotations, case studies, sketches, cartoons, photographs, charts and tables (e.g. #14-2 "Summary of Sexually

Transmitted Diseases" (p.261)). Chapter 1 is a good review of
nursing requirements pertaining to clients' sexual concerns (25
points listed, p.10-12). Chapter 2's historical overview is
useful.

b. Myths are constantly being debunked (e.g. #5 of 10 -
"Exhibitionists are latent homosexuals" (p.4)).

c. The Mims-Swenson Sexual Health Model is based on the Annon
Plissit model and is a useful construct (Figure 1-1, p.5).

d. The section on sex research dealing with its methodological
challenges, problems and issues, is useful (p.345-347).

Deficiencies

a. Insufficient cross-cultural information is offered. A list of
effective training programs and resources should have been
included in an appendix. The index does not correspond to the
text. (e.g. "amyl nitrite" (p.246) is called "amyl nitrate"
(p.244-245) in the index; also androgen and estrogen index-
references do not match the paged textual inclusions).

b. Chapter 7's "Taking a Sexual History" is deficient in scope and
in presentation.

c. The authors are not always neutral and objective (e.g. in the
section on sadomasochism, consensuality is poorly covered
(p.87); also transvestism and transsexualism are termed "Gender
Identity Disorders" (p.82)).

d. The medical-model approach to the treatment of atypical sexuality is overstressed. Cited studies usually refer only to anti-
social offenders (e.g. Groth and Birnbaum on pedophilic cases
(p.86)).

e. An error in defining pedophilia is noted. It is the sexual
preference of adults for children, not just "men for children"
(p.85).

54. Pomeroy, Wardell B. Boys and Sex: Girls and Sex (revised). New
York: Dell Publishing Co. Inc., 1981. 199 pp. & 184 pp.

Brief Summary - The author writes from his perspective of having
been a sexologist for over forty years and a former colleague of the
sex researcher Kinsey. These volumes are revised from the original
1968, 1969 editions, and Pomeroy acknowledges in a Preface to the
Second Edition that the interim "changed attitudes toward sex, and
the greater acceptance they imply,... made it necessary to revise
this volume and bring it up to date" (B&S - p.xii). Both volumes
accord a short Introduction to the youthful readers and their
parents. The book directed toward boys has chapters covering the
responsibility of any boy as a sexual being, anatomy and physiology,
sex play before adolescence, masturbation and homosexuality, the
realities of dating, coital intercourse, and typical questions and
their answers about sexual concerns a boy might raise. Similarly,
the book directed toward girls talks about the same subject-issues
although in a somewhat different sequence. An extra chapter (6) is
inserted dealing with "The Female Orgasm." Afterword in each volume
includes one sentence common to both books. "It isn't what you do
sexually that matters, as long as you're not hurting someone else"
(B&S - p.178; G&S - p.166).

Critique - Strengths

a. There are numerous anecdotal quotations and examples. The
prose has impact, yet is easy to understand. While these
volumes are of limited value to educators, health-care
professionals and sexologists, they are excellent books to
recommend to parents and/or these persons' young and teenage
progeny. Historical, cross-cultural and cross-species
background sexual material is especially prevalent in the "Boys
and Sex" volume (e.g. p.60-64; p.78).

b. Perceptive clarity is given about certain misconceptions and
myths (e.g. "Another popular belief is that a person who is
aroused physically by a member of the same sex and suppresses
the feeling is a 'latent homosexual'... The truth is that all
of us are potentially capable of doing every act imaginable..."
(B&S - p.74); also "No medical evidence exists that shows any
kind of relationship between masturbation and illness" (G&S -
p.127)). The "Questions and Answers" chapters (i.e. refer to
Summary above) are immense assets. Shock statements (e.g.
"We're still in the Dark Ages as far as solid research data on
sexual behavior is concerned" (G&S - p.7) and constructive
comments (e.g. "Sometimes men ... expose their penises ... to
provoke a reaction... The girl may think that it's the
exhibited penis that's ugly and repulsive. In reality, it's the
circumstances surrounding the incident that are repellent, not
the penis itself" (G&S - p.51)) are proffered.

c. The books are without subjective judgmentality and
pejorativity.

Deficiencies

a. The volumes lack cited research and other references as well as
graphs, charts and tables, statistical or otherwise. No general
bibliography is included.

b. Pertinent sketches, cartoons, or photographs along with a few
graphs or charts would have heightened the textual impact. The
"Girls and Sex" volume requires more input on historical and
cross-cultural perspectives.

55. Rowan, Robert L. Men and Their Sex. New York: Irvington
Publishers Inc., 1982. 171 pp.

Brief Summary - Rowan, a physician, in his Introduction states "this
book will help to explain your normal sexual function and the
problems that can develop among sexually active people" (p.1). The
text comes in four Parts. Part I describes the function of the male
sexual parts of the anatomy. This is followed by discussions of
atypical situations involving normal delayed ejaculation, premature
ejaculation, ejaculatory incompetence, retrograde ejaculation and
the presence of blood in the semen. A lengthy report about the
prostate gland is included. In Part II, various "Conditions and
Diseases of the Penis" are examined. These are "Peyronie's
Disease," priapism, phimosis, circumcision, the insertion of foreign
bodies, superficial venous thrombosis, wound traumas or injuries,
the human bite, congenital birth defects such as hypospadias or
epispadias, penile cancer, and penile skin diseases such as

psoriasis, eczma, or carbuncles. Part III's "Sexually Transmitted Diseases" describes gonorrhea, syphilis, genital herpes, hepatitis, genital warts, chancroid, non-specific urethritis such as chlamydia trachomatis, "Reiter's Disease," granuloma inguinale, lymphogranuloma venereum, trichomonas hominis, and molluscum contagiosum. A short Part IV termed "Examining Your Own Testicles" briefs the reader about signs of cancer. The book includes treatments, both effective and not so effective, that have been utilized for the various difficulties.

Critique - Strengths

a. Various anatomical sketches, other drawings, footnotes and anecdotal case studies (e.g. p.35) are of aid to the text.
b. Certain subjects are much better covered in this book than in almost all other such generalized books (e.g. "The Prostate Gland" (p.58); "Peyronie's Disease" (p.85)).
c. The book has a limited reference value for physicians. It is very useful for non-medically trained sexologists, students and as a reference volume from them to lay clients.
d. Some hypotheses are presented for other researchers to follow up (e.g. "... I believe that these patients have an ejaculatory mechanism that is tuned differently than the norm... This concept was developed during Dr. Thomas Howley's and my experiments on electro-ejaculation" (p.46)).
e. The author evinces a neutral position with regard to clients (e.g. "... the physician should not sit in judgment in relation to patients' behavior..." (p.18)).

Deficiencies

a. No bibliography or photographs are included. Research alluded to is never cited (e.g. "... some recent studies show that high blood pressure itself can cause impotency or ejaculatory problems" (p.53). Even cursory historical and cross-cultural data appropriate to many topics are absent. Discussion is over-simplified at times (e.g. "The process of erection is directed by one type of nerve and its chemical, the process of ejaculation by another" (p.51). Terms such as autonomic nervous system, parasympathetic, sympathetic, cholinergic and adrenergic are not mentioned here).
b. Factual claims are often made which are unsubstantiated by references (e.g. "... because of this pattern, sexually active men can be particularly prone to prostatitis" (p.35)).
c. Misemphasis on certain points can lead to myth-productions (e.g. "men with large organs may well be asked back..." (p.11); also "... in many cases the question is just talk because the patient is in his seventies or older..." (p.79)).
d. An occasional inherent moralization can be detected (e.g. "One should try to have relaxed, unpressured and regular, steady sexual relationships. This allows for the necessary emotional adjustment that good sexual relations require..." (p.41)).

56. Sarnoff, Suzanne & Irving. Sexual Excitement: Sexual Peace. New York: M. Evans & Co. Inc., 1979. 333 pp.

Brief Summary - In three Parts, these two married professionals explore the continuum of masturbation in men and women as this pertains to fantasy and interpersonal relationships. After an Introduction in which the authors state "everyone is involved in masturbation - physically or mentally - throughout life" (p.1), they turn in Part I to "The Experience of Masturbation" through orgasm and fantasy. Part II delineates "Masturbation and Child Development" from the infant to the adolescent. Part III details "Masturbation and Adult Fulfillment" in couples and singles. An Epilogue entitled "From Confusion to Understanding" imparts a philosophical rationale to the practice of masturbation in a modern complex world.

Critique - Strengths

a. The case histories plus the personal revelations of the authors' masturbatory evolution impart integrity to the book. Footnoted references of sexological experts and historically relevant personages are included.
b. A positive approach to masturbation permeates through the book. The historical roots of societal hostility toward its practice are explored (e.g. Tissot, p.288).

Deficiencies

a. No visual aids assist the text. Relevant cross-cultural data are missing.
b. Some sentences make little sense (e.g. "Who knows what would have happened if Irv had been a real masturbator, too?"(p.220)).
c. Unproven hypotheses are often repeated (e.g. references to the "Oedipus Complex," pages 96, 110, 115, 119, 121, 128, 135, 187).
d. Biased judgmentality and unsubstantiated assumptions are evident (e.g. "There are some people whose childhood development has made it extremely difficult for them to accept responsibility for expressing their feelings of sexual love: people for whom such expression is so guilt-arousing that they have a need to punish or be punished by their sexual partners; people who are drawn to the impersonality of group sex with strangers; people who feel it necessary to use various costumes and implements to blot out their personal identities or to pierce their emotional numbness" (p.294-295)).

57. Woods, Nancy Fugate. Human Sexuality in Health and Illness. (2nd Ed.). St. Louis: The C.V. Mosby Co., 1979. 412 pp.

Brief Summary - Seven other health professionals collaborated with the author in order to produce this book. As Woods states in her Preface, the book is divided into three Units. "Unit 1 ... examines the biopsychosocial nature of human sexuality, including sexual response patterns, the wide variation possible in human sexual behavior, and the changing nature of sexuality throughout the life cycle. Unit II is devoted to sexual health and health care. Assessment of sexual health, roles for professional nurses in the delivery of sexual health services, preventive and restorative intervention, and sexual dysfunction are explored. Unit III explores clinical aspects of human sexuality" (p.ix). Unit I termed

"Human Sexuality: A Holistic Perspective," summarizes in particular the physiological findings and theories of Masters & Johnson and Helen Kaplan. Unit III delves into "Sexuality during Pregnancy and Lactation," "Sexuality and Abortion," "Sexuality, Fertility and Infertility," "Aftermath of Sexual Assault - Rape," "Adaptation to Hospitalization and Illness," "Sexuality and Chronic Illness," "Sexual Adaptation to Changed Body Image," "Sexual Adaptation to Trauma-Paraplegia," and "Drug Effects on Human Sexual Behavior."

Critique - Strengths

a. The book has illustrations, cited references, charts, tables, graphs and boxed synopses of key subjects. A Summary at the end of each chapter is useful. An innovative section entitled Questions for Review terminates each chapter in Unit III. Comparative research statistics are employed (e.g. "Table 3-3. Incidence and Frequencies of Sexual Behaviors among Research Populations of Well Aging Persons" (p.65)). Topics are well covered. Historical-anthropological input is included (e.g. p.20-21)).

b. Good critical statements proliferate (e.g. "Masters & Johnson described only one sexual response pattern for males, although it is highly unlikely that it is invariant" (p.4); also "In some instances, health professionals need to acknowledge that their sexual feelings are interfering with their practice" (p.283)). The authors objectively dissect unsubstantiated claims (e.g. "It has been suggested by groups opposed to abortion that its availability will increase nonmarital intercourse. The validity of this statement has not yet been established" (p.225)).

c. The text is basically objective and non-judgmental (e.g. "Finally, the alternative approaches to marital sex, such as mate swapping and group sex, are not generally well understood. All these areas may provoke questions with which clinicians may be confronted" (p.109)).

Deficiencies

a. The method of obtaining a sex history of a patient is not emphasized properly and is inadequately discussed (p.79-82).

b. A poorly-worded statement occurs once (i.e. "Particularly sensitive areas are masturbation, incest, and promiscuity. It should be made clear that an indiscriminate, all-permissive analytic attitude to all types of sexual behavior is irresponsible" (p.143)). Co-author Fogel does not enlarge upon or explain this pejorative generalization.

Sex Education

58. Ayres, T., Lyon, P., McIlvenna, T., Myers, F., Rila, M., Rubenstein, M., Smith, C., & Sutton, L. <u>SAR Guide for a Better Sex Life</u>. San Francisco: The National Sex Forum, 1975. 128 pp.

<u>Brief Summary</u> - In its Preface, the book states "the SARguide ... is currently a required text in numerous college and university human sexuality courses; many counselors and therapists use the book with their clients" (p.5). Five Sections comprise the book. Section A is the Introduction and lists the twelve SAR process steps (p.13-14). Next a questionnaire is detailed asking about the reader's sex-history and fantasy. Home exercises are outlined beginning with this Section and continuing throughout the book. Section B describes the anatomy and physiology of the sexual response cycle, and includes sub-sections on fantasies and on masturbation. Video films are recommended beginning with this Section. In Section C, myths and facts about male sexuality, homosexuality, female sexuality and lesbianism are explored. A "desensitization" (p.77) sub-section refers to specific sex-slang words after which the concepts of bisexuality and androgyny are differentiated and explained. Section D discusses the benefits of massage while Section E talks about sexual issues with persons having disabilities, these representing "one of the sexual minorities" (p.116).

Critique - Strengths

a. Excellent quotations, instructional sketches, diagrams, photographs, charts (e.g. "Kinsey's Heterosexual-Homosexual Rating Scale" (p.110)), specific video recommendations, descriptive at-home exercises and interpersonal enrichment aids are found in this manual. Bibliographic references follow certain key subjects (e.g. Female sexuality, p.86-87). An Appendix lists lubricants, recommendations for genital hygiene and the male-female dysfunctional "sexual concerns" (p.125-127).
b. The book utilizes comparative research and experientially developed information (e.g. the Masters & Johnson sexual

response cycle model, p48-55 with additional acknowledged input by Wilhelm Reich; also adaptations from Hartman and Fithian's Sexological Exam, p.66-67 and 112).

c. SAR is an acronym for "Sexual Attitudes Restructuring" and this is accomplished with ingenuity, originality and flair. "Myths and Societal Messages" (p.72) are commented upon (e.g. Men must "have a big cock" (p.72) and "fuck only young attractive women" (p.72)). Innovative exercises demythologize sex-negative societal roles (e.g. "At Home Exercise 23 - Masturbation with Something in your Vagina/Around your Penis" (p.110)).

d. Pejorativity and moral judgmentality are not in evidence.

e. The book can serve as a base model from which a professional can tailor adaptations for use in sex-educating any particular group of persons.

Deficiencies

a. No subject index is provided. References are not cited. Insufficient historical and cross-cultural references are provided.

b. Unreferenced generalized statements represent subjective forms of proselytization (e.g. "bisexuality is ... perhaps the most enriching and fulfilling - the most human - option of all" (p.91)).

c. The methodological history behind developing this SAR process is insufficiently dwelt upon by the authors. Mistakes made and corrected would have been a most useful input for other sex educators.

59. Bruess, Clint E. & Greenberg, Jerrold S. _Sex Education: Theory and Practice_. Belmont: Wadsworth Publishing Co. Inc., 1981. 335 pp.

Brief Summary - Part I is an "Introduction to Sex Education." Part II is termed "Instituting and Expanding Sex Education Programs." Its chapter 4 gives a historical overview while the following two chapters detail current controversies and scopes in connection with implementing sex educational programs. In Part III, the "Biological, Psychological, and Sociological Aspects of Sex Education" are explored. Part IV termed "Sexual Decision Making" includes "Alternative Sexual Behaviors." "Conducting Sex Education" makes up Part V. Part VI is called "Evaluation and Research" and rates the effectiveness of sex education and the sex educator. In closing, the authors caution that "conscientious, caring sex educators (must be) taking charge of their professional growth" (p.264). Eight Appendixes deal with resource information, guidelines and references. Some contributions by other educational specialists are included.

Critique - Strenths

a. The book is rich in support-systems such as the aforementioned Appendixes, quotations, cited references, charts, photographs, sketches and tables. A Summary and a Suggested Readings section close out each chapter. Innovative and constructive ideas abound. These include Key Concepts at the beginning of each chapter, exercises including questionnaire charts (e.g.

p.198-203) suitable as learning devices for both educators and their students, and a Cases section after each Part. Humorous anecdotal stories (e.g. on masturbation - p.25) and cartoons are also provided. Historically apt background-material is presented (e.g. Psychosexual development theories (Freud and Erikson, p.106-108)).

b. Certain chapters exhibit strong support-mechanisms for the embryonic sex educator (e.g. "Implementing Learning Strategies for Sex Education"; also "The Controversy" which lists fifteen rebuttals to opposing arguments against sex education).

c. Non-judgmental posture is usually maintained (e.g. in the section on swinging: "The personal values of the educators should not be imposed on students; rather, the sex educator's role is to help students be aware of possibilities and be more secure in their own decisions" (p.147). "... Many sexual behaviors should be considered on a continuum; it is difficult to judge when a specific behavior is 'abnormal' or a 'perversion' " (p.178)).

Deficiencies

a. Cross-cultural input is not given.

b. The authors betray qualification biases in suggesting who should be a sex educator. In Appendix D they leave out certain resource facilities and training institutions (e.g. The Institute for Advanced Study of Human Sexuality, San Francisco); also in Appendix F, the "AASECT Code of Ethics" is fraught with value-judgments and ambiguities (e.g. "Candidates should not be ... accepted for admission to a training or educational program ... if they are known to be unqualified in matters of education, training, or personal character" (p.301)).

c. Some subjects are inadequately discussed (e.g. The sexual alternatives, p.178-180). Inadequate choices of cited references are sometimes offered (e.g. on swinging, the only reference given is that of Denfeld's "Dropouts from Swinging" (1974)).

d. One sexual myth is described in a potentially misleading way (e.g. "6. It is not necessary to masturbate in order to be healthy" (p.7)). Pejorativity can be seen (e.g. "Promiscuity, broken marriages, illicit love affairs" (p.19)).

60. Burt, John & Meeks, Linda. Education for Sexuality: Concepts and Programs for Teaching. Philadelphia: W.B. Saunders Co., 1975. 550 pp.

Brief Summary - Section 1, "Introduction to Sex Education," states "since sexual relationships are intimate forms of social relationships, it seems entirely appropriate to begin this book with a discussion of ... love" (p.4). Three other Sections complete the book. Section 2 discusses "The Biological Aspects of Human Sexuality" including the topics of the male, the female, human sexual response, pregnancy and childbirth, contraception, abortion, and venereal diseases. Section 3 details "Philosophical, Psychological, and Social Aspects of Human Sexuality" with regard to "Intelligent Choice of a Sexual Lifestyle," "Masturbation," "Homosexuality," and "Population Stabilization." Section 4 discusses "Educational Aspects of Human Sexuality" as they concern "Sex Education of the First Grade Child" (3 units), the "Second,"

"Third," and "Fourth Grade Child" (2 units each), the "Fifth" and
"Sixth Grade Child" (1 unit each), and "Sex Education in the Junior
and Senior High School" (in 11 units).

Critique - Strengths

a. An accompanying Instructor's Manual includes useful assignments
    such as reading and essay homework; good defensive rationales to
    use in promoting sex education as a concept and in situation
    ethics (p.3); Reading Lists (p.24-32); and suggested examination
    questions (p.42-64). Appropriate sketches, tables, charts, and
    quotations are presented for the various levels of student (e.g.
    "Atlas of Teaching Illustrations" (Appendix 4, p.429-537).
    Other useful Appendixes are the "Glossary of Terms," a typical
    speech useful for introducing sex education to the community,
    and an exercise termed "What is Your Intimacy Quotient?"
    (p.413)). After all chapters, a proper-level Suggested Reading
    List is offered.
b. Well-structured segments separate each chapter (e.g. the eleven
    units in chapter 19 pertaining to material for junior and senior
    high school students (p.338-384)).
c. Many myths are effectively discounted (e.g. the chapter on
    Contraception, p.81-110).
d. Alternative viewpoints are presented in an objective manner
    (e.g. Five positions on homosexuality with a positive emphasis
    on position #5, p.175-177).

Deficiencies

a. No index is included. The text lacks tools suitable for young
    readers. No graphs or photographs are evidenced. Furthermore
    some exercises are apt to become embarrassing and conformity-
    seeking to any student studying in class with his/her peers
    (e.g. "Several students can explain the rationale behind the
    criteria they used" (p.376)). Improper and inadequate
    historical and cross-cultural perspectives are included (e.g.
    Three slanted and generalized references from Sweden, Masters &
    Johnson, and Russia, p.8-9).
b. Controversial subjects dealing with many of the sexual varia-
    tions and sexual minorities (e.g. sadomasochism, transvestism)
    are basically ignored.
c. Biased moralizing is sometimes in evidence (e.g. "I sincerely
    hope that you do not participate in coitus or become pregnant
    until after marriage, but if you should..." (p.121)).
d. Occasional errors surface (e.g. "Estrogen" (p.35) is character-
    ized as a single hormone).

61. Calderone, Mary S., & Johnson, Eric W. _The Family Book About
Sexuality. New York: Harper & Row, 1981. 349 pp.

Brief Summary - After a short Preface entitled "Is This Book for
You?", the authors comment upon "Understanding Ourselves as Sexual
Persons" by utilizing environmental arguments. This is followed by
"The Human Sexual Response Systems: How They Develop and How They
Work." Subsequent chapters deal with the human reproductive
systems, family planning options, life-cycle sexual patterns such as

gay lifestyles, aging and pair-breaking events, marital sexuality, familial sexuality issues, socially and physically handicapped persons' sexual needs, sociosexual problems of a legal and personal nature, information about various "Planned Sex Education Programs," and a final chapter termed "Making Sexual Decisions".

Critique - Strengths

a. A 70-page "Concise A-to-Z Encyclopedia" effectively defines concepts and terms. Resource information is provided through "Other Family Reading about Sexuality" (p.299) and "Sources of Help" (p.315). Innovative drawings, anatomical sketches, tables using cited research (e.g. p.95) and charts (e.g. p.50) aid textual comprehension. Anecdotal quotations are common. Some percentage statistics are included.
b. Many discerning sections are provided (e.g. Ten variations in sexuality with regard to "Parents as Role Models" (p.27)). Constructive advice is often available (e.g. Eight points to follow "If you are raped" (p.192)).
c. The book is recommended both for professional sexologists and educators and also as a reference resource for their clients and students.
d. Pejorativity is virtually non-existent except for the dubious title "Sexual Problems" (p.167) which covers certain sexual-minority activity. Contrasting viewpoints are objectively presented (e.g. "In favor of decriminalizing prostitution ... against..." (p.189)). Biased belief-systems are challenged (e.g. " ' Crimes' that have no true victims ... seem to many people examples of misuse of law-enforcement facilities" (p.173)).

Deficiencies

a. Some resource organizations are not listed (e.g. educational institutions specializing in graduate or certificate human sexuality programs). No graphs are shown and more cited research should have been utilized.
b. Certain topics are insufficiently and inaccurately covered (e.g. sadomasochism, p.193; also the limiting definition that "a transvestite is a person who dresses in clothes of the opposite sex in order to be able to perform sexually and achieve orgasm" (p.194)).
c. Some mistakes of commission and omission occur (e.g. "androgen-the hormone that..." (p.233) implies a single hormone rather than a class of hormones; also a similar mistake about "estrogen" (p.247); also the Kinsey 0-6 scale definition (p.256) should specify that any individual's rating combines willing overtness with fantasy arousal).

62. Carrera, Michael. _Sex: The Facts, The Acts & Your Feelings_. New York: Crown Publishers Inc., 1981. 448 pp.

Brief Summary - Carrera in his Preface states his book does not "equate sexuality with genital acts only" (p.9). Each topic depicts Facts, Myths (in the form of questions and answers), often the pertinent Feelings arising therefrom, the Relationships aspects and the impacts of Culture and Religion. Occasionally sub-sections entitled Problems or Techniques are added. The two parts of the book are termed "Facts and Feelings," and "Acts and Feelings." Included in the former are childhood-adult "Ages and Stages," "Birth Control," "Body Image," "Desire and Response," Disability," "Drugs," "Erotica," "Fetishism," "Gender and Sexual Orientation," "Incest," "Infertility," "Love," "Men's Sexual Systems," "Normality," "Pregnancy," "Pregnancy Termination," "Prostitution," "Rape," "Sex Education," "Sexually Transmitted Diseases," and "Women's Sexual Systems." The second section discusses "Kissing," "Masturbation," "Oral Sex," "Positions for Intercourse," "Sex During Pregnancy," and "Touching and Caressing."

Critique - Strengths

a. The format of the book is innovative and very useful (refer to Summary). The Myths, Culture and Religion sections are especially relevant in giving cross-cultural and historical input. The text is well referenced. The 2-page Further Reading List (p.435) divides its content. The sketches, graphs and photographs are valuable additions. Even the 12-page Glossary/Index includes pictures pertinent to certain key topics. Resource organizations are listed (i.e. "Help" (p.448)).
b. Recent research is cited (e.g. the Perry-Whipple observations about female ejaculation during orgasm (p.95)).
c. The topic of "Normality" is well-covered. Creative terminology is used (e.g. "pregnancy termination" (p.283) for abortion). The sections termed "Ages and Stages" and "Sex Education" are outstanding.

Deficiencies

a. Objective judgmentality is not always maintained (e.g. "a compulsive masturbator" (p.387); also "most mental health professionals find it difficult to believe that swinging is as emotionally benign as some swinging couples have claimed" (p.31) is one-sided and not cited; similarly "many experts believe that regular, prolonged or frequent extramarital affairs are unhealthy and that they are an immature, neurotic adaptation to marriage" (p.33)). The author's ambivalence on key issues of interest is of little assistance to devout Roman Catholics caught in personal tragedy or confusion (e.g. "Catholics therefore believe that not only is abortion murder, but it also condemns the unborn person to hell" (p.290)).
b. The author by inference evokes the medical model upon the variation of sadomasochism. Consensual behavior is not discussed (e.g. "psychoanalysis is generally not successful, nor is group therapy or drug therapy. Aversion therapy has ... no long-term studies to suggest that it is effective on a large scale" (p.153)).
c. When discussing hormones, a mistake is twice made in terming "estrogen the female hormone" (p.195, 361). "Estrogen" is a family of hormones.

63. Crooks, Robert & Baur, Karla. <u>Our Sexuality</u>. Menlo Park: The Benjamin/Cummings Publishing Co. Inc., 1980. 607 pp., plus Instructor's Guide, 240 pp.

<u>Brief Summary</u> - The authors in their Preface state that the book's orientation is psychosocial in direction rather than being biologically focused and accords a student "an opportunity to learn about sexuality in a personally meaningful way" (p.vii). The text is divided into six Parts. Part I introduces the philosophical parameters of the subject along with the current methodologies and problems of doing sex research. Part II deals with biological data while Part III describes "Sexual Behavior" patterns, both normative and atypical. In Part IV, "Sexual Problems," both physical and psychological, are delineated with a chapter on "Increasing Sexual Satisfaction" being included. "Sexuality and the Life Cycle" follows and describes this aspect from infancy to old-age. Part VI concerns itself with "Social Aspects of Sexual Behavior" and their options; in the conception of children, birth control, sex and the law, and "Cross-Cultural Variations in Sexual Expression."

<u>Critique - Strengths</u>

a. References are often comparably cited together. Anecdotal examples, photographs, sketches, graphs, tables and a Summary with Suggested Readings after each chapter are appropriately utilized. In addition, a 9-page Glossary and 11-page Bibliography are included. Cross-cultural data are supplied (e.g. see Summary). The Instructor's Guide has short-answer essay plus true-false questions (giving page references), suggestions for classroom activities, and audio-visual resources. In the back of the Guide are located the addresses of "Media Resources."
b. Seldom-discussed topics such as anal intercourse (p.159) are described.
c. There is a balanced and objective criticism of research-subject limitations (e.g. "There are also some limitations to cross-cultural studies that pertain to the biases of the ethnographers..." (p.545)).
d. Pejorativity and judgmentality are essentially not in evidence (e.g. "It is important to note that the term <u>atypical</u> is largely culturally defined... The terms we use in this chapter refer to behaviors, not to people. While it may be convenient to label people as transvestites, voyeurs, fetishists, and the like, such labeling is inappropriate and potentially oppressive" (p.239-240)).

<u>Deficiencies</u>

a. More emphasis should have been given to the historical roots of our culture's sexual development. Many eminent sex historians are not cited in the Bibliography.
b. The weakest chapter describes "Atypical Sexual Behavior." The section on "Sadomasochism" (p.245-246) is inadequate. Transvestism is insufficiently defined (i.e. "The term transvestism is applied to behaviors whereby an individual obtains sexual excitement from putting on the clothes of the

opposite sex" (p.247)).

c. In three places, the chemical compound "amyl nitrite" is
erroneously stated as being "amyl nitrate" (p.199-201).

64. DeLora, Joann S. & Warren, Carol A. B. <u>Understanding Sexual
Interaction</u>. Boston: Houghton Mifflin Co., 1977. 660 pp.

Brief Summary - The authors are educators who point out in their
Preface that this book "is designed for use in any human sexuality
course, regardless of the specific discipline within which the
course is taught" (p.xvii). Five Parts comprise the text. Part I
termed "Perspectives in Human Sexuality" presents scenarios in the
contexts of physiological (18th century), psychological (19th
century) and sociological (20th century) sexual attitudes and
activities. Part II, "Sexuality and the Life Cycle: Typical
Patterns," covers gender identity considerations and the sociosexuality of children through to the very old. Part III entitled
"Alternative Sexual Patterns" defines "normality and abnormality"
(p.238) in various ways and then covers patterns of incest,
nonmonogamy, homosexuality, bisexuality, transsexualism, some lesser
practiced variations, prostitution, and pornography. Chapter 14
called "Sex and Consent" deals with legal nonconsensual issues and
sexual violence. In Part IV, "Sexuality and Reproduction: Medical
and Social Aspects," the topics of menstruation, pregnancy, childbirth, contraception, sterilization, abortion, and venereal diseases
are discussed. Chapter 18 concerns itself with "Sex Therapy," its
causes, types, and the varying modalities developed for treatment.
Part V, "Sexuality in Society: Dimensions of Change," discusses
present-day alternatives, the concepts of love, sexual values and
ethics, current trends and future possibilities.

Critique - Strengths

a. A vast array of anecdotal plus other-expert quotations, cited
references and studies are of great help. A 30-page
Bibliography and an 11-page Glossary are included. The many
sketches, diagrams, cartoons, photographs, tables and simple
statistics are also useful. Cross-cultural and historical data
are extensively reported (e.g. "Among the Balinese ... babies
are comforted by manipulating their genitals... (cited reference
given). The ancient Greeks considered it an older man's duty to
have sexual relations with boys..." (p.348)). A Conclusion
terminates the Appendix and each chapter. Italics emphasize key
concepts.

b. Appendix A titled "The Methods and Methodological Problems of
Sex Research" by Kirby is excellent in describing and giving
examples of the four types of research done (i.e. surveys,
direct observations, in-depth interviews, and specialized-
population direct-observation). Biases and weaknesses of
research design are carefully documented (e.g. "... are those
people who do not respond significantly different from those who
do respond?... Whether this capability and motivation are
linked to sexual behavior is not known" (p.565)). Comparative
methodologies are contrasted and critiqued (e.g. "... others
have found that aversion therapy alone does not diminish
interest in the original sexual behavior pattern (Barlow, 1974)"

(p.486); also "we include ... criticisms of the medical approach" (p.241)).
c. Myths and misconceptions are explained and clarified (e.g. "Many people erroneously believe that masturbation is physically harmful..." (p.166 with historical references, p.167-168)). Role stereotypes are discounted and properly examined (e.g. "Sexual Activities of Older People..." (p.232)).
d. Controversial subjects are treated with objectivity (e.g. "... Examination of these arguments for incest taboos reveals a lack of solid foundation for them..." (247); also "sadomasochistic behavior with a consenting adult partner ... poses no social problem" (p.368)).
e. Chapters 20 and 21 on sexual values and ethics, and trends (i.e. refer to Summary) are usefully presented as to alternatives and possibilities.

Deficiencies

a. Some important subjects are inadequately discussed (e.g. transvestism is covered in only seven lines (p.307-308); also certain STD's, such as chancroid, hepatitis, are not included.)
b. Pejorativity, though rare, does occur (e.g. "... the promiscuous" (p.317)).
c. Overt and inferential mistakes pop up at times (e.g. "Androgen A hormone..." (p.587); also concerning trichomoniasis, the statement "Most infected males are carriers with no symptoms" (p.452) is unreferenced and over-exaggerated).

65. Diamond, Milton & Karlen, Arno. Sexual Decisions. Boston: Little, Brown & Co., 1980. 573 pp.

Brief Summary - A Foreword by Lief recommends this book as a college text. Part I termed "The Foundation" discusses the scope of sexuality with its sexual-learning and decision-making processes. In Part II entitled "The Person," the authors explore the body, its functions, its development, the effect of drugs and hormones on it, and physical illness. Part III, "Sex Behavior," delves into these aspects and variables. "The Couple" is the topic of Part IV and discusses "Love," "Relationships and Marriage," "Sexual Techniques" and "Psychosexual Health and Dysfunction." Part V is called "Reproduction" and makes up three chapters. Part VI, "Society," explores cross-cultural sexual mores, gender roles, and legal, moral and ethical sexual considerations.

Critique - Strengths

a. Photographs, sketches, tables and graphs supplement the text. Thorough referencing is offered. An 18-page Glossary and a 25-page References section terminate the book. A succinct Overview summarizes each chapter after which a student-aimed section concludes with Review, Discuss, Decide. Pertinent and incisive questions head each chapter. Extensive usage of historical and cross-cultural data including anecdotal information and quotations heighten the book's effectiveness immensely (e.g. "Male and Female" (p.115)).
b. Research is critically examined and analyzed (e.g. "A

questionnaire may ask clumsy or vague questions... For example, Hite's study (1976)..." (p.25)).
c. Frank acknowledgement of differing points of view is given. (e.g. "One of us (Karlen) considers dysfunctional any sex behavior that largely or completely displaces coitus... The other (Diamond) considers dysfunctional only behaviors that are not voluntary or that are destructive to partners" (p.327)).
d. Myths are clarified and corrected (e.g. penis size, p.37).
e. The text is objective (e.g. concerning pedophiliac acts: "Such conclusions surprise many people; perhaps they forget that genital acts may not greatly startle a child, may satisfy his or her curiosity, may even be sought after. Kinsey et al. (1953) noted..." (p.184)). Minimal pejorative bias is evident (i.e. "We believe that the terms discussed in this section are best avoided unless they can be better defined" (p.238)).

Deficiencies

a. Occasional topics are inadequately covered (e.g. "Sadomasochism" (p.242) avoids describing the intricacies of consensual situations).
b. Unsubstantiated and uncited claims sometimes surface (e.g. "Despite evidence to the contrary, many homosexual groups informed the public that changing from homosexuality to hetero-sexuality is impossible" (p.233)).
c. A few errors can be discerned (e.g. "amyl nitrate ... butyl nitrate" (p.83) should read "... nitrite"; also the Kinsey scale (p.220) neglects to include fantasy as the second necessary component.

66. Francoeur, Robert T. Becoming a Sexual Person. New York: John Wiley & Sons, 1982. 836 pp. (A Teacher's Manual and a separate 3-Part Student Guide are also available.)

Brief Summary - Fifteen chapters cover "Sexual Customs in America" from Columbus to the present time, "Sexual Customs in Other Cultures," "The Genetic and Psychosocial Origins of our Sexuality," "Enriching your Sexual Health and Responses" with anatomical and self-health knowledge, "Sexual Maturation," "Pregnancy, and Childbirth," "Responsible Sexuality - Contraception and Abortion" as well as "Reducing the Risk of Sexually Transmitted Diseases," "... How to Become a Sex Researcher," information concerning "The Quest for Intimacy," "The Breakdown of Intimacy - Coping with Sexual Assault," "Intimate Lifestyles Today," "Sexual Orientations and Affectional Preferences," "Achieving Sexual Health and Maturity" through the solving of sexual problems and dysfunctions, "Some Legal Implications of Sexual Behavior and Relationships," "Sexual Values and Moral Development" with an examination of values and ethics in "Developing a Moral Awareness" (p.670) through social scripting and/or religion, and "Our Sexual and Reproductive Future." This last chapter features three potential scenarios of future possible sociosexual evolvements; the cyclic, traditionalist one, "a transitional scenario: slowly toward pluralism" (p.743), or an innovative "countercyclic scenario" (p.744).

Critique - Strengths

a. An impressive array of appropriate photographs, drawings, cartoons, anatomical diagrams, quotations, anecdotal stories, footnotes, and cited references dot the text. Useful student aids include Key Concepts to Remember, Thinking It Through, Key Terms to Remember, and the Bookshelf. Numerous tables with statistics can be found along with flow charts and graphs. Some sections are colored in multi-shades for added emphasis. Headings often appear in red ink, and italics are utilized for contrast. A 20-page Bibliography and 22-page Glossary of terms terminate the text. Historical and cross-cultural information is prevalent, especially in the first two chapters. This material is tied into "Models of Sexual Deviance" (Table 11.2, p.528-529).
b. Sexual myths are often exposed (e.g. "Penis Myths" (p.137)).
c. Innovative concepts and topics abound (e.g. "The Hot and Cool sex model" (p.473); also "Figure 11.3 Relationships and Potential Erotic Responses" (521)).
d. Comparative cited research studies are often offered (e.g. "Table 10.8 Sexual Desire, Frequency, and Satisfaction in Married Women" (p.481)). Valid criticism of theoretical models of sexuality is given (e.g. "Freud's View of Women's Sexuality" (p.101)). Recent research developments are acknowledged (e.g. the " 'female ejaculation' " (p.156) phenomenon). The text is objective in presenting viewpoints, behaviors and therapies (e.g. "James Ramey, who takes a positive view of incest, has found..." (p.428); also "A Catholic Process View of Sexual Values" (p.687)).
e. This is a student-oriented text and asks many challenging questions (e.g. "Will there be new laws protecting the civil rights of homosexuals...? Should there be?" (p.554)). The book is also eminently suited as a general reference text on human sexuality.

Deficiencies

a. Occasionally, an injudicious choice of dubious research is cited (e.g. "For those homosexuals who are uncomfortable with their orientation, behavioral modification is sometimes successful... (Masters & Johnson 1979)" (p.546)).
b. Information about certain of the sexual-minority lifestyles is omitted (e.g. sadomasochism is insufficiently explained in terms of its being a consensual activity. Basic terminology is not included.)
c. Both in the text (p.515) and in the Glossary (p.G-10), the Kinsey 0-6 Scale is insufficiently defined as being behavioral only.
d. A few assumptive phrases can be found (e.g. "The sociopathic... (and) the pathological pornographer" (p.427)).

67. Gagnon, John. Human Sexualities. Glenview: Scott, Foresman & Company, 1977. 432 pp.

Brief Summary - In his Preface, Gagnon admits " 'Human Sexualities' may seem to be an odd title... The choice of the plural centers on my belief that there are many ways to become, to be, to act, to feel sexual" (p.i). The central theme of this book revolves around psychosocial-sexual "scripts" (p.5) which all humans acquire and which tend to activate themselves through the individually unique imprinting mechanism. Gagnon next emphasizes various aspects of societal evolution which have resulted in "changing purposes of sexuality" (p.22). The third chapter evaluates sex research. From Chapters 4 through 13, Gagnon details how individuals of each sex evolve through attaining various "gender identities and roles" (p.58). Chapter 14 delineates "Prostitution of Women." Congruent to this topic is the subsequent chapter "Sexual Offenses and Offenders." In Chapter 16, "Sexual Minorities," Gagnon describes sadomasochism, animal contacts, fetishism, transvestism and transsexualism. The concept of pornography is headlined by the title "Erotic Environment." "Sex Therapies" next discusses sexual dysfunctions and the treatment options. "Physical Health and Sexual Conduct" investigates problems surrounding venereal diseases, contraception and abortion. Five proposals for "maintaining sexual health" (p.404) are advanced. The final chapter "Epilogue: Future of Sexuality," explores possible future sociosexual patterns.

Critique - Strengths

a. Photographs, charts and tables supplement the text. A 4-page References and a 6-page Glossary complete the book. Some historical and cross-cultural background material is presented (refer to Summary above). The book's constructs and format are innovative and positive in their impact (refer to Summary). Gagnon criticizes traditional logic and assumption by keeping a non-judgmental attitude. This introductory textbook is of particular benefit for beginning students professionally interested in sexology.
b. Myths are attacked (e.g. "One function of science is to debunk the old myths..." (p.55)).
c. Perceptive insights abound (e.g. "Nonorgasmic sexuality has its own validities and delights" (p.135); also "pornography is fantasy sex, consumed by people who know its fantasy... They are released from responsibiliity" (p.357)).
d. Sex research is analyzed (e.g. "The tendency to turn findings into rules should evoke a strong sense of caution. Findings may be wrong" (p.56)) and constructively critiqued (e.g. Masters & Johnson, p.130-139; also Kinsey, p.235-255)).
e. The text is basically free from serious subjective moralizings.

Deficiencies

a. Unreferenced information is prevalent (e.g. "There is, however, some evidence in the reports of clothing fetishes that they may have something to do with strong attachments to mothers" (p.334)). Inaccuracies are often transposed intact into Gagnon's textual message (e.g. uncited Marshall & Suggs data, p.10-11)).
b. Some mistakes occur (e.g. While the Kinsey 0-6 Scale is accurately portrayed in Table 2, p.263, Gagnon wrongly states earlier that the scale cannot be used for "comparing fantasies with sex acts" (p.261); also the androgenic and estrogenic

classes of hormones are referred to in the singular tenses
(p.398, 420, 421, 422)).

68. Gordow, Annette G. Human Sexuality. St. Louis: The C.V. Mosby
Co., 1982. 685 pp.

Brief Summary - The author, a clinical psychologist, acknowledges in
her Preface that the book is "intended to be used as a primary text
for undergraduate courses in human sexuality... The book has a
strong interdisciplinary focus" (p.viii). Part I entitled "History
and Culture" reflects "Historical Perspectives of Sexuality" as well
as "Sex Roles in a Changing Culture." Part II, "The Basic
Elements," deals with "Sexual Anatomy and Physiology," "An Overview
of Sexual Behavior," "Birth Control and the Reproductive Systems:
The Male Hormonal System," "The Menstrual Cycle, Pregnancy and
Childbirth." Part III details sexuality from an individual's
prenatal period through to the aging adult. Part IV, "Sexual
Complications," encompasses "Sexual Dysfunction and Sex Therapy,"
"Sexually Transmissible Diseases and Sexual Health Problems" and
"Sex Offenses, Paraphilias, and Commercialized Sex." An Epilogue
summarizes "the old shoulds have been replaced by new shoulds, which
also are repressive but in a different way... The major problem
with our culture's present preoccupation with sex as performance is
that it removes sexual functioning from its natural context and
destroys its potential as a unique form of communication"
(p.607-608).

Critique - Strengths

a. Many photographs, sketches, tables, charts and cited quotes
complement each chapter. A Glossary and a 9-page References
section conclude the text. Summaries follow each major sub-
topic. Briefly abstracted Suggested Readings terminate each
chapter. The historical overview is adequate but a real
strength stems from the continual cross-cultural input (e.g. the
section "Cross-Cultural Research" (p.425-426) concerns
extramarital sexuality).
b. Not only is research often competently examined (e.g. Money &
Ehrhardt - p.56), it is also often comparably cited (e.g. Table
4-1, Kinsey versus Hunt, p.131) and adequately critiqued (e.g.
Freud, p.103; Kinsey, p.109). Recent problem-areas as well as
new theoretical concepts are included (e.g. Box 6-1, "Toxic
shock syndrome" (p.221); also the limerence theory of Tennov
(p.340-344)).
c. Innovative sections aid the reader (e.g. The chart called
"Which aches and pains may be warnings of serious trouble?" (Box
5-1, p.162) concerning birth control pills). Myths are often
exposed (e.g. "2. Myth: That girls are more 'suggestible' than
boys..." (p.48)).
d. Pejorativity is non-existent (e.g. "Because of the imprecise
usage and potentially harmful effects of the frigidity label, I
recommend that the use of this term by avoided" (p.497)).
Controversial sexual behaviors are objectively acknowledged
(e.g. "Ultimately, extramarital sexuality must be dealt with on
an individual basis..." (p.437)).

Deficiencies

a. No graphs are utilized. The occasional erroneous terminology
    surfaces (e.g. "estrogen" (p.86, 161) is termed a sex hormone,
    and not as representing a family of sex hormones).
b. Fetishism, transvestism, transsexualism, consensual incest, and
    consensual sadomasochism are deemed to be generally less than
    positive manifestations of human sexuality (e.g. "the general
    functioning of transvestites may not be greatly hindered by
    their cross dressing" (p.567); also "the public has reason to be
    concerned about sadomasochism..." (p.581)).
c. The author accepts everything published by Masters & Johnson.
    Their constant medical-model approach and methodological design
    biases and shortcomings are never acknowledged (e.g. "Treatment
    of homosexual dissatisfaction... Certainly these results are
    positive enough to warrant greater optimism regarding the
    treatment of sexual dissatisfaction" (p.524-526) (also p.400)).

69. Goldstein, Bernard. Introduction to Human Sexuality. New York:
McGraw-Hill Inc., 1976. 303 pp.

Brief Summary - The author in his Preface concedes "clinical
impressions often do not reflect the situation found in a random
sample of people" (p.vii). This book illustrates such a difference
throughout its length. Fifteen chapters follow depicting the biological functioning of male and female sexuality as well as their
homologous and differentiated differences. Endocrinological and
genetic dispositions are also explored. Puberty is discussed as are
sexual motivations, courtship procedures, precoital and coital
activities, the topics of pregnancy, contraception, abortion, and
artificial insemination. The final two chapters concern themselves
with homosexuality and "problematic" (p.249) sexual behavior.

Critique - Strengths

a. Cited references, graphs, sketches and tables proliferate
    throughout the text. Additional sketches appear in the
    Appendixes. An extensive Bibliography and Glossary terminate
    the book. Some cross-cultural and cross-species data are
    offered.
b. Textual qualifiers are properly used (e.g. Concerning male
    circumcision "no definitive statement one way or the other has
    ever been published by either the American Pediatric Society or
    the American College of Surgeons" (p.21-22)). Theoretical disa-
    greements are also cited (e.g. "Other researchers, although
    accepting most of Masters' & Johnson's conclusions, are not
    willing to accept this one (Fox and Fox, 1969)" (p.155)).
    Comparative statistics are utilized in an effective manner (e.g.
    concerning premarital intercourse, the data from Kinsey (1953),
    Sorenson (1973), and Kanter & Zelnick (1973) are compared
    (p.121)).
c. Pejorativity is minimal.

Deficiencies

a. Not all references are cited. This book is designed as an

introductory text only and a high emphasis is placed on the
physiological aspects of human sexuality. The historical roots
of our culture's approach to sexuality plus certain contemporary
alternative lifestyles (e.g. open-marriage models) are
neglected. Furthermore, subjects such as transvestism and
transsexualism are minimally discussed.

b. The medical-model approach is employed by which a specific
    sexual variation is something to be cured by therapy (e.g.
    "perhaps the person who best fits the definition of a trans-
    vestite would be one who is so concerned about cross-dressing
    that he seeks out help in some form of therapy" (p.234)).
    Generalizations occur. No data backing up certain comments are
    forthcoming (e.g. "The sadist generally is male, unmarried, and
    possesses deep feelings of inadequacy" (p.255). The subject of
    incest, both coercive and consensual, is poorly covered.

70. Haeberle, Erwin J. _The Sex Atlas_. New York: The Seabury Press,
Inc., 1978. 523 pp.

Brief Summary - Part I, "The Human Body," deals with "The Process of
Sexual Differentiation," "The Male Body," "The Female Body," "Human
Reproduction," and "Some Physical Problems" such as "Infertility,"
"Genetic Defects," "Sexual Malformations," "Pain during Sexual
Intercourse," and "Venereal Diseases." In Part II termed "Human
Sexual Behavior," sexual behavior is delineated from infancy to
adulthood, types of sexual activity are described and "Sexual
Maladjustment" is analyzed. Treatment suggestions are offered
utilizing the Masters & Johnson format. Part III, "Sex and
Society," delves into the philosophical and historical background
and rationale of how western civilization sociosexually evolved.
Three models have gripped our western culture, beginning with the
natural-unnatural religious model of sexual conformity-deviance,
followed by the legal-illegal model, and more recently, the healthy-
sick treatment-approach model. Other topical discussions include
"Marriage and the Family," and "The Sexually Oppressed." In the
final chapter "Sexual Revolution," the subjects of sex research, sex
education, and sexual ethics are investigated.

Critique - Strengths

a. Numerous photographs, artistic reproductions, sketches, charts
    (e.g. "Models of Sexual Deviance" (p.399)), tables, diagrams and
    graphs augment the text. Each chapter is concluded by a
    Reference and Recommended Reading section. The sections "A
    Glossary of Sexual Slang" (p.491-494) plus the Bibliography and
    a 6-page Resource Guide are most useful.

b. Although the book is directed at the layperson, it is novel
    and thought-provoking enough in its approach to be of immense
    value to the professional (e.g. the three models of conformity-
    deviance - see Summary). Furthermore its theme of emphasizing
    the historical antecedents plus its many cross-cultural
    references (e.g. Current psychiatric "cross-cultural
    perspectives" (p.384-386)) are assets seldom found in comparable
    texts. A clarity of expression is derived from a precision of
    definition (e.g. "embryo (Greek: swelling within)" (p.72)).

c. Contemporary imperfections are incisively analyzed (e.g.

" 'Genitality' still reigns as the supreme sexual ideal"
(p.252); also "once we accept recreation as a legitimate purpose
of sex, many of our traditional moral standards, criminal laws,
and psychiatric assumptions no longer make sense" (p.486)).
d. Pejorative remarks are not in evidence. Catchy phraseology
often surfaces (e.g. modern psychiatrists when referring to any
disease of the mind, are really talking about "a metaphorical
disease of a theoretical proposition" (p.392)).

Deficiencies

a. Many references are not cited. Unwarranted conclusions at
times needlessly polarize the author's arguments (e.g. "where
needed reforms are consistently blocked, revolution becomes
inevitable" (p.299); also in terming exhibitionism "an
unacceptable nuisance" (p.272) and voyeurism "an intolerable
invasion of privacy" (p.272), the continuum approach to these
sexual variations is essentially ignored). Sadism and masochism
are arbitrarily lumped under "Some Examples of Compulsive and
Destructive Sexual Behavior" (p.272). The author does correct
this impression, but the heading is misleading.
b. The chart termed "Heterosexual and Homosexual Behavior" (p.231)
in describing the Kinsey 0-6 Scale, neglects to include Kinsey's
concept of a fantasy quotient. Also the claim that of all
people, only "a minority are erotically attracted to both men
and women" (p.138) is not accurate if one goes by the 1-5
portion of the Kinsey scale.
c. Haeberle implies that Christian sexual asceticism stemmed
mainly from its adoption of "most of the Jewish legal tradition"
(p.348). Other historians such as Bullough present convincing
evidence that many early Greek ascetic sects also had a major
influence on Christians.
d. Some mistakes occur (e.g. "estrogen, a hormone..." (p.48)
should be "a family of hormones"); also in an error of omission,
Haeberle neglects to mention that androgens are also produced by
the male and female adrenal cortex (p.30, 46).

71. Hyde, Janet Shibley. Understanding Human Sexuality. New York:
McGraw-Hill Inc., 1979. 587 pp.

Brief Summary - Hyde asserts in the Preface that the book is
designed as a basic text for college undergraduates and "assumes no
prior college courses in biology, psychology or sociology" (p.xix).
Twenty-three chapters follow. The opening chapter termed "Sexuality
in Perspective" accords a brief historical overview coupled with
current theoretical, cross-cultural and cross-species perspectives.
The text then discusses the topics of "Sexual Anatomy," "Sex
Hormones and Sexual Differentiation," "Menstruation and Menopause,"
"Conception, Pregnancy and Childbirth," "Birth Control," "The
Physiology of Sexual Response," "Techniques of Arousal," "Sex
Research," "Sexuality and the Life Cycle-Childhood and Adolescence,
then Adulthood," "Gender Roles," "Female and Male Sexuality,"
"Homosexuality and Bisexuality," "Variations in Sexual Behavior,"
"Rape," "Love," "Sexual Dysfunction and Sex Therapy," "Sexual
Diseases," "Ethics, Religion and Sexuality," "Sex and the Law," and
"Sex Education." The final chapter entitled "Sexuality in the

Future" examines areas such as embryo transplants, cloning and choosing a baby's gender. The author concludes that society must "shape technology to our values, rather than the reverse" (p.530).

Critique - Strengths

a. The text has many cited references, appropriate photographs, sketches, graphs and tables. An innovative section termed "Cited" details an apt quotation from an expert on the subject to follow. An additional section called "Focus" imparts a personal anecdotal or historical story about the topic. A Summary and Suggestions for Further Reading terminate each chapter. A 6-page Glossary and 15-page Bibliography conclude the book. The historical background is well covered (e.g. "Figure 1.2 The History of Scientific Research on Sex" (p.5)). Cross-cultural information is often forthcoming (e.g. photographs, p.14-15). Unusual diagrams are sometimes utilized (e.g. six colored diagrams denoting steps required for a vasectomy (Figure 6.6, p.147)).
b. An excellent section called "Issues in Sex Research" (p.206) includes a critical analysis, both positive and negative, on the procedures of sampling, self-reports versus direct observations as well as the ethical issues involved.

Deficiencies

a. Personal bias interferes with an attempted objectivity (e.g. While Hyde can state "the 'respectable deviant' ... who is skillful enough ... not to get caught is not studied in such research. Thus the picture that research provides us of these variations may be very biased" (p.362), Hyde also generalizes without citations that "transvestism ... is a problem only when it becomes so extreme that it is a person's only source of erotic gratification" (p.359-360)).
b. Contemporary ethics are offered with moralistic value-judgments (e.g. "Few ethical thinkers today take the position that either promiscuity or impersonal sex is a good thing..." (p.479); also "the physical and sexual side of human nature ... is helpful, but if it is pushed too far, it can also leave people under the control of their impulses and thus less than fully human" (p.485)).
c. The section on "Consensual Extramarital Sex" is poorly done. Group Marriage is not discussed. References and statistics from Bartell and Gilmartin are slanted in order to cast a judgmental tone on swinging (e.g. "Although they describe themselves ... as exciting people with many interests, in fact they engage in few activities and have few hobbies" (p.265)).
d. Textual inaccuracies occur (e.g. "Estrogen" (p.50, 52) means a class of female sex hormones; also "amyl nitrate" (p.200) should read "amyl nitrite"; also the Kinsey 0-6 Scale is stated "experience only" (Figure 14.6, p.333) and omits the component of fantasy).

72. Julian, Cloyd J., Jackson, Elizabeth N. & Simon, Nancy S. _Modern Sex Education (3rd Ed.)_. New York: Holt, Rinehart and Winston, Inc., 1980. 95 pp.

Brief Summary - The Preface states this book "was written to meet the demands by parents, teachers, school administrators, boards of education, guidance counselors, and students for an authoritative and personal approach to sexuality" (p.iii). Eight chapters explore sexual issues as they pertain to the family, the pre-pubertal to the immediate post-pubertal period, "Relationships" involving dating, love and marital considerations, "Reproduction" in both its creative and preventative aspects, "Family Planning," "Sexual Variance," "Sexually Transmitted Diseases," and a final chapter entitled "Healthy Sexuality" which delves into the reasons for sex education and where to turn for resource help.

Critique - Strengths

a. Appropriate photographs, sketches and student exercises (e.g. p.21) dot the text. The format is sharp with color and headings, including those in margins. A 4-page Glossary of terms and some Suggested Further Reading references after most chapters are further assets.
b. The preamble to each chapter takes the form of a series of factual statements in the forms of rhetorical questions. These are effective myth debunkers (e.g. "Did you know that the average pregnant teenager is a high health risk?" (p.57)).
c. The book is basically free from moral judgmentality (e.g. "In 1970, the President's Commission ... concluded that there was no evidence to suggest that exposure to pornography had a harmful effect upon moral character, sexual orientation, or attitudes" (p.61)).

Deficiencies

a. There are no graphs, charts or cited references and any furnished statistics are sparse and most elemental. Many statements require much more amplification and referencing (e.g. "Incest occurs in families more often than one might imagine" (p.64)). Historical references are too few and too recent in time. Cross-cultural information is almost totally lacking.
b. The book is designed to fit a weekend or mini-course format. Large amounts of important material are left out of major sections, such as the chapters on "Sexual Variance" and "Sexually Transmitted Diseases." Controversial subjects are avoided (e.g. the words transvestism, transsexualism, sado-masochism, and fetishism, amongst others, are not even mentioned).
c. Errors and inadequate definitions sometimes are in evidence (e.g. "estrogen, a female hormone" (p.86); also "Incest, a form of child abuse..." (p.64)).

73. Katchadourian, H.A. & Lunde, D.T. Fundamentals of Human Sexuality (3rd Ed.). New York: Holt, Rinehart & Winston, Inc., 1980. 544 pp. (with Instructor's Manual 191 pp.) (Also Human Sexuality, Brief Edition (2nd Ed.). (Katchadourian, Lunde & R. Trotter), 1975. 350 pp. with Instructor's Manual 158 pp. is a simplified version of the major text. Additionally, Biological Aspects of Human Sexuality (2nd Ed.). (Katchadourian & Lunde), 1980, 207 pp. represents Chapters 2 through 7

of the major text's 3rd Ed.).

Brief Summary - The book is divided into three Parts, termed
"Biology," "Behavior" and "Culture," after an introductory chapter
by Katchadourian on "Fundamental Questions About Human Sexuality."
Part I covers sexual anatomy, physiology, sex hormones, the
conception to childbirth process, contraceptive techniques, and
"Sexual Disorders." Part II deals with psychosexual development,
autoeroticism, normative as well as variations in sexuality, and
"Sexual Malfunction and Therapy." Three chapters termed "Sex and
Society" (discussing cross-cultural patterns), "Sex and the Law"
(with mainly U.S. but including some foreign input), and "Sex and
Morality" (utilizing Judeo-Christian historical information plus
contemporary "situation ethics" (p.484)) comprise Part III.

Critique - Strengths

a. Excellent biological sketches along with photographs, cartoon-
type drawings, tables, graphs and charts with simple statistics
complement the text. Many references exist (e.g. Three
references from Money (Box 13.5 "Raising a Male as a Female"
(p.429)). A 20-page Selected Bibliography plus an 8-page
Glossary are included. Both a Name Index and a Subject Index
are offered. The Instructor's Manual lists source materials,
periodicals, plus many types of possible examination questions
along with their answers.
b. The Part termed "Biology" is the best one while the one on
"Behavior" is almost as useful with care being taken to describe
conflicting historical and current sexual theories, models and
postulates from a host of back-up references (e.g. Freud's
"Psychoanalytic States of Psychosexual Development" (Box 8.6,
p.236-237) and including a cited reference from Salzman
critiquing Freud). Cross-cultural data are often supplied (e.g.
Box 8.16, p.271)). Historical background material is plentiful
(e.g. refer to Summary above).
c. The text is easy to follow. Some phrases stand out (e.g.
"prepill morality" (p.485)).

Deficiencies

a. Misinformation sometimes occurs (e.g. Fantasy is not stressed
as comprising part of the Kinsey 0-6 Scale - "a person with ...
experience would be placed close to the heterosexual end of the
scale" (p.357)).
b. Medical-model conclusions surface which stem from assumptions
(e.g. "Some people who originally had a strong homosexual orientation may change to a more heterosexual orientation. Some of
these changes ... are made with therapeutic assistance" (p.359).
Here the authors cite the Masters & Johnson research which
itself is methodologically unsound). The continuum approach to
variations of sexuality is basically ignored in favour of
emphasizing the societally unacceptable end of the spectrum
(e.g. regarding voyeurism, exhibitionism, sadomasochism
(p.374-377)). Considerable ignorance of these variations is
displayed (e.g. "At their mildest, sadistic men soil women..."
(p.377)).

c. Subjective moralizing occasionally occurs (e.g. "One of the major practical difficulties with the new morality is how easily it is perverted... Fletcher points out that 'liking' does not equal 'loving'..." (p.490)).

74. Kelly, Gary F. _Sexuality: The Human Perspective_. Woodbury: Barron's Educational Series, Inc., 1980. 320 pp.

Brief Summary - The author, a college educator, in his Preface admits "it is my hope that this book will be suitable for use in human sexuality courses that emphasize increased self-awareness to some degree" (p.vi). Part 1 termed "Male/Female, Women/Men" describes the "roots of change" (p.3) in sociosexual attitudes, the biological "Sexual Systems and Sexual Responses," and the critical relationships existing between "Gender Identity and Society." Part 2, "Human Sexual Behavior," discusses one's "Learning to be Sexual," types of "Shared Sexual Behavior," the process of "Reproduction," "Birth Control" methods, "Homosexuality and Bisexuality," and "Other Forms of Sexual Behavior." Part 3's "Dealing with Sexual Problems" dissect the subjects of "Problematic Sex" as exemplified by uncomfortable personal extremes, socially exploitive acts, sex-change etiology, handicapped persons' sexual difficulties, sexual diseases, and genetic malformations; the educating requirements necessary for qualifying interested professionals, and "Sexual Dysfunctions and their Treatment." Part 4 entitled "Sex and Contemporary Society," has three chapters devoted to issues involving "Sex, Art, the Media and the Law," sociosexual trends and possibilities, and a final chapter outlining some exercises to ascertain "Who Are You as a Sexual Person?"

Critique - Strengths

a. An abundance of apt photographs, sketches, anatomical diagrams, charts, graphs and tables highlight the text. Citations are continually used and References terminate each chapter. Many appropriate case studies are included and a 5-page Appendix lists resource organizations. Particularly helpful are questionnaires (e.g. "Your Sexual History" (p.17)). Considerable historical (e.g. Figure 1.1, p.6) and cross-cultural (e.g. Figure 11.2, p.249) data are included.
b. Many myths and cultural misconceptions are attacked (e.g. case study, p.32; also "Facts and Fallacies about Masturbation" (p.76); also the various definitions involved in "The Normalcy-Abnormalcy Issue" (p.200)).
c. Past sex research is both critiqued and compared (e.g. "Published information about sexuality is largely opinion, prejudice, and conclusions drawn from very limited, poorly designed research studies..." (p.vii); also homosexual "Hypotheses" (p.115)). Discerning postulations at times are presented (e.g. "Table VIII Factors Inhibiting the Persistence of Monogamy as a Dominant Form" (p.277)).
d. The medical-model approach is critiqued (e.g. "It is also unfortunate that so much of human sexual behavior has been studied by ... people who have tended to view much of it in the context of pathology" (p.vii)). Objectivity is constantly maintained (e.g. case studies on bestiality (p.142) and sadomaso-

chism (p.147); also "many psychotherapists feel that incest, per se, does not necessarily constitute a 'sick' act..." (p.173, two cited references given)). Value-judgments are attacked (e.g. "Promiscuity... This term is emotionally and morally loaded..." (p.166)).

Deficiencies

a. More cross-cultural and historical background would have helped.
b. An occasional unwarranted assumption surfaces (e.g. "It is probably safe to assume that most group sexual contacts represent a once-in-a-lifetime or very occasional episode for most of the participants..." (p.157)).
c. A few mistakes occur (e.g. the Kinsey 0-6 Scale is represented as that of behavior only - "... this continuum ... does not adequately reflect the inner interests and needs of individuals" (p.112); also "estrogen" (p.25) is a class-name for a family of such hormones; also "amyl nitrate" (p.86) should read "amyl nitrite").

75. McCary, James Leslie. McCary's Human Sexuality (3rd Ed.). New York: D. Van Nostrand Co., 1978. 512 pp.

Brief Summary - This book is a revision of earlier 1967 and 1973 editions. Part 1's "By Way of Introduction" deals with the rationales for sex education plus the preponderance of sexual myths and fallacies. Part 2's "The Human Sexual System" details male-female sexual physiology, including prenatal development. Part 3 entitled "The Sexual Act" delves into the concepts of love, techniques of sexual arousal, drugs and sex, variations in sexual intercourse, orgasm, birth control, and "Sex in the Later Years." Part 4 describes "Present-Day Sexual Attitudes and Behavior." Part 5's "Sexual Complications" discusses sexual dysfunctions, variance, diseases, and disorders. Part 6 is called "Sex and Society" and analyzes the legal implications of illegitimacy and societal sex offenses and boundaries. The book closes with some "model sex laws" (p.434).

Critique - Strengths

a. An extensive 31-page References section plus a 19-page Glossary close out the text. Cited references, quotations, photographs, cartoons, drawings, anatomical diagrams, pertinent statistics, graphs and tables all usefully complement the text. Resource organizations are occasionally suggested (e.g. p.19). Historical, especially religious, background material is provided (e.g. p.8-11). Some cross-cultural information is included (e.g. "A study of 76 primitive societies (Ford & Beach 1951) showed that 64% approved of homosexual relations" (p.344)).
b. Research is compared and cited (e.g. Table 16.3 - 21 studies (1948-1975) on "Incidence of Premarital Intercourse among the College Educated Aged 18-22 (Gunderson 1977)" (p.273)). Seldom-cited references occur at times (e.g. "Some women experience status orgasmus, which is a sustained orgasmic

response lasting at least 20 seconds... (Jobaris and Money 1976)" (p.181)).

c. Chapter 2 (refer to Summary above) is innovative in dealing with sexual myths and fallacies. They are itemized by section with later references being included as to their explanation and exposure.

d. Certain topics are unusually complete (e.g. sexual physical disorders; also sex-law proposed and suggested changes (refer to Summary)).

Deficiencies

a. Sex-research methodology and bias controls are minimally discussed. More historical and cross-cultural research data should have been included (e.g. the German sexologist Hirschfeld is not even mentioned).

b. Subjective and selective value-judgments are in evidence (e.g. "Studies involving personality ... of promiscuous women indicate that they have generally made an uneven progression to physical, emotional, intellectual, and social maturity..." (p.362, cited reference included)). Erroneous conclusions are derived at times from idiosyncratic studies (e.g. "Fang (1967) ... showed that swinging is on the decline..." (p.360)). Certain topics display a medical-model analysis in which mutual consensuality of behavior is insufficiently explored (e.g. sadism and masochism - p.330-332). Other sub-topics are totally excluded (e.g. the disease called nonspecific urethritis).

c. Some mistakes occur (e.g. the Glossary - "androgen A steroid hormone..." (p.468); "Estrogen A steroid hormone..." (p.471) should both read "a family of hormones"; also "Trichomoniasis an infection of the vagina..." (p.484) omits the male-infection possibility).

76. Money, J. & Musaph, H. Handbook of Sexology (5-volume). New York: Elsevier North Holland Inc., 1978. 1448 pp.

Brief Summary - The authors, acting as both editors and contributors. have analyzed the basic aspects of human sexuality from the various disciplinary perspectives. Book I entitled "History and Ideology" explores "History and theory of sexology," "Youth and sex," "Customs of family formation and marriage," and "Religion, ideology and sex." Book II termed "Genetics, Hormones and Behavior" is sectioned into three parts; "Genetics, cytogenetics, sex reversal and behavior," "Prenatal hormones and the central nervous system," and "Hormones and sexual behavior in adulthood." Book III, "Procreation and Parenthood," refers to "Regulation of procreation," "Pregnancy and childbirth," and "On parenthood." Book IV deals with "Selected Personal and Social Issues" which covers the sections "Special issues-personal" ("Masturbation," "Masked sexual adjustment problems," "Skin, touch and sex," "Unusual sexual behavior of non-human primates"), and "Geriatric sexual relationships." Book V, "Selected Syndromes and Therapy," concerns itself with "Psychosexual impairment," "Sexual problems of the chronically impaired...," "Personal and social implications of diseases of the genital tract," and "Treatment and counseling for sexual problems."

Critique - Strengths

a. A complete Author Index, Subject Index and Contents are listed in each book. Each chapter has a summary and bibliography by the contributor and each section is co-ordinated by an overall expert in that area. Tables, references, photographs, sketches, graphs and case studies are used at appropriate times. A table of acronyms at the beginning of each book is also an asset for the reader deficient in biochemistry. Book I in particular provides historical and cross-cultural material (see Summary).
b. Highlights are the excellently described seldom-investigated topics (e.g. Chapter 20 on "sociohistorical perspectives" (p.269), especially as they pertain to the linkages of industrialization, sexual repression and the revolution in eroticism).
c. Interdisciplinary sexology is well documented.

Deficiencies

a. Minimal or no mention or discussion ensues on key sexological issues (e.g. Group sex, consensual sadomasochism).
b. Some chapters are poorly done with an overemphasis on neofreudian theoretical dogma (e.g. Chapter 92 by Frijling-Schreuder on masturbation - "The vicissitudes of masturbation during childhood development form a pivot for development towards either mental health or neurosis... Obsessive masturbation may be an expression of a neurotic conflict as may be the complete inhibition of masturbation" (p.1143-1144)).
c. Certain authors show pejorativity and judgmentality (e.g. Chapter 67 by Friedman on "Psychogynology" - "Greedy, insatiable demands are made, leading to promiscuity and unfaithfulness... A hostile attachment to a mother ... may lead to a homosexual potentiality" (p.882)).
d. At times, assumptive unproven hypotheses are offered as uncited facts (e.g. Chapter 93 by Pierloot on "Masked sexual adjustment problems..." - "Some sadomasochistic partner relations ... function temporarily quite well but almost invariably lead eventually to the arousal of serious tensions" (p.1148); also "other 'female complaints' occurring in connection with initial sexual relations ... are due to infantile fixations..." (p.1152)).

77. Nass, Gilbert D., Libby, Roger W. & Fisher, Mary Pat. Sexual Choices. Belmont: Wadsworth Publishing Co. Inc., 1981. 729 pp.

Brief Summary - This book begins with "Our Sexual Identity," then proceeds into "Gender Identity and Gender Role" and from there moves on through the topics of sexual scripting, physiology, fantasies, dreams, chemical mood modifiers, masturbation and then into "Developing Sexual Relationships." Then the book progresses to "Sexmaking with Others" followed by "Homosexual and Bisexual Preferences." At this point it steps back to "Early Sexual Learning" which includes inhibitory patterns before getting into "Adult Sexual Careers" which covers various lifestyle options. After "Intimacy and Older People" comes "Women's Liberation and Sexual Choices," after which "Sexual Assault" is examined. The subjects of "Sex for Sale" and "Dealing with Genital Infections" are fitted around the issue of "Enhancing Sexual Health" (with a side-topic of "Sexuality and Disability"). The many concerns governing conception, contraception, abortion, pregnancy and birth complete the factual presentation of the book. The final chapter entitled "Toward Sex-Positive Futures" deals with futuristic sociopolitical, ethical and moral sexual possibilities.

Critique - Strengths

a. Three Appendixes termed "An Inventory for Self-Evaluation," "A Brief Look at Sex Research," and "The Yellow Pages of Informed Sexual Choices" are useful. The last Appendix furnishes resource addresses. Topical anecdotal stories are utilized and often accompanied by relevant photographs. Excellent diagrams also abound. Research is cited. Some historical input is provided.
b. Unknowns are properly acknowledged (e.g. "Just how androgen-estrogen-progesterone levels affect female sexual desire is therefore unclear" (p.11)). Research ambiguities are clearly pointed out (e.g. Concerning the Masters & Johnson 4-phase orgasmic cycle, the authors also describe "several points of view other than that of Masters & Johnson" (p.182)).
c. Innovative terminology is often employed (e.g. "visual rape" (p.380) in describing peeping tomism). Not-often found but informative sections are sometimes proffered (e.g. "Profiles of Rapists" (p.391)).
d. Controversial issues are usually discussed from both perspectives (e.g. A Feminist's Ambivalence Toward Pornography (p.404); also "Some (scholars) ... even feel that incest may be okay under certain circumstances" (p.265)).

Deficiencies

a. Appendix C lacks the listing of "Graduate School Programs." Cross-cultural perspectives are basically ignored.
b. Transsexualism is dismissed in one line (p.11). Some alternative lifestyles and sexual minorities are inferentially criticized by quoting an expert with only one viewpoint (e.g. Sammons "conjectures that swinging arrangements don't work very well" (p.301). Transvestism is not even mentioned. Many atypical behaviors are minimally discussed (e.g. fetishism (p.84)), or are slanted in coverage (e.g. A journalist Santini states after interviewing "almost a thousand women that behavior like 'bondage and discipline' are an indirect acting-out of anger and a dangerous exaggeration of traditional gender roles" (p.381). The authors present no scientific evidence to back up this layperson's conclusion).

78. Read, Donald A. *Healthy Sexuality*. New York: Macmillan Publishing Co. Inc., 1979. 280 pp.

Brief Summary - The author, an educator, relates in his Preface that this book emphasizes "a more 'humanistically' oriented course" (p.vi). Indeed "this is not a fact-oriented, but a feeling- and values-oriented book" (p.132). The first three chapters termed

"Changing Sexual Attitudes," "Healthy Sexuality," and "Sex and Human Values," discuss sociosexual trends, sex as a learned behavior, and issues around sexual values-clarification in developing sexual self-options. Chapters 4 through 6 describe female and male sexual anatomical systems and focus on masturbatory patterns. The following chapter describes sexual arousal as researched by Masters & Johnson. The subsequent three chapters deal with "Intimate Behavior," traditional and alternative "Sexual Lifestyling," and the many variations of "Sexual Expression." Chapters 11 through 13 diagnose contraceptive techniques, issues around "Pregnancy and Birth," and "Some Potential Problem Areas" as evidenced in sexual dysfunctions, infertility, rape, abortion, and the sexually transmitted diseases. A final chapter is entitled "Keeping Sex and Sexuality Alive Throughout the Life Span."

Critique - Strengths

a. Apt photographic depictions (e.g. Lifestyle ads (p.133)), drawings, anatomical diagrams, anecdotal stories, quotations and references dot the text. Marginal headings are in red ink and certain areas are italicized for effect. Statistics are often quoted and cited (e.g. p.5). Four Appendixes list two bibliographies (twelve pages), a Glossary of Terms (seven pages) and eight pages of typical student questions and answers.
b. Constructive innovations include posed rhetorical questions (e.g. Three about "Jane's autobiographical sketch" (p.41)), and challenging value-system exercises (e.g. some continuums of sexual behaviors (p.32)).
c. Sexual myths are often exploded (e.g. "penis size" (p.74)). On occasion, accepted ideas are questioned (e.g. " 'Premature' ejaculation is not only difficult to define but may, in fact, not be a valid concept" (p.258)).
d. The text sticks assiduously to its humanistic approach (e.g. the quoting verbatim of the nine points developed in Kirkendall's "Bill of Sexual Rights and Responsibilities" (p.7)).
e. The book gives sound philosophical advice (e.g. "Another answer may be ... to allow ourselves to grow beyond any myths or stereotypes" (p.17)). It is also non-judgmental (e.g. "I believe that there is virtually no expression of sexual loving and caring that could be called 'abnormal' " (p.141); also "It makes no sense to label such people 'latent homosexuals' " (p.134)).

Deficiencies

a. Some essential topics are neglected (e.g. a historical input, also cross-cultural comparisons) or are minimally covered (e.g. sex research; also coercive as well as consensual incest; also consensual sadomasochism except for a brief section on bondage (p.147)). Anti-sociosexual behavior is also not properly delved into except for rape (p.211-212).
b. At one point there is an unsubstantiated assumption (e.g. "Anything in excess can be harmful. When it comes to masturbation..." (p.255)).
c. A few minor mistakes occur (e.g. "estrogen" (p.50) should read

"the estrogens"; also "The Oneida commune has a system..."
(p.129) should read in the past tense).

79. Roberts, Elizabeth J. ed. Childhood Sexual Learning: The
Unwritten Curriculum. Cambridge: Ballinger Publishing Co., 1980. 303
pp.

Brief Summary - Roberts in her Preface states "this book is based on
the premise that human sexuality and the ways in which we express it
are not entirely inborn. Instead, maleness and femaleness are made
up of a complex set of roles and attitudes that are developed and
limited by family, society and culture" (p.xi). The topics include
"Dimensions of Sexual Learning in Childhood," "Toward an
Understanding of Sexual Learning and Communication - An Examination
of Social Learning Theory and Non-School Learning Environments,"
"Work, the Family and Children's Sexual Learning," "Television as a
Sphere of Influence on the Child's Learning about Sexuality,"
"Sexual Learning in the Elementary School," "Peer Communication and
Sexuality," "Social Services and Sexual Learning," "Religion and the
Sexual Learning of Children," "Human Sexuality - Messages in Public
Environments" (such as in the People's Republic of China and also
covering the "Sources of Messages" such as body language, clothing,
sports, work roles, political demonstrations, museum exhibits,
advertising, adult entertainment, the newsstand, graffiti, and
toilets).

Critique - Strengths

a. Textual aids include cited references, anecdotal stories,
   tables and useful charts (e.g. "Figure 3-1. Connections Between
   the Work World and the Family and Sexual Teaching and Learning"
   (Greenblat, p.69)).
b. The book is a good one for scholars and educators to examine in
   depth due to its profound analysis of a seldom-focused component
   of childhood learning.
c. At times, certain authors display useful, sophisticated
   theories of children's sexual learning patterns (e.g. "...
   Responsibility for an individual's health ... has been left
   almost entirely to the doctor... Children may transfer such an
   abdication of general health responsibility to matters of sexual
   health and understanding as well" (Bane and Holt, p.200-201)).
d. "Religion and the Sexual Learning of Children" is extremely
   well-written and analyzed. Collins presents a recounting of how
   religion has influenced countless generations of persons in
   their learned childhood sexual patterns. The chapter accords
   both a historical and a contemporary perspective (e.g.
   "Scientifically erroneous information about the body is
   apparently still being conveyed to children - especially girls -
   through the (Roman Catholic) church's inculcation of the virtue
   of virginity..." (p.224 including a cited reference)).

Deficiencies

a. Visual aids are minimally present. No general bibliography is
   included. Little cross-cultural data are presented.
b. Little attention has been paid to why some children who acquire

negative messages still manage to emerge totally sex-positive in attitude toward the sexual continuum of behavior, including the sexual minorities.

80. Rosen, Raymond & Rosen, Linda Reich. _Human Sexuality_. New York: Alfred A. Knopf, 1981. 566 pp.

Brief Summary - The authors, both psychologists, state this book "has grown out of our experiences in sex education, sex research, and sex therapy during the 1970's" (p.ix). Part I details cross-cultural sexual mores, historical and contemporary research, sexual physiological and psychosexual development, and sexual relationships and lifestyles. Part 2, "Human Sexual Response," discusses sexual anatomy, sexual psychophysiology, and endocrinological sexuality. Part 3 termed "Sexual Function and Dysfunction" describes masturbation, variations of sexuality, and male and female sex-dysfunctional problems. Part 4 entitled "Reproductive Issues" covers pregnancy, childbirth, contraception, and abortion. Part 5 deals with sex offenders and offenses plus sexual health issues such as venereal diseases, disabilities, mental retardation, and drug side-effects. In the Epilogue called "Sex Education and Personal Growth," the authors conclude "sex education must, by definition, address the needs of the whole person..." (p.525).

Critique - Strengths

a. A 13-page References section plus a 3-page referenced Glossary terminate the book. Apt photographs, anatomical sketches, cartoons, charts, tables (e.g. "Table 2.1 The Bem Sex-Role Inventory" (p.37)), graphs and histograms dot the text. Key phrases and concepts are printed in italics and bold print. Cited references, boxed anecdotal stories and cited case examples (e.g. "Case Study of a Transvestite Exhibitionist..." (p.456)) are usefully provided. An Overview precedes and a Summary concludes each chapter and a pertinent colored-page essay concludes each Part (e.g. Ending Part I, "Sex and Aging" (p.121-127)). Cross-cultural (e.g. p.4) and historical (e.g. p.13) data are specifically provided in many chapters.

b. Research is often cited, compared and statistics furnished (e.g. "Table 7.1 Comparison of Kinsey and Hunt Data on Masturbation Incidence and Frequency" (p.238)). Up-to-date research concepts are acknowledged (e.g. "Female Ejaculation-Fact or Fantasy?..." (p.146)). Research inadequacies are postulated (e.g. Concerning behavioral approaches to sex-offender treatment, "our own experience suggests unless treatment is continued over several months, perhaps even years, the possibility of a relapse always exists (Rosen and Kopel, 1977)" (p.468)).

c. Sexual misconceptions and myths are denounced (e.g. "... people (sometimes) abstain from masturbation ... (in) the mistaken notion that it will 'use up' sexual desire" (p.236); also the innovative "Phallic Facts and Fallacies: Cross-Cultural Images of the Penis..." (p.158)).

d. Controversial topics are usually analyzed from both positive and negative biases (e.g. swinging (p.102-103); also incest (p.449-450)).

    e. The text is basically free from pejorativity and subjective
       value-judgments (e.g. "Basic Values for Sex Education" (p.524)
       as stated by Calderone (1977)).

Deficiencies

    a. Inaccurate assumptions about certain techniques are emotionally
       biased and misleading (e.g. "During the so-called sexological
       examination, therapists will touch and stimulate the breasts and
       genitals of the patient..." (p.330)).
    b. Some subjects are either minimally explained or are not covered
       at all (e.g. transsexualism (brief references only, p.35,
       p.456); also pubic lice; also sadomasochism).
    c. Sexual research-design methodology and bias controls are selec-
       tively addressed (e.g. "survey limitations" (p.18)), but should
       have more thoroughly covered other areas.

81. Rosenzweig, Norman & Pearsall, Paul, ed. _Sex Education for the
Health Professional: A Curriculum Guide._ New York: Grune & Stratton,
Inc., 1978. 351 pp.

    Brief Summary - In the Preface. the editors expound the view that
"we believe this book is the first attempt to bring together in a
systematic fashion the various pedagogical approaches of our contemporary leaders in sex education as they relate to the training and
work of health care professionals" (p.x). Six Parts make up the
text with the final Part being the Appendix of audio-visual aids
with some available listed resources. In Part I, historical,
current medical, and legal perspectives are explored in relation to
"Developing a Pedogogical Approach..." Part II features topics useful in "Designing a Curriculum" from theological, medical, and
anthropological perspectives. Part III describes the various
teaching methodologies covering small-group, audio-visual, and
assessment-instrument programs. "... Special Target Audiences,"
namely psychiatrists, gynecologists, urologists, physiotherapists
and nurses, are addressed in Part IV. In Part V, eleven special
programs are detailed by their respective local designers.

Critique - Strengths

    a. The text contains useful cited references, tables, charts and
       the Appendix (see above). Innovative key charts are often in
       evidence (e.g. "Relationship of physical disability to
       sexuality" (Cole, p.92-93)). Apt case examples are frequently
       to be found. Historical (e.g. Calderone, p.7) and anthro-
       pological (e.g. Gebhard, p.103) background information is
       included.
    b. There are research-data comparisons (e.g. "Table 11-1
       Instruments for Assessment of Sex Education Curricula" (Williams
       and Miller, p.140-141) which includes reliability and validity
       data).
    c. The medical-model approach. while acknowledged, is tempered by
       some authors who emphasize the multidisciplinary model (e.g.
       "Sexuality Curriculum for the Gynecologist" (Priver); also "The
       National Sex Forum Model" (McIlvenna)).
    d. As of the date of publication, the text is a relatively com-

plete cross-section of North American professional sex-education programs.

Deficiencies

a. No photographs or sketches complement the text.
b. Not enough actual examples of programs are proffered and thus the embryonic sex educator is ill-prepared on how to handle controversial subjects such as incest, sadomasochism, or co-marital sexuality, both from his/her own personal bias and also as to how to prevent projecting that bias onto his/her students.

82. Sandler, Jack, Myerson, Marilyn & Kinder, Bill N. <u>Human Sexuality: Current Perspectives</u>. Tampa: Mariner Publishing Co. Inc., 1980. 264 pp.

Brief Summary - Seventeen chapters detail the book as follows: "Sexuality - A Historical Perspective," "The Sexual Revolution," "Cross-Cultural and Cross-Species Comparisons," "The Sex Researchers," "Sexual Anatomy and Sexual Response," "Psychosexual Development," "Sexuality Through the Life Cycle." "Birth Control and Infertility," "Other Dimensions in Sexual Behavior," "Variations in Sexual Orientation," "Sex and the Law," "Pornography," "Sexual Problem Behaviors," "Sexual Dysfunctions and Treatment," "Sexual Health," "Sexuality in Special Populations," and "Sexuality: Personal Perspectives." This final chapter emphasizes sex and values, alienation, the synthesis of sexuality as a concept, and interpersonal relationships, as they deal with the components of sex, love and intimacy.

Critique - Strengths

a. Assets such as cited references, sketches. quotations and a 14-page References section augment the text. Historical and cross-cultural input is provided (refer to Summary). The book is well-designed. Content-emphasis is balanced and sensible. Although it is a basic book for students and laypersons, it is still a good supplemental reference book for the professionals.
b. The text is usually unbiased, citing facts and not assumptions (e.g. "Their facts supported those of Gebhard et al. (1965)... Exposure to pornography was not cited by the sex offenders as important factors in the commission of their offenses"(p.159)). Certain concepts are handled with ingenuity (e.g. Even though classifying incest as a first-order problem behavior, a qualifier is added stating "incest may also be regarded as occupying one end of a continuum, with normal familial interactions at the other end" (p.167)).
c. Constructive criticism of research is often presented (e.g. Masters & Johnson (p.44)). Myths are exposed through references (e.g. penis size (p.61)).
d. The final chapter is excellent in non-judgmentally recounting options and choices one can exercise. Cultural pitfalls are succinctly portrayed (e.g. " 'The American way of sex' is preoccupied with orgasms" (p.216)).

Deficiencies

a. Graphs, charts and photographs are insufficient for such a
    text (e.g. the Kinsey 0-6 scale is not displayed and it is
    wrongly described as measuring "actual behavior" (p.138) only,
    when in fact the scale also includes the component of fantasy).
b. The authors overly emphasize the medical model of treatment for
    atypical behavior (e.g. "treatment of the fetishist may
    involve..." (p.171)). Also concerning transvestism, the claim
    "aversion therapy has been quite successful" (p.172) is undocu-
    mented. Generally aversion therapy has proven of dubious value
    in long-term redefinement of a person's sexual desires and
    preferences. Speculative statements which ignore available
    research findings occasionally occur (e.g. "group sex appears to
    be of a transient and episodic nature engaged in by a relatively
    few individuals perhaps only a few times" (p.134)).
c. The book is not completely and objectively non-judgmental (e.g.
    "It seems as if sex now exerts another kind of tyrannical hold
    on us: there is a tendency to confuse quantity with quality and
    to equate promiscuity with sexual freedom" (p.216)).

83. Shope, David F. Interpersonal Sexuality. Philadelphia: W.B.
Saunders Company, 1975. 360 pp.

Brief Summary - Chapters 1 and 2 discuss types and limitations of
sex research and a few recent researchers as well as "Theories of
Sexuality" from biological, social-psychological, learning and
substantive perspectives. In chapter 3, "Love and Sexuality," Shope
states that "sexuality refers to the total characteristics of an
individual - social, personality, and emotional - that are manifest
in his or her relationships with others and that reflect his or
gender-genital orientation" (p.36). The next few chapters cover
"General Sexuality" with reference to biology, the needs of
"Psychosexual Partners" whether heterosexual or homosexual, some
aspects of "Marriage and Sexuality," the psychological factors and
physical methods of "Sexual Techniques," the stages of "Childhood
Sexuality" and the parental support-systems required, male and
female sexuality, and premarital and extramarital sex. The next two
chapters explore "Sexual Morality," and "Atypical Sexual Behavior."
"Specific Sexual Variants" (p.286) such as "Pressuring" (p.287),
"Moral Guilt" (p.287) and "Sexual Irresponsibility" (p.288) are
discussed. The final chapter is an "Epilogue."

Critique - Strengths

a. Tasteful photographs, appropriate anatomical diagrams (in
    Appendix A), cited references, graphs, tables and footnotes
    assist the text. Quotations and anecdotal case examples are
    further aids. A 6-page Glossary and 13-page References as well
    as three Appendixes on "Anatomy and Physiology,"
    "Contraceptives," and "The Venereal Diseases" serve as further
    supplemental material. A summary concludes each chapter.
b. Sex research with its historical background is well covered and
    critically examined (e.g. refer to Summary above). Methodology
    and theory are effectively analyzed (e.g. "One result of a
    theory opening up new avenues of investigation is the necessity

of continually modifying it in the light of new evidence"
(p.9)). Original research is presented (e.g. Table 10-1
including probability statistics - "Some Dating Characteristics
of Male Virgins and Nonvirgins" (p.193)).

c. Chapter 14 on "Atypical Sexual Behavior" provides an excellent
objective and original approach (e.g. refer to Summary above)
and is also non-judgmental (e.g. "Acts such as sadomasochism,...
transvestism, anal intercourse, and bondage and discipline also
have not been considered separately because they are part of
many successful relationships" (p.292)). The text is objective
in impact (e.g. "Experimentation with new family forms will and
should continue..." (p.144); also "moral individuality demands
that the final decision to include or exclude behavior be the
responsibility of the behaving person" (p.272)).

d. Insights are often given (e.g. "the preceding evidence clearly
demonstrates that virginity... is a continuum" (p.197); also "1.
Both nonmarital sex itself and society in general would benefit
if a workable set of norms could be established for sexual
activity outside the marital bond" (p.257)).

e. Although the book is useful for professionals as well as laypersons, it is ideal for students because it approaches its
subject from an unusual, yet appropriate, perspective.

Deficiencies

a. Although the sin-illegality-sickness progression of western
cultural historical approaches to unconventional sexuality is
mentioned (e.g. p.275-277), not enough historical and cross-
cultural antecedents are given. Furthermore, analogies to other
cross-cultural contemporary societies are lacking.

b. Pejorativity occurs occasionally (e.g. the definition of
"Promiscuity" (p.317); also "a sexually promiscuous girl"
(p.206)).

c. The phrase "Estrogen: a hormone..." (p.314) is erroneous.
Additionally, cautions about "estrogen replacement therapy"
(p.230) are not forthcoming. Appendix C (p.309-312) should be
more complete in its brief outline of sexually transmitted
diseases. Many of these, such as trichomoniasis, are not
acknowledged.

84. Wilson, Janice. <u>Sexpression: Improving Your Sexual
Communication</u>. Englewood Cliffs: Prentice-Hall Inc., 1980. 238 pp.

<u>Brief Summary</u> - The book is divided into three Parts; "Sexpression:
Images and Roles," "... Society and You," and "Communication and
Sexual Discovery." Wilson's thesis is that "sex is communication "
(p.5). In Part I, she coaches the reader into evaluating her/his
personal sexpression while being aware of sexual gamesmanship toward
othess. Chapter 4 descsibes the pitfalls of traditional masculine-
feminine sex-role stereotypes. Part II details "Your Sexual
Heritage" which encompasses the historical sexual double standard
and the church-inspired negative sexual messages. Parental, peer,
media, and so-called expert sexpressions are next scrutinized. Part
III describes "The Language of Coitus" and the necessity of
"Creating Facilitative Sexpressions." This latter ability "thereby
encourages your sexual equipment to stay in the most cooperative

working order. Hidden innuendoes, manipulations, and other dishonest strategies go by the wayside..." (p.212-213).

Critique - Strengths

a. The book is an excellent resource for a client lacking in communication skills. The vernacular case-studies are effective. Sexual myths and societal sociosexual shortcomings are explained (e.g. The seventeen points concerning "Double Standard Roles" (p.48-49) of male-female sexual issues). Selected References after each chapter are helpful. Historical background is given.

b. Positive recommendations occur (e.g. the eleven points of coital communication etiquette (p.214-218)). Chapter 2 ("Sexual Gamesmanship") is outstanding as it lists twenty-three such points.

c. There is a good analysis of key concepts (e.g. the "normal" (p.55) definition of sexual activity).

Deficiencies

a. The book has no visual aids, graphs or charts. Cross-cultural references are also not in evidence.

b. Chapter 4, which deals with masculine-feminine roles, should have discussed the concept of androgyny. Even the word "androgyny" is not mentioned.

c. Occasional mixed messages of a judgmental vein are noticeable (e.g. "7. The more parents talk to their children about sexual matters, the less likely their children are to engage in promiscuous sexual activity" (p.12)).

85. Wilson, Sam, Strong, Bryan, Robbins, Mina & Johns, Thomas. Human Sexuality (2nd Ed.). St. Paul: West Publishing Co., 1980. 512 pp. (with Instructor's Manual 149 pp.; plus Study Guide - prepared by Bryan Strong & Bruce Linenberg 346 pp.)

Brief Summary - The book begins with an Introduction and Readings excerpted from Plato's Symposium, the Bible, Augustine, and The Song of Roland. Six Units comprise the book. Unit 1 entitled "Sexuality in America" presents an overview of the historical roots begetting our contemporary American sexual attitudes. In Unit 2, "Sexual Structure and Function," conception and pregnancy, and "Sexual Maturation" are examined. "Birth Control and Sexual Diseases" information comprises Unit 3 while Unit 4 deals with "The Sexual Person" in analyzing sex roles, psychosexual development and change, "Intimate Relationships" and "Sexual Communication." Unit 5 delves into "Sexual Behavior," "Sexual Dysfunctions," "Homosexuality," and "Sexual Variations." Unit 6 relates sex to society in the areas of politics, the law, pornography, rape and abortion. An Epilogue defining the various concepts of sexual normality terminates the text. An abridged Human Sexuality - Essentials (2nd Ed.) is also available (1981, 359 pp. with Instructor's Manual, 149 pp., and Study Guide, 346 pp.). The authors explain that this version "is similar to the larger text except that the readings have been deleted, and more quotations have been added to open boxes at the top of the pages... (and which) offers flexibility for those

teachers who want to use their own supplementary materials..."
(p.1).

Critique - Strengths

a. Photographs, sketches, a Glossary, tables and references
(including a Bibliography) aid the written material.
Additionally, anecdotal quotations, Questions and Readings are
mostly useful in balancing perspectives. These Readings are
broadly excerpted (e.g. "Sexuality and the Aged" (Barrow,
p.268-271)). Also some resource information is given (e.g.
"Federal Information Centers" (p.54-57)). The accompanying
Study Guide and Instructor's Manual are innovative and present
easy-to-use material and exercises pertinent to the text.
Simplified but extensive historical and cross-cultural
information is provided.
b. Pejorativity is minimal.
c. Research comparisons are offered (e.g. "In the years since
Masters & Johnson first published their interpretation of the
human sexual response cycle, other researchers have published
what they feel are the physiological highlights of the
phenomenon..." (p.81)). Good constructive criticism of controversial research is sometimes proffered (e.g. the Masters &
Johnson homosexuality research (p.389, cited references
included)).

Deficiencies

a. Few graphs are presented. Little material is available for the
student interested in research methodology and bias control.
There are occasional poor choices of Readings excerpts where
misinformation is presented (e.g. "... Los Angeles scientists
have found they could correctly identify the homosexuals in a
group of males merely by measuring the traces of the male
hormone, testosterone in human samples" (p.151)).
b. The words "estrogen" (p.487) and "androgen" (p.150) are
referred to as a hormone, and not as representing a family of
hormones.
c. The concept of androgyny has been omitted from the section on
sex roles (p.225-233).
d. Judgmental input surfaces around a major philosophical issue
(i.e. "... as we examine the most common forms of sexual
variations, ... they exist in some form in most of us; what
makes them aberrant is when they become excessive or dominant in
our sexual behavior" (p.414)).

86. Yates, Alayne. _Sex Without Shame: Encouraging the Child's Healthy
Sexual Development_. New York: William Morrow and Co., Inc., 1978. 252
pp.

Brief Summary - The author, a child-oriented physician, divides her
book into two sections. Part I is "Understanding the Child's
Sexuality." Children from birth and through all ages are sensuous,
erotic beings, but parental mixed messages, cultural myths and
parents' reticence to be positive about the subject do incalculable
damage and foster later adult sexual dysfunctions. Current popular

books about rearing children either avoid or promote misconceptions about topics such as masturbation. A few children become manipulators while slum living can infuse many of its children with a sex-anger symbiosis which becomes most destructive in adulthood and perpetuates itself from one generation to the next. Coercive incest and anti-body religious proscribations are additional causes of such misery. In Part II, "Enriching the Child's Sexual Response," Yates recommends a practical, low-key, sex-positive sex-education program for all children and adolescents be instituted by their parents or guardians. In a brief Epilogue, the author advises that "once a firm erotic foundation is laid, sexual expression can be gently shaped through principles of honesty and responsibility" (p.230).

Critique - Strengths

a. Copious quotations and case examples (e.g. p.36) assist the text. Cited references, including research ones (e.g. "Thirty-six percent of year-old infants are reported by their mothers to play with their genitals. (Newson, 1968)" (p.13)) are plentiful. A 17÷page Bibliography completes the text.
b. Myths are exposed (e.g. p.21). Historical (e.g. on masturbation hysteria in the 19th century (p.22-24)) and cross-cultural (e.g. Chapter 6 (p.67-76)) background material is covered.
c. Many useful generalized observations and insights are proffered (e.g. "Masturbation culminating in climax may occur as early as the first month of life" (p.12); also "another sexual dysfunction, performance anxiety, is rooted in our early attempts to educate children, such as toilet training" (p.172-173)).
d. Constructive criticism is levelled at occasional other experts (e.g. Dr. Spock (p.26-27); also Freud (p.46-47)).

Deficiencies

a. No photographs, drawings, charts or tables reinforce the text. Research data and statistics are limited.
b. Some pejorativity surfaces (e.g. "Mothers who seduce their sons ... may ... be promiscuous" (p.114); also the concept of childhood "compulsive masturbation" (p.174)). Neofreudian jargon seems overworked (e.g. "Jacqueline's oedipal struggle..." (p.190)).
c. Methodologically unsound research references occur (e.g. "Parents with a skewed or deficient relationship can predispose their offspring to homosexuality. (Marmor, 1965)" (p.192)).
d. Yates claims "incest is always indicative of family pathology... Society is quite correct in seeking to prevent or abolish incest" (p.112) without offering any research proof to back up such a sweeping statement. On the other hand, she cites three references in asserting "mutual sex play among siblings does not prove harmful, and could foster a robust, healthy, nonincestuous stance later in life" (p.114). Also one mother-son incident reported by Finch (p.114) is claimed to have been positive in scope. The author needs to clarify her position on consensual incest.

Sex Research

87. Bancroft, John. <u>Deviant Sexual Behaviour: Modification and Assessment</u>. Oxford: Oxford University Press, 1974. 265 pp.

<u>Brief Summary</u> - Bancroft, a physician, in his Introduction opines that "the goals fall into three main categories" (p.1-2). These are suppression of the activity, or a better individual adjustment to it, or "a lessening of the deviant pattern and a change towards a 'normal' conforming sexual role... It is in this third category, which provides the subject matter of this book, that ethical and scientific issues are most likely to become confused" (p.2). Instead of evocative psychoanalytic and psychotherapeutic methods, the book details directive methods. Chapter 1 historically reviews "The Concept of Sexual Deviance" and is followed by the more recent procedures involving "The Modification of Sexually Deviant Behaviour." Chapter 3 describes some "Techniques of Modification." Next follows "Comparative Studies" after which "The Effects of Treatment, Predicted and Observed" are delineated. Chapter 6 is termed "Clinical Findings and Prognostic Factors." Chapter 7's "Theoretical Conclusions" states the three approaches are stimulus-response learning, operant learning, and cognitive attitude change. "Various Measures of Change" discuss gender identity, sexual preferences, sexual attitudes, sexual arousability, and sexual activity. The concluding Chapter 9 is called "Clinical Conclusions."

<u>Critique - Strengths</u>

a. A 28-page Bibliography and Author Index plus an Appendix termed "Technical Aspects of Penile Plethysmography" (which includes graphs and one plate photograph) are of aid. Quotations, cited references, footnotes, graphs, tables, histograms and charts (e.g. "Figure 7.2 Complex Factorial Design" (p.180)) are also of immense value. Well researched historical (e.g. refer to Summary above) and cross-cultural (e.g. p.7) background material puts the book into proper perspective.
b. Clear concepts emerge (e.g. "Sexual deviance is most appro-

priately considered in this sociological sense. It may also be defined ... in terms of statistical abnormality or of psycho-pathology" (p.5)).

c.   Contemporary research inadequacies are acknowledged (e.g. "not only have selection criteria varied or been unspecified but criteria of improvement and duration of follow-up have also varied considerably" (p.32)). Research improvements are suggested (e.g. refer to Summary).

d.   Pejorativity and emotional value-judgments are absent.

Deficiencies

a.   Inadequate visual aids complement the text. Also, more cross-cultural material would have been helpful.

b.   Methodological shortcomings are never thoroughly explored (e.g. the various "Measures of Change" (p.184)). This also applies to aversion therapy (p.33-42) which also is ethically dubious. By inference, while Bancroft admits results are uniformly poor (e.g. Table 6.1-13 studies (p.146)), he still assumes that so-called deviants (e.g. homosexually oriented persons) can in theory be behaviorally reoriented. No conclusive evidence is forthcoming to justify this assumption.

c.   The final chapter omits reporting on the necessity of taking a client sex history.

d.   Unsubstantiated conclusions occur (e.g. "Paedophilia, although most commonly homosexual..." (p.156)). The statement "the behavioural approach ... allows one to escape from the medical model" (p.22) is not totally valid.

88. Beyer, Carlos ed. Endocrine Control of Sexual Behavior. New York: Raven Press, Pubs., 1979. 421 pp.

Brief Summary - This book, part of the "Comprehensive Endocrinology Series," consists of three sections: "Biology of Sexual Behavior" (three chapters), "Reproductive Behavior in Some Specific Vertebrate Groups" (threee chapters), and "Perspective in the Biochemical and Physiological Correlates of Sexual Behavior" (five chapters). The articles are summaries of various animal-experiment results in the androgen-estrogen area of hormonal research.

Critique - Strengths

a.   The book is an excellent reference source for the scientist specializing in endocrinology, neurobiology or physiological psychology. Each chapter is thoroughly appendixed by references. Chapter 3 by Larsson has 497 references alone. Graphs, ring-structure charts, tables and schematic diagrams augment the text and seem consistent and accurate.

b.   At times, interesting but as yet unexplained questions are posed (e.g. Larsson notes many species of male animals persist in sexual activity long after castration. He postulates four answers to the phenomena (p.97-98) and then rationally counter-argues against all four solutions leaving the answer still unresolved).

c.   Levels of activity of androgens, estrogens, antiandrogens and antiestrogens, both overt and inhibitory, are compared (e.g.

"only three androgens, all aromatizable, were effective in producing sexual behavior: testosterone, androstenedione and androstenediol... Testosterone was the most potent androgen and androstenedione the least potent" (p.103)).

Deficiencies

a. All the work discussed is animal experimentation and as such, cannot always be extrapolated to human endocrine and metabolic activity. This is the major weakness of all such research from the perspective of the sexologist-scientist dealing only in issues concerning human sexuality.
b. Some research described is repetitive (e.g. Larsson (p.92) and Luttge (p.341)).

89. Butler, Sandra. Conspiracy of Silence: The Trauma of Incest. San Francisco: New Glide Publications, 1978. 220 pp.

Brief Summary - The author defines incest in terms of "incestuous assault" (p.4) and is not concerned with consensual incest between adults or siblings. This, she asserts, is overwhelmingly an older male relative with a younger child. Non-touching voyeuristic exploitation is categorized as trauma-producing and is also included. After describing "The Scope of the Problem," Butler delves into the problem from the viewpoint of "The Children," then "The Aggressors," followed by "The Mothers." Rationalizations of the adults (the father, sometimes the mother) are noted. The American nuclear-family structure is next dissected and causal hypotheses are proffered. Health-care, legal and religious professionals are castigated as generally disinterested. The book concludes by offering guideline letters for the concerned persons to emulate when writing victims, aggressors, mothers or involved professionals.

Critique - Strengths

a. Two Appendixes detail the California penal codes and the "Mandatory Child-Abuse Reporting Law for California." The text is well cited with many appropriate case histories. Statistical and other footnoted references are provided (e.g. Of "103 cases of sexual molestation of juveniles ... 80 of that number were incestuously based" (p.13-14)). A 2-page Selected Bibliography is included.
b. The difference between consensual and manipulative non-consensual incest is noted. Clear concepts are presented (e.g. "incest is relentlessly democratic" (p.28)).
c. Unsubstantiated professional theories are attacked (e.g. the blaming of some child victims as evincing "seductive behavior" (p.35)). Hypotheses emerge (refer to Summary).
d. Advice is offered (e.g. The hypothetical guideline letters are supportive and useful devices)).

Deficiencies

a. No visual aids are included. Historical and anthropological input and data are missing. Only limited constructive specific

suggestions are offered as possibilities for the important
cultural changes necessary to forestall the creation of a
continuous new series of incipient incest-assault cases.
b. Although adult sex-attitude negativity and sex-role stereotyping are noted in many individual cases, their collective
build-up is not properly researched and explored.

90. Ciba Foundation. Sex, Hormones and Behaviour. Amsterdam:
Excerpta Medica, 1979. 390 pp.

Brief Summary - Twenty-one distinguished scientists participated in
this symposium by offering fifteen presentations. The Chairman,
E.J. Sachar, initially asks "by what mechanisms and under what
conditions do hormones pre- and postnatally play a role as determinants of sexual behaviour in human beings?" (p.1). This
conference intersperses animal-research topics with their human-
research counterparts. Other than one chapter each on male homosexuality and transsexuality, the book focuses on hormonal-
biochemical modes of primate sexual interaction. In the closing
chapter entitled "Final General Discussion," Sacher enumerates some
undiscussed hormonal-research areas and evokes comments on future
trends from his colleagues.

Critique - Strengths

a. Good textual support is furnished by graphs, charts, tables,
photographs and thorough referencing. Historical background and
cross-cultural research is provided. Because of the discussion-
interaction of the participants, the correlation between the
animal research and the human research is often clearly brought
out (e.g. "this observation indicates that - in contrast to the
rat - testosterone cannot be replaced by estrogens in human
males" (Pirke, p.39)).
b. Topical findings and tentative postulates are mentioned (e.g.
"there seems to be a certain testosterone level above which
sexual activity is independent of the absolute concentration of
the hormone" (Nieschlag, p.197)). Healthy debate surfaces which
is informative (e.g. when Dorner terms "genuine homosexuality an
inborn deviation of sex drive" (p.121) and directly relates rat
experiments to human appropriateness (p.134)), Beach counters by
saying "it seems to me you are using different rules" (p.135)).
c. Insights into human experimental difficulties are noted (e.g.
"in contrast to animal experimentalists, human researchers
typically are unable to design ideal experimental studies, but
rather depend on ..." (Ehrhardt, p.42)).

Deficiencies

a. The Crown paper entitled "Male Homosexuality: Perversion,
Deviation or Variant?" is not relevant. It is overly
speculative and offers no original new research.
b. Dorner and Crown allow themselves occasionally to be judgmental
(e.g. "this seems to me to represent the promiscuous end of the
spectrum of homosexual behaviour" (Crown, p.136)).
c. The Dorner presentation termed "Hormones and Sexual
Differentiation of the Brain" is methodologically unsound. He

bases much of his research on effeminate homosexuals who are
defined as being chosen on "the basis of their general
behavioural patterns" (p.104). Thus his conclusion "we have
found significantly increased ... FSH and LH levels associated
with decreased plasma free testosterone levels in homosexual
men, but only in effeminate homosexuals" (p.81) is based on an
imprecise experimental design.

91. Cox, Daniel & Daitzman, Reid, ed. Exhibitionism: Description,
Assessment and Treatment. New York: Garland STPM Press, 1980. 431 pp.

Brief Summary - In the Preface, Daitzman explains that "the book is
written for law students, attorneys, and judges as a sourcebook on
how to communicate with mental health professionals; and as a primer
... involved with treating the sexual deviate..." (p.xii-xiii).
Four sections comprise the book. In Section One, a medical and
legal overview is presented. Section Two elucidates the
psychodynamic treatments of group therapy and psychoanalysis. This
is followed in Section Three by the behavioral models of treatment
which are electrical aversion therapy, aversive behavioral
rehearsal, and covert sensitization. Section Four concludes the
book by discussing victims, the integration of theory with
therapeutics, the dilemma of the therapist dealing with the legal
system, and "Future Research Issues."

Critique - Strengths

a. Cited references, case studies, graphs and tables are well
   utilized. The four Inventory Appendixes (Evans, p.119-122) are
   most useful. Referenced conclusions are aptly included (e.g.
   "Cox and Daitzman (1979) conclude..." (Cox, p.8)).
b. Research shortcomings are examined (e.g. "It is necessary to
   point out that all research investigating the exhibitionist
   suffers from the same shortcoming - sample selection bias. All
   of these studies have worked with arrested exhibitionists" (Cox,
   p.6)). Discerning positive criticism of present methodologies
   is offered (e.g. "There is neither evidence to suggest that ...
   (electrical aversion therapy) is better than no treatment, nor
   any substantial evidence to suggest how it compares with other
   modes of treatment" (Evans, p.98).
c. New research possibilities are adequately presented (e.g. "For
   example, teenage exhibitionists and their parents might be
   analyzed" (Allen, p.79)).
d. Insights are appropriately stated (e.g. "An important issue is
   whether exhibitionism is culture-bound" (References follow,
   Rhoads, p.298)).

Deficiencies

a. Much material is repetitive (e.g. Many authors cite the pioneer
   work of Lasegue (p.3, 61, 68, 82, 152, 184, 295, 308)). Visual
   aids are lacking. Historical and cross-cultural input is
   minimal.
b. Occasional pejorativity is noted (e.g. "Her husband was promiscuous..." (Allen (p.74)).
c. Evans admits "there is a paucity of controlled studies indi-

cating the relative efficacy of these methods" (p.89) concerning electrical aversion therapy. Aside from the ethical issues involved, not enough attention is paid to the implied coercive aspects of offenders' treatment in this modality. No proper longitudinal studies are presented for any treatment method on the recidivism rate. The caution stated that "the advisability of booster sessions was recognized early (Wolpe, 1969)" (Maletzky, p.223) is not reassuring.

92. Ellis, Havelock. _Psychology of Sex_. New York: The New American Library, 1954.   272 pp.

Brief Summary - Ellis in his Preface directs his book to "ordinary medical practitioners and students" (p.6) who are unable to find time to peruse his 7-volume work "Studies in the Psychology of Sex." After a brief introductory chapter, Ellis in Chapter 2 details "The Biology of Sex." In "The Sexual Impulse in Youth," the author critiques Freud's hypotheses. Chapter 4 delves intp "Sexual Deviations and Erotic Symbolisms." Childhood often germinates the resultant deviation. Topics discussed are urolagnia, coprolagnia, erotic zoophilia, kleptolagnia, exhibitionism, algolagnia (sadomasochism) and sexual senility. "Homosexuality," the next subject, also includes comments about eonism (transvestism). Chapter 6, "Marriage," discusses its sexual component through the phases from early marriage to post-menopause. Next follows "The Art of Love," a descriptive format for adding spiritual components to sexual lust. The final chapter emphasizes "that the erotic personality rests on a triangular association between the cerebrum, the endocrine system, and the autonomic nervous apparatus" (p.256).

Critique - Strengths

a.   Numerous statistical and descriptive references to other researchers are helpful. A 3-page Glossary concludes the book. Some historical and cross-species observations occur (e.g. "Neumann, who watched elephants love-making, observed..." (p.39)).

b.   Constructive criticism of contemporary researchers is valuable (e.g. refer to Summary). At times, Ellis seems to anticipate later research (e.g. Kinsey's 0-6 Scale in stating "in psychic health ... the range of what may be considered normal variation is very wide" (p.12); also "... The clitoris is a normal focus of sexual sensation and tends so to continue, frequently as the chief if not the only focus" (p.251)).

c.   Clever philosophical insights abound (e.g. "Any sexual devia-tion which has always given satisfaction without injury to a particular individual must be considered normal for that individual" (p.160)).

Deficiencies

a.   No visual aids or bibliography complement the text.

b.   Subjective judgmentality occurs (e.g. The variations of oral sex "become deviations ... when they replace the desire for coitus" (p.43-44); also "... has sometimes led to the other extreme - equally unnatural and undesirable - of license and promiscuity as an ideal, if not even a practice" (p.229)).

c. A few serious errors exist (e.g. "The heredity of inversion is
well-marked" (p.169); also "when early masturbation is a factor
in developing sexual inversion..." (p.100)).

93. Ford, C.S. & Beach, F.A. Patterns of Sexual Behavior. New York:
Harper Bros., 1951. 316 pp.

Brief Summary - The authors present anthropological data on human
sexuality from 190 different human societies. In addition, other
primates such as apes and monkeys and non-primate mammals are
discussed and compared as to sexual behavior. In the first as well
as the final chapter, the authors identify the sexual variables from
the triple perspectives of human cross-cultural studies,
human-animal infra and interspecies behavior, and the physiological-
behavioral-causal determinants. Chapters 2 through 9 discuss the
sexual customs, habits and tendencies of these human societies and
animals. Atypical sexuality, such as homosexuality, is noted as
common. Chapters 10 through 12 describe pubertal maturation and
adolescent development, after which "feminine fertility cycles"
(p.199) are elucidated. Other physiological components of sexuality
are reported upon, and theoretical concepts are proposed concerning
hormonal influences, the nervous system and the glandular roles of
functioning.

Critique - Strengths

a. An extensive Bibliography plus a Glossary are definitive aids.
Tables, diagrams, footnotes and charts along with pertinent
photographs are also important adjuncts.
b. Comparative cross-cultural data are furnished (e.g. Concerning
two polygynous Siberian tribes, the Yakut man tends to prefer
females with "narrow pelvis and slim hips ... (while the
Chukchee male usually requires woman of) broad pelvis and wide
hips" (Table 5, p.88)).
c. Well-reasoned conclusions occur (e.g. In cultures approving of
bilateral painful stimulation, the sexual behavior of immature
persons is allowed "to be relatively free and nonrestrictive ...
(and such cultures also envisage) the woman as an active,
vigorous participant in all things sexual..." (p.64)).
d. Although dated, the book is still the most comprehensive work
of its kind.

Deficiencies

a. One must accept the empirical reports of the authors derived in
turn often from unscientifically trained sources. There is no
way today of verifying what they have claimed as sociosexual
fact; indeed the emergence from isolation of many tribes and
sub-races has permanently altered their sexual mores and
attitudes. This begins to put the book into a historical
perspective rather than as any contemporary explanation of
cross-cultural sexuality.
b. Less useful is that portion of the text devoted to physiological theorizing. Much of what is postulated has since become
untenable (e.g. "Human males who lack any source of testicular

hormone ... (find that this) is not indispensable to coital performance" (p.231-232). Such a statement implies the authors' ignorance that the adrenal cortex produces testosterone as well).

94. Forward, Susan & Buck, Craig. Betrayal of Innocence: Incest & Its Devastation. Harmondsworth: Penguin Books Ltd., 1979. 204 pp.

Brief Summary - The major author Forward, a social worker, was herself a childhood victim of paternal incest-aggression which she describes in an opening introductory chapter. A brief resume of anthropological-historical-theoretical issues of the incest taboo itself is followed by chapters written from the perspectives of "The Victim's Anguish," "The Aggressor's Bitter Victory" and "The Silent Partner" (usually the wife of the aggressor and mother of the victim). The next six chapters denote the types of incest; father-daughter, mother-son, sibling, grandfather-granddaughter, mother-daughter and father-son. It is stated "seventy-five percent of all reported incest cases involve fathers and daughters" (p.55). The book closes by scrutinizing the legal ramifications of incest and concludes by offering solutions for aiding affected families, victims and aggressors in developing mutual trust and understanding.

Critique - Strengths

a. An excellent Appendix entitled "Treatment Resources" is most useful to laypersons, offenders, victims, students and professionals. A 5-page Bibliography is a further asset. Historical and cross-cultural issues are explored (refer to Summary). The many case histories portrayed are superb. Such subtleties as reverse role-playing (p.175) in therapy are exemplified constructively.
b. The chapter "Incest and the Law" graphically demonstrates problems inherent in this area.
c. Forward is objective and supportive toward the problems of the incest-aggressors.

Deficiencies

a. No visual aids are included. Statistical data are totally lacking. Unsubstantiated and unreferenced generalities abound (e.g. "some experts estimate that at least casual sibling sexual contact occurs in nine out of ten families with more than one child" (p.85)).
b. The statement is proffered that "in reality the dynamics of mother-son incest are ... the most subtly traumatic of all forms of incest" (p.73). No proof is presented to back up this conclusion. Consensual incest seldom surfaces in therapy or in the courts, and these authors have not attempted any investigation in this area.
c. The writers of this book emphasize the psychoanalytic approach (e.g. "the fulfillment of his Oedipal desires" (p.75)). Such theory is always presented basically as fact.
d. Judgmental bias occurs at times (e.g. "not only was she compulsively promiscuous..." (p.175)) as does unproductive speculation (e.g. "I think her homosexuality is a defensive flight from men"

(p.95)).

e. The book does not address any societal solution for minimizing coercive incest in the future.

95. Freud, Sigmund (James Strachey, translator). <u>Three Essays on the Theory of Sexuality</u>. New York: Basic Books, Inc., 1975. 172 pp.

<u>Brief Summary</u> - This translation of the original (1905) through fourth edition (1920) also has a 23-page Introduction by Steven Marcus. The first essay entitled "The Sexual Aberrations" introduces the concept of the sexual object and the sexual instinct or aim. The "innate constitutional roots of the sexual instinct" (p.37) can lead into so-called perversions, neuroses or a normal sex life. In the second essay called "Infantile Sexuality," Freud traces sexual childhood development through the sensual oral-anal-genital phases of discovery on to masturbatory activity. Indeed, "under the influence of seduction children can become polymorphously perverse, and can be led into all possible kinds of sexual irregularities" (p.57). The third essay "The Transformations of Puberty" categorizes the changes "destined to give infantile sexual life its final normal shape" (p.73). Erotogenic zones exist and in the normal adult female, "susceptibility to stimulation (must be) transferred from the clitoris to the vaginal orifice" (p.87). As well, fantasies including incestuous ones must be traversed in the pubertal stage as a part of severing the parental cord. A Summary capsulates various concepts such as "Repression," "Sublimation," "Precocity" and "Fixation."

<u>Critique - Strengths</u>

a. Cited references, footnotes and an 8-page Bibliography are most useful. An Editor's Note, Prefaces to the various editions and an Appendix listing the predominant writings of Freud are helpful.

b. The book is required reading for its historical value for all students and practitioners of sexology. Freud's concepts on the sexual bases for neuroses, on infantile sexuality, and his implied continuum of a universal bisexuality component (e.g. "all human beings are capable of making a homosexual object-choice and have in fact made one in their inconscious" (footnote, p.11)) are examples of Freud's intuitive and predictive genius. The last example might be termed an accurate precursor of Kinsey's 0-6 homo-heterosexual rating scale.

c. Homosexuality is discussed dispassionately. Causal judgmental-ity is avoided (e.g. "we are not in a position to base a satisfactory explanation of the origin of inversion..." (p.12) and cross-cultural references given (e.g. "it is remarkably widespread among many savage and primitive races, whereas the concept of degeneracy is usually restricted to states of high civilization (cf. Bloch)" (p.5)).

d. Descriptively innovative phrases abound (e.g. "psychical herma-phroditism" (p.8); also "psycho-analytic investigation" (p.55)).

<u>Deficiencies</u>

a. No visual aids are included. A lack of historical antecedents

and case histories (except for a few in footnotes) are noted.
The scientific method has been essentially reduced to intuitive
speculations.

b. Some concepts of female sexuality are erroneous (e.g. refer to
    Summary; also "if she is led on by a clever seducer she will
    find every sort of perversion to her taste, and will retain them
    as part of her own sexual activities" (p.57)).

c. Assumptive conclusions sometimes are evident (e.g. "inversion
    can be removed by hypnotic suggestion" (p.6)).

d. Pejorativity is often apparent (e.g. "perversion" (p.27)).

96. Friedman, Richard C., Richart, Ralph M. & Vande Wiele, Raymond L.,
ed. <u>Sex Differences in Behavior</u>. Huntington: Robert E. Krieger
Publishing Company, Inc., 1978. 511 pp.

<u>Brief Summary</u> - This volume is an accounting of a conference of
forty participants. Section 1 entitled "Effect of Hormones on the
Development of Behavior" delves into nonhuman and human prenatal
hormonal influences as well as the role of fetal androgens in human
central nervous system differentiation. Section 2's "Stress and
Early Life Experience in Nonhumans" deals with experiments on rats
and monkeys. Section 3's "Early Mother-Child Interaction in Humans"
discusses early sex-differences and "socioemotional development"
(Lewis and Weinraub, p. 165). Section 4 describes "Development of
Sex Differences in Behavioral Functioning." In Section 5's "Gender
Identity," such development is reviewed of children with cryptor-
chidism, or male children displaying signs of transsexualism or
behavioral feminism. Section 6 called "Aggression, Adaptation, and
Evolution" reports on sex-difference aggression in certain animals
and in humans. Section 7 concerns "Perspectives on Psychoendocrine
Differences." Whalen cautions more knowledge is necessary "about
which hormones are normally effective in bringing about
differentiation and about the mechanisms by which they work"
(p.480).

<u>Critique - Strengths</u>

a. Detailed References terminate each chapter and cover all cita-
    tions. A proliferation of graphs, histograms, tables, charts,
    and statistics including probability figures are included. Some
    footnotes, sketches and photographs also complement the text.
    Case studies are presented.

b. There are many research-study comparisons (e.g. Table 1, nine
    studies, p.264). After each Section, an all-participant
    Discussion is of immense benefit in its clarifying key issues
    and suggesting future avenues of investigation. Interesting
    research postulates are often examined (e.g. "The question under
    study is whether the central nervous system that is exposed to
    abnormally high levels of androgen favors advanced intellectual
    development..." (Baker and Ehrhardt, p.54)). Hypotheses are
    suggested (e.g. "Our data suggests that boys tend to continue
    using the genital zone for ... discharge of the genital drives
    ... (while) girls tend toward the inhibition of direct and
    conscious genital zonal discharge..." (Galenson and Roiphe,
    p.230)). Future research directions are acknowledged (e.g. "Our
    findings ... answer several questions... In other respects they

are puzzling and raise new issues..." (Baker and Ehrhardt, p.72)). Conclusions are carefully qualified and assessed (e.g. "There appears to be a distinct increase above the newborn rate of the XYY syndrome in mental-penal ... institutions. The possibility of a higher risk for aggressive behavior has not been settled satisfactorily..." (Meyer-Bahlburg, p.449)).
c. The text is essentially objective and non-judgmental.

Deficiencies

a. Insufficient background historical, cross-species, and cross-cultural research is summarized. The book presupposes initial expert subject-knowledge of its readers, thus being of limited value to many sexologists.
b. Many chapters on animal research, while interesting, cannot be extrapolated to human application and are confined to being modalities designed for basic research only. Certain subjects are of minimal use to the professional sexologist (e.g. "An Ethological Study of Children Approaching a Strange Adult (Stern & Bender, p.233)).

97. Gagnon, John H. & Simon, William. Sexual Conduct: The Social Sources of Human Sexuality. Chicago: Aldine Publishing Company, 1973. 328 pp.

Brief Summary - The authors who are social scientists, present their book from the twin perspectives of sociology and psychology. The opening chapter termed "The Social Origins of Sexual Development" traces a historical and research background along with an exposition on "Scripts and the Attribution of Meaning" (p.19). The following two chapters describe sociosexual maturing in "Childhood and Adolescence" and their "Postadolescence Sexual Development." Chapter 4 deals with various modes of "The Pedagogy of Sex." The subsequent five chapters cover "Male Homosexuality," "A Conformity Greater than Deviance - The Lesbian," "The Prostitution of Females," "Homosexual Conduct in Prison," and "Pornography-Social Scripts and Legal Dilemmas." The final Chapter 10 entitled "Social Change and Sexual Conduct" discusses contemporary sociosexual trends in terms of futuristic possibilities.

Critique - Strengths

a. Cited references, footnotes, anecdotal and other-expert quotations assist the text. Some tables and one valuable chart (i.e. "Heuristic Stages of Conventional Stages of Sexual Development" (p.100) also aid comprehension. Conclusions, Summaries and Afterwords complete most chapters. Considerable and appropriate historical (e.g. p.220 on prostitution) and cross-cultural (e.g. Figure 10.1, p.306) data are provided.
b. Good insights and innovative concepts are found (e.g. "Rarely do we turn from a consideration of the organs themselves to the sources of the meanings that are attached to them ... where meaning and sexual behavior come together to create sexual conduct" (p.5 - cited reference given); also "The term script might properly be invoked to describe virtually all human behavior..." (p.19)).

c. Constructive criticism of sex researchers is objectively and
    astutely offered (e.g. Freud and Kinsey, p.5-6). Research
    problems are acknowledged (e.g. "the other major problem of data
    quality control results from attempting to gather data ... from
    children..." (p.13)). By inference unresolved research
    questions are posed (e.g. "there is no evidence that differing
    androgen levels in the two sexes will account for differing
    rates of overt sexual behavior ... and no evidence that these
    same biological events produce variations in meanings attributed
    to these behaviors" (p.49)). Research studies are reported
    (e.g. "Homosexual Adjustments in Male Institutions" (p.244, four
    studies cited)).

Deficiencies

a. No visual aids and no general bibliography are included.
b. Certain important sexual variations are not properly covered
    (e.g. transvestism, transsexualism, sadomasochism, fetishism,
    incest).
c. Some statements given as fact are not referenced (e.g. "In
    nearly all male youth cultures, cunnilingus is viewed either
    ambivalently or negatively" (p.88)).
d. Confusing and pejorative phraseology occurs at times (e.g.
    "Normal sexual deviance" (p.93); also "premarital promiscuity"
    (p.226)).

98. Goldstein, Michael J. & Kant, Harold. Pornography and Sexual
Deviance. Berkeley: University of California Press, 1973. 200 pp.

Brief Summary - The authors in their Introduction state "this book
... developed as an extension of a pilot study supported by the U.S.
Commission on Pornography and Obscenity" (p.1). The first two
chapters define what is meant by pornography and review the
literature as to its effects. Beginning with Chapter 3, the actual
research study is documented. After detailing the development of
the clinical research instrument, the method of sample selection of
male sex offenders is given. This study is compared with the
Gebhard et al. (1956) and Frisbie (1969) groups. The next six
chapters furnish the experimental findings in the areas of frequency
of exposure to erotica in preadolescence, adolescence and adulthood,
peak adolescent and adult experience with erotica (for sex offenders
as well as homosexuals, transsexuals and users), and the role of
fantasy in the use of erotica. The final two chapters sum up the
psychological implications of the study and the legal history
concerning its definition and control in our western English and
American culture.

Critique - Strengths

a. Aids include references, tables, graphs and Appendixes of the
    clinical research instrument as well as demographic information
    from its findings. Extensive interview-excerpts and a Summary
    and Conclusions after each chapter fortify the textual content.
    Historical and some cross-cultural input is provided. A
    pertinent quotation begins each chapter. The use of statistics
    in analyzing experimental versus control groups is properly

done.

b. Acknowledgment of inherent research bias is admitted (e.g. "might the sex offenders play down their degree of exposure to erotica in order to emphasize their psychological health...? (p.141)). Future research possibilities are given (Nine areas specified (p.139-140)).

c. Most conclusions are logical and useful (e.g. "Erotica, then, does not seem to be a major stimulus for anti-social sexual behavior in the potential sex offender" (p.152); also "In general, little overt imitation of behavior displayed in erotica is noted" (p.150)).

Deficiencies

a. No photographs assist the text. The experimental samples of subgroups ranging from thirteen transsexuals to thirty-seven homosexuals are much too small in numbers to constitute more than a pilot-study analysis of the subject.

b. There are occasional lapses into subjective judgmentality (e.g. "While their crimes indicated ... sex perversion..." (p.47)). Pornography is seemingly viewed as a necessary evil (e.g. "The difficulties enlightened educators have experienced ... makes it very unlikely that we will see this devaluation of pornography come to pass in the near future" (p.153)).

c. Some conclusions given cannot be generalized from this limited study (e.g. "Most sex offenders appeared to carry through the pattern of arousal and masturbation ... into their adult lives... (A) normally developing male, by contrast, readily substituted real women for symbolic women and intercourse for masturbation, but not for other forms of overt sexual behavior" (p.152)).

99. Hart, John. Social Work and Sexual Conduct. London: Routledge & Kegan Paul, 1979. 215 pp.

Brief Summary - Hart warns in his Introduction "the book is not about such matters as techniques of counselling in sexual dysfunctioning, family planning, sex education" (p.2). Part I entitled "Sexual Conduct" explores "Ways of Understanding Sex" from physiological, psychological, sociological and moral perspectives. This is followed by contemporary deviancy theory, and the societal and philosophical conflicts between the sex offender and the social worker. Part II is a collated study of case histories of atypical sexual conduct from the biases of various probation officers. Part III draws conclusions from this study and then directs the thesis of how social work and sexual conduct might be positively integrated.

Critique - Strengths

a. Aids include a chart (p.65), an Appendix of methodological experience, a Further Sources of resources and a 6-page References section. Research citations and relevant case studies are provided. Some historical and cross-cultural input is given (e.g. p.19).

b. Controversial topics are examined objectively (e.g. "paedophilia" (p.57); also "... At present there is no way of defining a cut-off point on a continuum which at one end denies children sexuality whilst at the other exploits it in barbaric prostitution" (p.59, three cited references)).

c. Traditional roles of social workers with regard to sex offenders are criticized (e.g. "None of the workers in the study saw it as their task to achieve the alleviation of this major social pressure on the women... Is this the appropriate stance for social work?..." (p.170)).

d. Subjective value-judgments in the text are minimal.

Deficiencies

a. No visual aids, graphs or tables complement the text.

b. An implied negative bias stems from a lone reference (e.g. "(For an evaluation of the physical dangers of youthful and/or promiscuous sexual activity, see Schofield (1976, pp.111-12))" (p.178)).

c. The study, while useful in describing its subject in a qualitative way, is of little value to the researcher who requires replicatable criteria, bias controls and methodological parameters.

100. Henslin, James M. & Sagarin, Edward, ed. The Sociology of Sex (revised edition). New York: Schocken Books, Inc., 1978. 294 pp.

Brief Summary - The opening chapter by Henslin acknowledges "the effects of social group membership in shaping, directing, influencing, or otherwise patterning human sexual behavior" (p.1). Other sub-topics follow: "The New Sexual Morality - A Society Comes of Age" (Moneymaker and Montanimo), "Factors Affecting Permissive and Nonpermissive Rules Regarding Premarital Sex" (Goethals), "From an Unfortunate Necessity to a Cult of Mutual Orgasm - Sex in America Marital Education Literature, 1830-1940" (Michael Gordon), "Aspects of the Campus Abortion Search" (Manning) for data in a midwestern university, "Forcible Rape - A Comparative Study of Offenses Known to the Police in Boston and Los Angeles" (Chappell, Geis, Schafer and Siegel), "Police and Petting - Informal Enforcement of Sexual Standards" (Cummins), "Dramaturgical Desexualization - The Sociology of the Vaginal Examination" (Henslin and Biggs), "Teasing, Flashing, and Visual Sex-Stripping for a Living" (Skipper and McCaghy), "Prostitution - Identity, Career, and Legal-Economic Enterprise" (Davis), "Homosexuality - The Scene and Its Students" (Karlen), and the final essay by Sagarin termed "Sex Research and Sociology - Retrospective and Prospective."

Critique - Strengths

a. Cited references, useful footnotes, charts, tables, quotations and anecdotal stories abound. Statistical research studies are sometimes presented (e.g. Tables 1-5, Chappell et al., p.117-119). Some topical cross-cultural (e.g. Henslin, p.114) and historical (e.g. Gordon (p.59-83)) information is given.

b. Some essays compare alternative philosophical viewpoints (e.g. concerning premarital sex, "Four Theoretical Positions" (Goethals, p.42)).

c. Future research cautions and possibilities are presented (e.g.

"The degree to which sexual behavior is affected by such matters as climate, intricacies of family organization, or sexual training in childhood needs to be considered carefully in any study undertaken" (Goethals, p.54-55); also "Impediments to Sex Research" (Sagarin, p.268)). Past research is effectively critiqued by Sagarin (e.g. Kinsey - p.259-261).

d. Myths are occasionally recounted (e.g. "Prostitution myths, the notion that sexual vice is linked to ... have been attacked as enforcement ideologies" (Davis, p.219, cited references given)).

Deficiencies

a. Only a few chapters list References. No visual aids are employed.

b. Value-judgments are at times subjectively postulated (e.g. "On the ideal level no one commits adultery" (Henslin, p.18); also "the male gay world ... seems sex-obsessed" (Karlen, p.228)). Unproven generalized statements are offered as facts (e.g. "The three most obvious and common roles one sees in the male homosexual scene are swish, butch, and boyish" (Karlen, p.231)).

c. The sub-topics chosen for inclusion are very dissimilar and impart a lack of cohesiveness and direction to the book. Many other suitable sub-topics are selectively ignored (e.g. alternative marital lifestyles; peer pressure to try atypical sexuality).

101. Herman, Judith Lewis. Father-Daughter Incest. Cambridge: Harvard University Press, 1981. 294 pp.

Brief Summary - The author, a physician, acknowledges in her Preface that "incest has been rediscovered as a major social problem... This growing awareness is largely a result of the women's liberation movement" (p.vii). Three Parts make up the text. A short Introduction shows how such relationships have permeated into our culture's awareness through past millenia. Part 1, "The Incest Secret," explores the prevalence of such father-daughter activity, society's tendency to blame such children and the authoritarian stances of these fathers. It includes hypothetical constructs for the all-cultural incest taboo. Part 2, called "Two Daughters' Lives," details some demographics about such families, destructive emotional impact from such experiences, and "Seductive Fathers and Their Families." This latter group do not overtly sexualize with their daughters, but still exhibits "behavior that was clearly sexually motivated" (p.109). "Breaking Secrecy," Part 3, describes "The Crisis of Disclosure," support systems necessary to "Restoring Families," the "Criminal Justice" system with its many failings, the pitfalls and benefits of therapists' "Remedies for Victims," and "Preventing Sexual Abuse." Herman concludes "Only a basic change in the power relations of mothers and fathers can prevent the sexual exploitation of children" (p.206).

Critique - Strengths

a. Useful tables giving simple but meaningful statistics, historical, professional and familial quotations, and case histories provide immense benefit. Copious footnotes are available. An

Appendix lists the 50-state "Incest Statutes" and "Parallel
Statutory Provisions." This addition usefully serves all
professionals connected with the legal system and legislators
anxious for reform.
b. Famous topical research is constructively criticized and
analyzed (e.g. Freud, p.9).
c. Plausible hypotheses and suggestions are provided (refer to
Summary above).

Deficiencies

a. Visual aids, graphs and a bibliography are lacking.
Cross-cultural input is minimal, and historical input neglects
to discuss examples of incest-taboo violation in the past, along
with any attendant speculative reasons for such behavior.
b. Herman has a methodologically flawed study, including an inadequate sample of forty incest victims, twenty victims of
so-termed seductive fathers, and twenty controls. Thus her
conclusions must be treated as hypotheses. Furthermore, all
forty cases were in therapy as were the twenty covert cases.
c. Generalized statements abound (e.g. "Incest, the most extreme
form of sexual abuse..." (p.vii)). Objective researchers (e.g.
Ramey, Pomeroy) are erroneously categorized as belonging to "the
pro-incest school of thought" (p.23). Table 5.5 (p.93) gives
meaningless statistics on "Promiscuity," a pejorative concept.

102. Hunt, Morton. Sexual Behavior in the 1970's. Chicago: Playboy
Press, 1974. 410 pp.

Brief Summary - This book is based on a survey undertaken by the
Playboy Foundation. Six chapters make up the book. The first one
entitled "Sexual Liberation: A Generation of Change" presents an
overview of the contemporary societal approach to sexual concerns.
Attitudinal tables by age are introduced on behavior such as
cunnilingus or anal intercourse. The next chapter details masturbatory patterns and selected respondent comments. Chapter 3 gets
into single-person premarital sexual behavior while the next chapter
deals with marital sexual preferences. In Chapter 5, postmarital
and extramarital sexual statistics are revealed while the final
chapter includes findings on homosexuality, sadomasochism, incest
and bestiality. A brief Epilogue concludes that "sexual liberalism
... is the emergent ideal upon which the great majority of young
Americans ... are patterning their beliefs and behavior" (p.361).

Critique - Strengths

a. Historical-anthropological data are provided (e.g. p.338).
Extensive referenced "Notes on sources" and a 10-page
Bibliography are very useful. Statistical tables and
respondent-quotations augment the text.
b. Objectivity is maintained (e.g. "This is said to be the great
advantage of the two swinging alternatives..." (p.270-271,
references given)).
c. The author compares his data with that of Kinsey's (e.g. Tables
38, 39, p.261).

Deficiencies

a. Visual aids are not included. Not enough tabled data are compared to other research.
b. The research questionnaire is not listed. Thus the research cannot be replicated. No validity or reliability constructs are presented. Methods of population selection are not good (e.g. "Using random selection of names, they initiated contact by telephone... About one out of five agreed" (p.16-17)). Volunteer bias is evident. Other biases also surface (e.g. Were the Research Guild interviewers professionally adept? Refer to p.16).

103. Lockwood, Daniel. __Prison Sexual Violence__. New York: Elsevier North Holland, 1980. 180 pp.

__Brief Summary__ - This book is based on a research dissertation by the author. Chapter 1 reviews the literature and describes the study. "I look at a continuum of actions, all perceived as aggressive, ranging from verbal propositions to gang rapes" (p.8). Next follows a chapter which outlines the types of sexual violence and some "Characteristics of Participants." Chapter 3 details "Target Violence" in its formation, victim-reaction and staff-reaction. The "Impact of Victimization" is then discussed. Emotional reactions such as fear, anger, and anxiety may lead to crisis situations which ultimately effect a victim's lifestyle, social relations, racial attitudes and sexual beliefs. In Chapter 5, "Victims of Prison Rape" are analyzed. This is followed by a chapter on "Aggressors" and some hypotheses are offered. The attitudes and support-issues involving the "Prison Staff" are next delved into while the final Chapter 8 discusses some "Alternatives to Prison Sexual Violence."

Critique - Strengths

a. Apt case studies interwoven with expert quotations and cited references accord strong support to the text. A 5-page References section terminates the book. Useful cross-cultural information is imparted (e.g. "Ethnicity..." (p.28); also "... an Indian prison" (p.6 - cited reference given)).
b. Myths are explained (e.g. "the myth widely prevalent among prisoners is that most varieties of sexual aggression pay off in erotic rewards" (p.81)). Constructive alternatives to violence are critiqued and evaluated in the final chapter (e.g. "the Alternatives to Violence Project (AVP)" (p.150)).
c. Research protocols are sensibly constructed (e.g. "Targets were compared statistically to 'nontargets', and aggressors were systematically compared to a control group" (p.2)). Limitations are acknowledged (e.g. "... Because of these reasons, there is a likely chance of underreporting of emotional reactions in our survey" (p.15)). Good definitions and vernacular explanations are included (e.g. "__Target__: the recipient of an approach perceived as aggressive..." (p.9); also "A man, they reason, who looks effeminate and weak, must be 'squeeze' " (p.117)). Conclusions and hypotheses are sometimes challenging in impact (e.g. "Paradoxical as it may strike us, aggressors can thus not only justify their acts but can argue that they, ultimately, are

the real victims" (p.128)).

Deficiencies

a. No visual aids, charts and graphs and only two tables (p.18, 21) are presented. Historical background material is minimal.
b. No appendix is included detailing the study-methodology. Statistical results are ignored except for rudimentary percentages. Inherent study-weaknesses detract from its overall usefulness (e.g. "a few interviews did yield rich material from the aggressor's point of view. Unfortunately, these are too few cases to construct any systematic analysis based on interview content" (p.13-14)). Considering the study resources available, the sample size should have been greater (i.e. "I examined 107 'targets' ... and 45 inmate 'aggressors' living in New York State male prisons" (p.2)).
c. Subjective judgmentality is displayed (e.g. "perverse sex" (p.115)).

104. Marshall, Donald S. & Suggs, Robert C., ed. **Human Sexual Behavior**. New York: Basic Books Inc., 1971. 320 pp.

Brief Summary - Seven cultures are examined ranging from the inhibited to the permissive. In order, Messenger discusses "Sex and Repression in an Irish Folk Community" island. Altschuler describes "Cayapa Personality and Sexual Motivation" which exists in Ecuador. Schneider outlines "Romantic Love Among the Turu," a tribe in Tanzania which tacitly condones "the institutionization" (p.69) of adultery for both sexes. Merriam elucidates "Aspects of Sexual Behavior Among the Bala" of the Congo and includes a summary on male and female transvestites termed bitesha. Marshall gives a lengthy resume about "Sexual Behavior on Mangaia," a sex-positive culture in Polynesia. Suggs critically attacks the earlier Linton-Kardiner studies of Marquesan culture in French Polynesia in "Sex and Personality in the Marquesas." Rainwater compares sexual roles of lower-social marital couples of Mexico, Puerto Rico, England and the U.S. in "Marital Sexuality in Four Cultures of Poverty." The editors in an Epilogue cross-culturally compare and critique these studies and provide certain anthropological methods and theory.

Critique - Strengths

a. Footnotes, references, some graphs (e.g. Marshall, p.141), and many apt quotations are included. Gebhard adds a summary in Chapter 8 in his role as an anthropological expert on sexuality. Two Appendixes act as a bibliography and provide "definitions, outline and a critique of method and theory" (p.250).
b. Suggs in particular critically evaluates previous research (see Summary) and in his section of Appendix II (e.g. in studying sexuality, "... standard anthropological field methods have serious drawbacks which are frequently unrecognized..." (p.272-273)).
c. The presented studies are descriptively informative, diversified, and reasonably free from patronizing judgmentality.

Deficiencies

a. The lack of photographs or sketches represents a loss of
    impact. Few graphs or tables enhance the text. The research is
    qualitative and cannot be substantiated. Insufficient
    historical background is offered (with the exceptions of
    Messenger and Marshall).
b. Conclusions often are derived from generalities which are
    quantitatively undocumented (e.g. "There are a very few
    individuals, perhaps two or three out of a population of 2,000
    who-at least socially and perhaps biologically - are
    intersexual" (Marshall, p.153); also "there is no doubt that
    Turu women, all of whom are clitoridectomized, can have
    orgasms... (Schneider, footnnote 2, p.62)). Some conclusions
    are of dubious conception (e.g. "My analysis of Cayapa drinking
    and sexual behavior is based on psychoanalytic theory, as the
    data seems to best fit within that framework" (Altschuler,
    p.148)).

105. Masters, William H. & Johnson, Virginia E. Human Sexual Response.
Boston: Little, Brown & Co., 1966. 379 pp.

   Brief Summary - Part I termed "Research in Sexual Response" outlines
   the authors' model of the sexual response cycle and gives the
   logistical, demographic and some medical determinants of the
   research population of "382 women and 312 men ... (of which) 276
   married couples have worked actively in the various programs"
   (p.15). Parts II and III elucidate the physiological components of
   the female and the male sexual response systems from the aspect of
   the 4-phase model of excitement, plateau, orgasm, and resolution.
   Genital and extragenital reactivity and responsivity are described
   in terms of anatomy and physiology. Part IV entitled "Geriatric
   Sexual Response" deals with aging females and males over forty and
   fifty respectively. Part V concerns "Generalities in Sexual
   Response." Chapter 17 compares similar female-male physiologic
   responses. The following chapter discusses "Myotonia in Sexual
   Response." The final chapter gives four examples of "Study-Subject
   Sexuality" and provides data concerning "failures of performance ...
   during the orientation program" (p.313).

Critique - Strengths

a. Many anatomical diagrams, photographs, tables, charts (e.g.
    "Sexual Response Cycle of the Human Female - Genital Reactions"
    (p.288-289)), and case studies complement the text. A 19-page
    References section plus a 10-page Glossary are useful.
    Statistics, mainly demographic in nature, are limited but
    appropriate.
b. The conceptual model of the 4-phase sexual response cycle is
    based on a substantial number of laboratory observations. It
    represents break-through knowledge which in turn has led to
    other research. This research is historically important and
    essential for all sexologists to understand.
c. Myths are often exposed (e.g. "The phallic fallacy that the
    uncircumcised male can establish ejaculatory control more
    effectively than his circumcised counterpart was accepted almost

universally as biologic fact..." (p.190); also the sections
titled "Penile Fallacies" (p.191-193) and "Vaginal Fallacies"
(p.193-195)).
d. The research is dispassionately presented and subjective bias
is not in evidence.

Deficiencies

a. No properly cited textual references or footnotes accord a con-
tinuity with earlier research. Additionally, some historical
and cross-cultural introductory information would have been
helpful.
b. Replication of the research as presented is impossible.
Appendixes covering all major aspects of research methodology,
bias controls, and equipment-design information are not given.
c. The research population has built-in biases (e.g. volunteers;
also "weighted toward average or above-averge intelligence"
(p.14)). Experiments and observations are conducted under
laboratory conditions with the subjects being aware of such
observations. These factors add unknown variables to the
results. Subsequent research by others indicates possible
modifications to the 4-phase model conceptualization.

106. McGill, Thomas E., Dewsbury, Donald A. & Sachs, Benjamin D. Sex
and Behavior: Status and Prospectus. New York: Plenum Press, 1978.
458 pp.

Brief Summary - "The volume has been divided into three sections,
representing three perspectives of sex and behavior: the
evolutionary view, the mechanistic view, and the perspective of
human sexuality" (p.xviii). Part I details "Evolution and Natural
History" from animal and human perspectives. Seven chapters
comprise Part II's "Mechanisms Controlling Reproductive Behavior";
and all provide animal data involving socio-environmental factors,
hormonal interactions, reflexive and neural mechanisms, and
copulatory patterns. Part III, "Human Sexuality and Sex
Differences," describes "Sex Differences in the Human Infant"
(Kagan), "Sex Differences in Cognition - Evidence from the Hawaii
Family Study" (Wilson and Vandenberg), "Gender and Reproductive
State Correlates of Taste Perception in Humans" (Doty), "The Context
and Consequences of Contemporary Sex Research - A Feminist
Perspective" (Tiefer), and "Inside the Human Sex Circus - Prospects
for an Ethology of Human Sexuality" (Bermant). Bermant's closing
chapter defines ethology on the basis that it must "provide
generalizations of species-wide significance" (p.393) in order "to
understand the behavior of organisms in their actual environments"
(p.403).

Critique - Strengths

a. A resource-varied 9-page Bibliography mainly featuring contributions by Beach, cited research, and articles with References
after each chapter are useful. Appropriate footnotes, graphs,
charts, statistical tables, diagrams, sketches and photographs
are included. Historical (e.g. Le Boeuf, p.3-33), cross-
cultural human (e.g. Bermant, p.389), and cross-species (e.g.

refer to Summary above) information is provided.
b. Interesting research is often proffered (e.g. refer to
    Summary). Future research possibilities are sometimes suggested
    (e.g. Kagan, p.315; also Tiefer, p.377). Research theoretical
    models are occasionally examined (e.g. the Trivers and Willard
    model (Le Boeuf, p.28)). Contemporary research is critically
    examined (e.g. "Are species differences in hormone-behavior
    interactions 'real' or are they the result of sampling error?"
    (McGill, p.183); also the section "Masculine Biases in the Study
    of Sexual Behavior" (Tiefer, p.367)).
c. The commentaries and research studies are basically objective.

Deficiencies

a. Much of the material presented concerns animal research (e.g.
    refer to Summary). While such research has intrinsic value, it
    has limited predictive value for any subsequent study-related
    research in human sexuality.
b. Bermant's chapter implies subjectively negative biases and
    unwarranted assumptions (e.g. "oral sex ... (in) its depiction
    in pictorial pornography tends to emphasize the power of men
    over women and in that sense has a definite hostile element.
    The perversity is relatively covert but present nevertheless"
    (p.401)). Unproductive phraseology also occurs in this chapter
    (e.g. "the ambience of scatological sexuality..." (p.402)).

107. Meiselman, Karin C. Incest. San Francisco: Jossey-Bass, Inc.,
Publishers, 1978. 384 pp.

Brief Summary - This book recounts the findings of prior research,
and integrates these with a 58-case original new study done by the
author who is a psychologist. A control group is also utilized.
After an opening resume of the probable taboo origins of incest,
Meiselman moves directly into summarizing the results of the
research literature and then listing her own findings. Chapters 4
to 6 describe in depth the father-daughter incestuous cases and
their aftereffects. The other less commonly reported forms of
incest complete the book's text, with Chapter 11 devoted to
"Treatment Recommendations."

Critique - Strengths

a. The text is well cited and cohesively structured with appropri-
    ate comparative research results. An 8-page References, tables
    and case histories also are included. Chapter 1 includes
    historical-anthropological materials.
b. Unlike most books on the subject, this one addresses both the
    societal long-term and the immediate prevention methods (e.g.
    "prevention of incest is tied to improvement in the functioning
    of society as a whole" (p.332).
c. A dispassionate criticism of past research is presented (e.g.
    "eleven adolescent girls ... makes it impossible to state that
    the family history and dynamics found in father-daughter incest
    is specific to incest cases" (p.50) as claimed by Kaufman, Peck
    and Tagiuri in 1954). Good analysis of potential research-
    design weaknesses is proffered (e.g. "if it were hypothesized

that incestuous experience leads to sexual promiscuity ... it would almost certainly be found that girls with incestuous case histories tend to be promiscuous" (p.33-34)). Assumptions are sometimes challenged (e.g. "if homosexuality is explained by psychoanalysts as being a 'flight from incest,' then how can they explain homosexual incest?" (p.42)). Hypotheses are offered (e.g. on homosexual incest, p.72). Good methodology with well-matched controls is utilized.

Deficiencies

a. No visual aids are included. Consensual incest is not effectively dealt with statistically or its proportion to coercive incest examined. The sample totally comes from a psychotherapeutic setting (e.g. p.55). Of the 58 cases cited in her research, Meiselman states only that two were consensual, two were uncertain and one shifted from early-consensual to later-coercive. A greater effort should have been made to find cases not originating from a legal or therapy background.
b. Subjective judgmentality is evidenced on occasion (e.g. "she had begun heavy drinking and promiscuous sexual acting out with both men and women" (p.307)).

108. Money, John & Ehrhardt, Anke. **Man & Woman: Boy & Girl**. New York: The New American Library Inc., 1974. 352 pp.

Brief Summary - The focal topic is "the sexual differentiation of man and woman from conception to maturity - (and) is presented ... in such a way as to integrate experimental and clinical data and concepts from each of the scientific specialties that have something to contribute: genetics, embryology, neuroendocrinology, neurosurgery, social, medical and clinical psychology, and social anthropology" (p.ix). Chapter I termed "Synopsis" abstracts the essentials of the text. Definitions are employed. Genetic dimorphism of the sexes, with both typical and atypical X and Y chromosome combinations, is detailed in Chapter 2. The following chapter goes into factors affecting sexual differentiation of the sex organs. Normative development and factors causing anomalies are discussed. Chapter 4 details the correlation of fetal hormones between the brain, the hypothalamus and pituitary glands. The next two chapters carry on the discussion, the first one relating to the brain's hormonal influences on sexual dimorphic animal behaviorism and the latter one delineating "human clinical syndromes" (p.97). Chapter 7 describes several cases where genitally malformed sex-reassigned infants easily assumed their sex-gender assignments. In Chapter 8, the differentiation procedure of gender identity is amplified. The following chapter discusses imprinting mechanisms in "Developmental Differentiation." Chapters 10 and 11 deal with pubertal hormones. The final chapter delves into the role of the postpubertal erotic dimorphism of the brain in influencing behavior.

Critique - Strengths

a. Cited references, apt photographs, diagrams, sketches, charts and graphs give tremendous impact to the book. Probability statistics are usefully employed in charts (e.g. p.113). A

23-page Bibliography and an 18-page Glossary are also included. Cross-species and cross-cultural information is often utilized (e.g. "the Batak people ... in northern Sumatra ... (where boys) participate in paired homosexual play" (p.136) before changing to normative heterosexuality after marriage).

b. Hypotheses, facts, future research possibilities and theories are posited in logical and challenging ways (refer to Summary). Speculations are acknowledged as such (e.g. "The etiology of ... transvestism ... is imperfectly understood. There may well be an as yet undiscovered fetal metabolic or hormonal component which acts to induce a predisposition to ambiguity..." (p.22)). Hypotheses are specific and narrow in focus.

c. Historical theorists are critically examined (e.g. "Freudian theory ... had no provision for differentiation of psychosexual development as male or female until the genital or Oedipal phase..." (p.190-191)).

Deficiencies

a. Much important research has taken place in that area since the book's publication. Certain conclusions about individual acceptance and sociosexual happiness after early sex-reassignment, seem open to re-evaluation.

b. Optional alternative hypotheses are not always objectively acknowledged (e.g. "The most likely explanation of the origins of homosexuality, bisexuality, and heterosexuality of gender identity is that certain sexually dimorphic traits or dispositions are laid down in the brain before birth..." (p.244)).

c. The definition of androgyny in the Glossary is incomplete and excludes psychocultural manifestations (p.295).

d. Some pejorative lapses occur (e.g. "... is in danger of becoming an obligative homosexual with a hang-up on having an older person as a partner" (p.207)).

109. Morneau, Robert H. & Rockwell, Robert R. Sex, Motivation, and the Criminal Offender. Springfield: Charles C. Thomas, Pub., 1980. 415 pp.

Brief Summary - The authors, both former FBI Special Agents, and now with degrees in the social sciences, Preface their book by stating that for "sex crimes, many times there are no little boxes where things fit easily and comfortably" (p.v). The authors direct its contents primarily at law enforcement officers. After a short Introduction giving some case examples and parameters, the authors focus on normative and atypical sexual patterns. Chapters 3 through 7 deal with those sexual variations which sometimes mentally or physically violate a victim or the perpetrator. Such acts, the authors claim, are pathological in that they involve "issues of incompleteness" (p.68). "Types of Sex Crimes Commonly Encountered by Police" include exhibitionism, voyeurism, frottage, kleptomania, manipulative troilism, and coercive incest. More "Dangerous Perversions" consist of pyromania, flagellation, necrophilia, lust mutilation, pedophilia, and rape. Chapter 5 talks about everyone's propensity for "Developing Fantasies," some of which involve danger and assault. Separate chapters are devoted to sadism and masochism,

including masochistic accidental hangings, bondage and infibulation.
Chapter 8 examines "Sex Symbols" while the following chapter
discusses "Sexual Fetishes." The final two chapters analyze the
controversial influences of pornography, erotic literature and
homosexual behavior.

Critique - Strengths

a. Excellent photographs, drawings, and flow charts are included.
   Quotations, footnotes, cited references and a 4-page
   Bibliography also exist. Many case studies reinforce topics.
   Historical (e.g. Herodotus, p.143) and cross-cultural (about
   incest (p.110)) input is provided.
b. The book is easy to follow. The authors strive to maintain a
   neutral tone (e.g. "We do not, in fact, know what normalcy is
   and, consequently, we cannot define abnormal" (p.67); also
   "While victimless crimes should perhaps be outside police
   purview..." (p.133)). The continuum of sexual behavior for each
   sexual variation is acknowledged (e.g. "Everyone fits on the
   chart at some point in sexual expression... All of us may be
   frotteurs. It is where we do it that counts" (p172).
c. Tolerance is advocated toward non-criminal sexual-minority
   persons (e.g. "A misguided personal vendetta against homosexuals
   must be viewed with abhorrence" (p.343)).

Deficiencies

a. The authors' mind-sets seem to imply that most sexual-minority
   persons of certain categories have a dangerous propensity for
   violence toward others (e.g. "The offenses committed by the
   pedophile ... range from exhibitionism to sadistic acts and
   rape-flagellation, and frequently end in murder" (p.155)).
   Elaborate justifications are offered for police raids on sex
   clubs (e.g. "... police seized shackles ... belts and whips...
   If death results, everyone at the party has a problem" (p.135)).
   Most sadomasochists practice consensuality, utilizing "safe
   words" with others. This is not properly emphasized and
   acknowledged. The book gives the impression that all devotees
   of sadism and masochism are dangerous to others as well as to
   themselves. Perhaps new terms should be devised by these
   authors to cover coercive non-consensual sadomasochistic
   practices. No documented studies using statistical research
   methods are ever offered to substantiate the authors'
   inferential biases and conclusions.
b. Too much explanation is offered in terms of neofreudian hypotheses (e.g. "This behavior is most easily explained in Freudian
   terms..." (p.145)).
c. Postulations and assumptions are either not supported by data
   or are erroneous (e.g. "Many such broadcasts seem to suggest
   that being overweight is associated with the inability to get an
   erection" (p.150); also "A person is not really a homosexual
   until he engages in a homosexual act" (p.354)). Myths are
   occasionally supported (e.g. "We presume that the ideal match is
   between a 'dyke' and a 'femme'... These are ... the patterns
   that are usually found" (p.359)). "The True Transvestite"
   (p.96) should seemingly be described as the pre-operative

transsexual.
d. Pejorativity is commonplace (e.g. "an aggressively promiscuous
    woman" (p.41); also "while the pervert watches" (p.73); also
    "dirty books" (p.328)).

110. Rubinstein, E.A., Green, R. & Brecher, E., ed. New Directions in
Sex Research. New York: Plenum Press, 1976. 180 pp.

Brief Summary - The subjects covered are as follows: "Early Sex
Differences in the Human - Studies of Socioemotional Development"
(Lewis), "Sexual Identity - Research Strategies" (Green),
"Male-Female Differences in Sexual Arousal and Behavior During and
After Exposure to Sexually Explicit Stimuli" (Schmidt),
"Heterosexual Dysfunction - Evaluation of Treatment Procedures"
(Fordney-Settlage), "Sexuality and Physical Disabilities" (Cole),
"Neuroendocrinology - Animal Models and Problems of Human Sexuality"
(Goy & Goldfoot), "Research in Homosexuality - Back to the Drawing
Board" (Bell), "Changing Sex Roles in American Culture - Future
Directions for Research" (Lipman - Blumen), and "Comprehensive Sex
Research Centers - Design and Operation for Effctive Functioning"
(Gebhard). A general discussion concerning "Ethical Issues" follows
these presentations. A section entitled "Summary and
Recommendations" is given with regard to methodology, ethics, and
subject-matter for future research. A brief humorous Epilogue
terminates the book.

Critique - Strengths

a. Numerous cited references, an 8-page References section and
    quotations complement the text. Some interesting diagrams and
    tables are included. The Group Discussion synopsis at the end
    of each presentation acts not only as a critical evaluatory
    process but also as a clarification mechanism for each topic.
b. Some useful research suggestions (e.g. "Many measures have a
    bell-shaped distribution. Males and females who fall at the
    ends of the distribution could be longitudinally studied to
    determine correlations between neonatal behavior and later
    developmental attributes" (Green, p.17)) as well as generalized
    criticisms of research (e.g. "Rigorous attention has not been
    paid to possibly confounding variables, especially stress, drug
    intake, and recency of sexual activity" (Green, p.25)) are
    proffered.
c. Interesting insights sometimes surface (e.g. "One person's
    homosexuality may amount chiefly to a political statement.
    Another's may represent a quest for intimacy. Still another's
    may be indistinguishable from a preoccupation with occupational
    needs, interests, and rewards" (Bell, p.104)).
d. The best topical presentations and ensuing discussions are
    embodied in Chapters 2 (Green) and 7 (Bell) (e.g. refer to
    Summary).
e. Pejorativity is minimal.

Deficiencies

a. No photographs, sketches or graphs accompany the text. No

generalized bibliography is included. Historically and cross-culturally related background issues are not covered.
b. Many of the book's ideas and postulations are now dated (e.g. Gebhard's proposals are no longer appropriate. New institutions such as The Institute for Advanced Study of Human Sexuality in San Francisco have formed since that time).

111. Sandler, Merton & Gessa, G.L., ed. Sexual Behavior: Pharmacology and Biochemistry. New York: Raven Press, Pubs., 1975. 363 pp.

Brief Summary - The primary emphasis of the book focuses on the hormonal-endocrinological aspects of sexuality as derived from both an endogenic and exogenic perspective. The clinical data on sexual pharmacology for both animals and humans suggest a generally "negative influence of drugs on fertility and ejaculation, with occasional anecdotal reports of positive effects on libido" (p.v). Two papers delve into the socio-legal and biochemical sides to anti-androgen treatment of sex offenders (p.197-208) and four chapters examine street-drug influence on sexual behavior patterns of users (p.63-80, p.85-98). The majority of the remaining chapters describe animal experiments.

Critique - Strengths

a. Cited references are extensive and appropriate. The highly technical biochemical names, compound formulae and ring-structures appear to be accurate and consistent. Charts, graphs, tables and photographs add positive impact to the book.
b. The book gives a reasonable cross-spectral evaluation of bio-chemical sex research.

Deficiencies

a. Animal experiments cannot be extrapolated to humans but indicate only a possible trend for human-experiment evaluation. Thus much of the animal work presented is of limited value (e.g. "castrated guinea pigs ... and rhesus monkeys ... exhibit copulatory behavior when administered 5a-DHT. However, castrated hamsters ... and rabbits ... failed to maintain male behavioral parameters after treatment with 5a-DHT." (Johnston et al., p.236)).
b. Two chapters seem irrelevant to the editorial topic (Shainess and Bieber). Additionally, both include judgmental, unproven hypotheses which are presented as fact (e.g. Shainess charts feminine erotic response which includes a claim that only six percent of women attain multiple orgasms and these are "not a sign of supercapacity but a fantasy misinterpretation of multiple erotic sensations never quite summing up to total satisfaction and orgasmic release" (p.285)).
c. The anti-androgen chapter by Saba et al. is based on a dubious etiology and the rationale for such drug use on a questionable philosophical justification (e.g. its use in Table 1 on a male "passive" homosexual with "reactive depressive illness" (p.198)).
d. A few authors utilize pejorative phraseology (e.g. "promiscuous or polymorphous sexual behavior" (Hollister, p.90)).

112. Schultz, Leroy G., ed. *The Sexual Victimology of Youth*.
Springfield: Charles C. Thomas, Pub., 1980. 432 pp.

Brief Summary - Section I termed "The Legal Control of the Sexual
Abuse of Children" details its history, furnishes a literature
survey and provides case examples. "Diagnosis and Treatment,"
Section II, suggests "Sexual Assault Center Emergency Room
Protocol." Section III deals with "Incest Policy Recommendations."
Section IV, "The Victim and the Justice System," is concerned with
interviewing victims, legal methods of protecting such victims, and
the proper preparation of hospital records for later courtroom
usage. Section V, entitled "The Child Sex Industry," explores its
societal ramifications. Rossman discusses "The Pederasts" and
Schultz gives twelve "Policy Recommendations on Child Pornography
Control." Section VI deals with the issue of children's rights.

Critique - Strengths

a. Many quotations, cited references, tables, research studies,
footnotes, and case studies are displayed. A 35-page
Bibliography with sub-headings and an Appendix giving rape laws
also are included. Abstracts sum up some chapters. Historical
(e.g. Schultz, Chapter 1) and some cross-cultural (e.g. Libai,
Chapter 16) input is made available.
b. Eclecticism is promoted (e.g. "Principal sources of the techniques comes from psychosynthesis, Gestalt therapy, conjoint
therapy, psychodrama, Transactional Analysis, and personal
journal keeping (Giarretto, p.156)). Advice is proffered (e.g.
"Incest Policy Recommendations" (Schultz, p.164)).
c. Insights appear (e.g. "are current approaches to the incest
victim themselves traumatogenic?" (Schultz, p.94)). Hypotheses
are presented utilizing cited studies (e.g. "... supporting the
hypothesis that affectional needs make these children more
vulnerable to victimization" (Swift, p.19)). Research qualifi-
cations abound (e.g. "We must make sure that the 'solutions' we
impose on children and their families do not become part of the
problem" (Brant and Tisza, p.58)).
d. Efforts are made to minimize cultural assumptions (e.g. "... we
feel the term 'sexual misuse' is preferable; it is less
pejorative and does not compel one to think only in terms of
victims and abusers" (Brant and Tisza, p.44)). Schultz dispels
cultural myths (e.g. "Most of the 'research' regarding incest
ends up being rhetorically manipulative, abounding in cliches
and myths... Many of the studies confuse moral damage with
psychological damage" (p.95)).

Deficiencies

a. Textual shortcomings are significant (e.g. "Four chapters ...
center on the 'medical-model' only" (p.viii)). Graphs, diagrams
and other visual aids are non-existent.
b. Unproven assumptions occur (e.g. "Usually the child escaped
into homosexuality as a characteristic outcome of incestuous
relations" (Yorukoglu and Kemph, p.125)).
c. Occasional subjective biases are in evidence (e.g. "the

'promiscuous pederast' type" (Rossman, p.342)).

113. Weinberg, Martin S., ed. <u>Sex Research: Studies from the Kinsey Institute</u>. New York: Oxford Univ. Press, 1976. 326 pp.

<u>Brief Summary</u> - After a brief Introduction, Chapter 2 recalls "Our History - How It All Began." Next follows the findings of the male and female volumes on sexual behavior. Chapter 4 describes "Pregnancy, Birth and Abortion" as well as "Sex Offenders: An Analysis of Types." So-called "think-pieces" (p.135) are presented on male homosexuality, fetishism and sadomasochism, and "First Coitus and the Double Standard." In Chapter 6, Bell's research is summarized ("The Personality of a Child Molester," "The Homosexual as Patient") after which the sociological works of Weinberg and Williams are outlined as "Social Reactions to Sexual Deviance." Chapter 8 concludes by discussing three Monographs ("The Other Victorians" (Marcus), "Sex and Repression in an Irish Folk Community" (Messenger), and "Picasso and the Anatomy of Eroticism" (Rosenblum)).

<u>Critique - Strengths</u>

a. A 6-page "Bibliography of Institute Work" terminates the text. Footnotes, photographs, tables, charts and boxed extracts are other aids. Anecdotal case studies are given (e.g. p.237).
b. The synthesis of these key works presented in book form serves as a focal reference book for the sexologist.
c. Further research possibilities are inferred (e.g. "we do have the impression that peepers who enter homes or other buildings in order to peep, and peepers who deliberately attract the female's attention ... are more likely to become rapists than are the others" (Gebhard et al., p.134)).
d. The text is non-judgmental (e.g. "When a ... patient announces his or her homosexuality to the physician, the doctor must conclude nothing more than that the patient becomes erotically aroused by persons of the same sex..." (Bell, p.202)).

<u>Deficiencies</u>

a. Pertinent research is not included ("Gagnon and Simon ... have requested that these articles not be reprinted here" (footnote, p.137)). An index is lacking.
b. An occasional pejorative remark surfaces (e.g. "... some of his promiscuous female in-laws" (Gebhard et al., p.124)).
c. Nothing is said as to the research directions into which the Institute found itself heading, or what financial or other problems might be inhibiting future growth.
d. Little critical self-analysis or acknowledgement of inherent project design-weaknesses is proffered.

Sex Therapy and Counseling

114. Annon, Jack S. The Behavioral Treatment of Sexual Problems.
Volumes 1 & 2. Honolulu: Enabling Systems Inc., 1975. 636 pp.

Brief Summary - Volume 1 is termed "Brief Therapy" and Volume 2 is
entitled "Intensive Therapy." Annon, a psychologist, informs the
reader in his Preface "I eventually evolved an approach that allows
for both brief and intensive therapy" (p.xviii). Volume 1 begins in
Part 1's "Introduction and Background" by exploring the behavioral
approach to the treatment of, as well as the behavioral view of,
sexual problems. Part 2's "Brief Therapy" begins by proposing the
"conceptual scheme" (p.53) of the PLISSIT Model, which in four
levels is an acronym for "Permission," "Limited Information,"
"Specific Suggestions," "Intensive Therapy." The final four
chapters in this volume delineate these four various levels of
treatment. Volume 2 begins with Part 3 and reiterates the PLISSIT
Model. Chapter 11 deals with an overview of "behavioral excesses"
(p.268) of the various paraphilias. This is followed by
"Difficulties in the Behavioral Treatment of Sexual Problems." The
next chapter discusses useful questionnaires and inventories. A
further conceptual scheme termed "The A.R.D. System" (p.390) which
stands for attitudinal or emotional function, the reinforcing
function, the discriminative or controlling function, is suggested
for intensive therapy. The final Chapter 17 cautions "that
intensive therapy does not mean an extended standardized program of
treatment" (p.463).

Critique - Strengths

a. Extensive References sections terminate each volume. Thirteen
    Appendices involving self-study programs, resource information,
    specific questionnaires and inventories, research data, and
    "Relaxation Procedures and Covert Treatment Techniques" (p.527)
    aid the researcher and clinician. A 10-page Glossary is also of
    benefit. Sketches, diagrams, graphs, cited references,
    anecdotal stories and actual case studies further reinforce the
    text. Some statistics are provided (e.g. Table 7, p.452).

b. The innovative conceptualizations (e.g. refer to Summary above) and original inventories (e.g. appendix H - "Composite Fear Inventory" (p.487)) are therapeutically valuable.

c. Research is intensively reviewed and cited on a broad, behavioristic base (e.g. Chapter 11, p.265-290).

d. Myths are exposed (e.g. "Figure 5. Foreshortened view of penis" (p.79)).

e. Pejorativity is not in evidence. Belief-principles are clearly expressed (e.g. "there is an obvious need for assessment procedures ... rather than the indiscriminate use of labels" (p.291)).

Deficiencies

a. Little historical-anthropological background information is provided.

b. Use of covert sensitization (and/or aversion) techniques to re-orientate homosexual interest to heterosexuality is of very dubious merit (e.g. case study of the bisexual Mr. Adam (p.351)). Insufficient case-studies' numbers with incomplete longitudinal (and other) data are presented to warrant justification in the efficacy of these methods over the long term. This is the weakness of Volume 2 and extends to all so-termed antisocial or atypical sexual behaviors even if applied to volunteers eager to change.

115. Barbach, Lonnie G. _For Yourself: The Fulfillment of Female Sexuality_. New York: Anchor Books, 1976. 218 pp.

Brief Summary - This book addresses itself to preorgasmic and situationally orgasmic women. Barbach's Introduction is a synopsis of her work in this area, utilizing the all-female group concept of patient treatment. The first section of the book explodes the sexual myths and imprinting which women (and their male partners) have acquired. These problems are coupled with communication failures. The first steps include demythologizing and re-educating such patients. Beginning with Chapter 7:termed "Why masturbation?," Barbach focuses on genital awareness. Each female must establish her own masturbatory pattern. Couple exercises are introduced. The final section discusses sex and pregnancy, aging, personal body health, and one's children. The last chapter enjoins all women to support "Personal Liberation."

Critique - Strengths

a. Footnotes, exercises, one diagram of female external genitalia, and an 8-page bibliography are included. The text is manual-stylized and is written in a positive, anecdotal way.

b. Sexual myths are often dissected (refer to Summary). Barbach is introspective and such an attitude accords authenticity to the text (e.g. "listening carefully to the women changed some of my own attitudes about traditional love-making and called into question some of the stereotypes under which I had unwittingly been operating" (p.xvi-xvii)). The therapy format is logical in its sequence. The group process is innovative.

c. Challenges at times occur (e.g. "Why don't we stop

psychoanalyzing our fantasies?" (p.82)).

Deficiencies

a. More cited references and diagrams would have been useful. A brief historical and cross-cultural overview would also have been helpful.
b. Minor improvements in the therapy regimen can be added (e.g. the yes-no exercises of Chapter 4 should emphasize that one should be firm yet diplomatic in an egalitarian way when one is involved in such exercises with one's partner and/or peers). The book tends to overstress the goal-inevitability and necessity of coital intercourse. Other forms of sexual expression are downplayed.
c. Actual research statistics of female groups using Barbach's techniques would have greatly strengthened the text. Only a few qualitative figures are forthcoming.
d. Occasional pejorative lapses occur (e.g. "... either promiscuous or over-sexed..." (p.78)).

116. Beigel, Hugo C. & Johnson, Warren R., ed. Application of Hypnosis in Sex Therapy. Springfield: Charles C. Thomas, Pub., 1980. 346 pp.

Brief Summary - Part 1 termed "Exploration" deals with client-interview and assessment methods. Part 2 is called "Brief Methods of Therapy" and directs itself at reeducation, direct suggestion-methods and indirect short-term therapies such as flooding and aversive imagery. Part 3's "Various Other Methods" stress relaxation, symptom transformation, symptom utilization, and abreaction techniques. Part 4, entitled "Drawing on the Power of Imagination," relates "Memory and Dreams" to hypnosis, "Hypnotic Regression Therapy" (Stickney), hypnotherapeutic uses of "Imagination and Imagery," "Hypnosis and Frigidity..." (Oystragh), "Posthypnotic Suggestions and Amnesia," and "Autohypnosis" as a therapeutic tool in sex therapy. Part 5's "Sexual Disorders in Females" covers the use of hypnotherapy in overcoming various dysfunctions, "The Role of Hypnosis in the Treatment of Infertility" (Wollman), and the results of a controlled experiment statistically proving that hypnosis can induce breast growth (Williams). Part 6 details hypnotherapeutic approaches to "Sexual Disorders in Males."

Critique - Strengths

a. Two Appendices titled "Some Favorite Induction Techniques" and "Some Legal Considerations" are most useful. An 8-page References section interrelates to citations throughout the text. Other support-aids include photographs, sketches, tables, quotations, editor's notes, case studies, and anecdotal stories.
b. Differing therapy methods and their proponents are described (e.g. "Hypnotherapy of Sexual Disorders in Women" (Dengrove)). Statistics are occasionally offered (e.g. Chapter 22 (Alexander, p.215)). Beigel's Chapter 33 termed "Premature Ejaculation" offers a good analysis of inherent therapeutic-cultural bias in defining and explaining this phenomenon (e.g. "Editor's note ... Albert Ellis, among others, has frequently referred to it as a true iatrogenic condition..." (p.282)).

Deficiencies

a. Chapter 1, "The Initial Interview," is not definitive enough as
to scope, technique, and method. There is a lack of historical
and cross-cultural input on this subject.
b. Research is poorly presented with no graphs or diagrams, and a
minimum of tables and statistics. Often, only idiosyncratic
case studies of one person are offered (e.g. Chapters 7, 17, and
32). Methodological bias controls are largely neglected. Some
chapters are too brief in explaining their subjects with no
corroborative evidence at all being presented (e.g. Chapter 26,
p.240-241). At times, generalized conclusions are given (e.g.
"I had found homosexuality and nymphomania more often connected
than I had expected" (Wollman, p.102)). Unwarranted assumptions
often occur (e.g. "Homosexuals who want to give up their
predilections are confronted with..." (p.135)). Alleged therapeutic results are not properly backed up by longitudinal
follow-up except for Chapter 31 (Ward).
c. Pejorative phraseology occurs (e.g. "compulsive promiscuity ...
addictive masturbation" (p.ix)).

117. Chapman, J. Dudley. The Sexual Equation - Woman:Man::Socially:
Sexually. New York: Philosophical Library Inc., 1977. 446 pp.

Brief Summary - Part I termed "The Genesis of Sexual Difficulties"
delves into the topics of "Understanding the Mind of Woman: Man,"
"Sexualization of Non-Sexual Relations," "Female-Male Gender
Identity," "Egalitarianism to Body-Mind," and "Monotony of
Matrimony." In Part II called "Treating Sexual Problems or
Dysfunction," Chapman begins with the mnemonic "Basics" in "Sexual
Problems-Dysfunction." This leads to the chapters entitled
"Behavior Modification; Affect-Love," "Sensual or Sensory Message,"
"Imagery-Imagination-Fantasy," "Cognitive - The Sex Education for
Sexual Dysfunction" and "Sexual-Sensual-Self" in which Chapman
concludes "if you can respect yourself, you will respect your
partners" (p.433).

Critique - Strengths

a. Aids such as the massage photographs (p.328-342), a graph
(p.93), the many composite case studies and the Bibliography and
Additional Reading after each chapter are included.
b. The book is easy to read. It can be recommended to clients.
The text describes how to achieve personal sexual esteem and how
to get in touch with one's own body and that of one's partner
(e.g. "The breast is as unique in its response to touch as is
the woman of whom it is but a part" (p.349)).
c. Myths are discounted (e.g. "Myth Six: The sex myth of
spontaneity..." (p.389)) and "Frequently Asked Questions - and
Some Stimulus Responses" (p.396) given.

Deficiencies

a. Since the text is directed at the lay public, it offers less of
value to the professional sexologist.

b. The author sometimes offers generalizations which tend to be pompous (e.g. " 'Sex' is a physiologic act, and in our technologic age, an act that amounts to a compulsive, mechanistic display" (p.7)). Unreferenced conclusions based on judgmental personal assumptions are at times provided (e.g. "Most swingers admit they meet but never engage the same couple more than once or twice... On close inspection, swingers are rigid, bigoted, simple people who seem to want something bigger than what they are: the expression of creativity" (p.64)).

118. Crown, Sidney, ed. Psychosexual Problems: Psychotherapy, Counselling and Behavioural Modification. London: Academic Press Inc. (London) Ltd. (also New York: Grune & Stratton Inc.), 1976. 484 pp.

Brief Summary - This text has four parts entitled "Sex Therapies," "Psychosexual Problems and the Life Cycle," "Psychosexual Problems in Medicine and Surgery," and "Sex Education." Crown in his Introduction states the book is directed from differing foci at "general practitioners, community-based counselling services and to specialised departments within a hospital" (p.3). Part I delves into "Individual Psychotherapy," "Group therapy," "Counselling," and "Modification of Sexual Behaviour." Part II discusses "Adolescent Sexuality and Chronic Handicap," "Sexual Problems of Young Adults," "Sexual Minorities," "Psychosexual Problems in Marriage," "Psychosexual Problems in a Religious Setting," and "Sexual Behaviour in the Elderly." In Part III, six chapters analyze psychosexual problems from the perspective of a general practitioner, untoward drug effects on sexuality and sexual problems of disabled people, the sexual work spheres of the obstetrician and gynecologist, the urologist, the person specializing in contraception and family planning, the venereologist, and the surgeon. A single chapter by Cole in Part IV explores issues necessary for a new approach to sex education. Crown summarizes a Conclusion.

Critique - Strengths

a. References and a usual Summary or Conclusion after each chapter are aids. Some case studies are well presented (e.g. Bloomfield and Marteau, p.282).
b. Parts III and IV are the best areas of the book and here the authors are factually comprehensive, non-judgmental and positive in their collective approaches. Certain earlier chapters are occasionally outstanding (e.g. Cameron (p.145-155) concerning the handicapped adolescent and sexuality). At times, a good presentation of all sides of an issue is given (e.g. MacKay (p.115) as to the use of sex surrogates).

Deficiencies

a. No visual aids, charts, tables or graphs assist the text.
b. Several authors present neofreudian theory as accepted fact (e.g. Crown & Lucas (p.13)). Uncited conclusions are often based on unproven assumptions (e.g. "In fact, on closer investigation, it is usually if not invariably, discovered that the promiscuous have weak libidinal drives" (Cauthery (p.177)).

c. Pejorative value-judgments are often presented (e.g.
    "Promiscuity ... may have very different causes" (Bloomfield &
    Marteau (p.281)). The book is oriented to the medical-model
    approach (except for Part IV). Material is often omitted when
    discussion of a particular sexual variation is offered (e.g.
    "sadomasochistic forms of behaviour are considered to reflect a
    perversion only when they become the actual sexual goal"
    (Hertoft (p.208)).

119. Gullick, Eugenia L. & Peed, Steven F., ed. The Health
Practitioner in Family Relationships: Sexual and Marital Issues.
Wesport: Technomic Publishing Co. Inc., 1978. 149 pp.

Brief Summary - A short Preface suggests that "this volume is
addressed primarily to the family physician... However, it is hoped
that other health care providers (e.g. nurses, psychologists, social
workers, ministers, etc.) ... will find the contents of this book
useful" (p.ii). Section 1 concerns sexual-marital dysfunction,
sociological changes evolving in the family, and various age-related
sexual clinical issues. Section 2 discusses sexual myths, the
psychophysiology of sexual response, sexuality as it relates to both
organic illness and to aging, and the definitions, etiology, and
treatment considerations of the various sexual dysfunctions. In
Section 3's "The Practitioner and Intervention," Peed covers the
mechanics of sexual interview-taking along with the office
management of any patient with psychogenic sexual dysfunction.
Section 4 deals with communication as this relates to marital
intimacy, the divorced patient, and clients who have predilections
for societally atypical sexual variations.

Critique - Strengths

a. References after each chapter, citations, quotations, anatomi-
    cal sketches, and an abstract before each Section assist textual
    comprehension. Some anecdotal examples are included (e.g.
    p.103), as are cross-cultural (e.g. Mathis, p.22 - cited
    reference given) and historical (e.g. Mathis, p.27 - cited
    reference given) data.
b. Sexual myths and stereotypes are exposed (e.g. Chapter 4
    (Mathis)). Guidance statements are proffered (e.g. "The
    physician's acceptance or rejection of the appropriateness of
    masturbation, homosexuality ... impacts on his relationship with
    the patient" (Wood, p.12)).
c. Goals and resource areas are emphasized (e.g. "time require-
    ments alone may dictate that the primary physician refer the
    patient exhibiting a sexual dysfunction to a sex therapy program
    or specialist" (Peed, p.93)). Research is compared and reviewed
    (e.g. Cooke, p.30-45).
d. The medical-model approach to sexual variations is downplayed
    (e.g. They "in most instances do not involve serious harm to
    others... Those who wish to remain as their predominant life
    long sexual fantasies and impulses have directed, can be helped
    to lead productive lives, avoiding acts and circumstances likely
    to cause them serious legal problems" (Mathis and King, p.128)).
    The text is mostly objective (e.g. "... numerous terms (are)
    based upon value judgments or labels ... used prejudicially...

For example: 'frigid' ... 'unfaithful' ... 'promiscuous'..."
(Peed, p.79)).

Deficiencies

a. Only one table (Peed, p.75) and no visual aids, graphs or
    charts reinforce the text.
b. Certain uncited assumptions are stated as fact (e.g.
    "Homosexuals can change their overt sexual behavior... Those
    who are strongly motivated to live as heterosexuals ... can
    often be helped in doing this by counseling or psychotherapy"
    (Mathis and King, p.123)). Some subjects are not defined
    properly and are incompletely covered (e.g. sadomasochism in its
    consensual aspect (Mathis and King, p.125)).
c. The book is very limited in its coverage of key concepts such
    as sexual dysfunctional treatment. Furthermore, many topics are
    ignored (e.g. sexually transmitted diseases).

120. Hartman, William E. & Fithian, Marilyn A. <u>Treatment of Sexual</u>
<u>Dysfunction</u>. San Diego: Center for Marital and Sexual Studies, 1972.
298 pp.

Brief Summary - After giving a tabled summary of the "Daily
Schedule" (of their) "Two-Week Intensive Sexual Therapy Program"
(with) "Treatment Procedure" (p.xi-xiv), the authors proceed with
their "bio-psycho-social approach" (p.1). A dual-sex team approach
is utilized dealing mainly with dysfunctionally bonded couples. The
referred couple undergoes psychological testing, sex histories,
physical examinations, a so-called "Sexological Examination," "Body
Imagery" exercises in self-concept and sensitivity, caress exercises, interspersed homework assignments beginning the fourth day,
and acquaintanceship with specific audio-visual aids including video
tapes of sexual intercourse. The final two chapters detail
miscellaneous techniques such as hypnosis, and a glimpse into the
ongoing research of the Center.

Critique - Strengths

a. Appropriate sketches, diagrams, respondent charts and case
    studies are included. A useful (if now dated) Annotated
    Bibliography and List of Publishers also aid the serious reader.
    Forms utilized are given throughout the book and in an Appendix
    (e.g. the sex history inventory of items (p.29-65)).
b. The authors use an eclectic approach where warranted (e.g. "Our
    history is a combination of the Kinsey and Masters & Johnson sex
    histories, with massive inclusion of our own items" (p.22)).
c. Innovative procedures stem from this text (e.g. "Sexological
    Examination" (p.77); also "Body Imagery Sensitivity Exercises"
    (p.134)).
d. Interesting insights often occur (e.g. "These people often
    function on an intellectual level and want to intellectualize
    sex rather than deal with it on an emotional level" (p.106)).
e. The authors tend to de-emphasize a medical-model approach.
f. No pejorativity is noticeable.
g. Some salient research information is sometimes offered (e.g.
    "The most significant finding of this research has been a

finger-printing phenonemon reflecting the wide variation between women's orgasms" (p.209)).

Deficiencies

a.   Some brief historical and cross-cultural background material would have been helpful. Cited references are minimal. Constructive criticism of comparable sex-therapy methods of treatment is not forthcoming. Rationales as to how the authors developed their methodology and what was discarded along the way are not given. Some inclusion of basic physiological infor- mation on male and female bodies would have furnished a more well-rounded text (e.g. "We do not elaborate on all of the rationale and theory in relation to our methods" (p.viii)).

b.   Some reported research findings are couched in brief general- ities. Such information should have been expanded upon and specifically analyzed by the inclusion of data, case studies and possibly some theoretical constructs (e.g. "We have found some women who report themselves to be non-orgasmic are in fact orgasmic, but have completely cut themselves off from their own sexual feelings. The biological response they are getting have not filtered into consciousness" (p.99)).

121. Heiman, Julia, LoPiccolo, Leslie & LoPiccolo, Joseph. Becoming Orgasmic : A Sexual Growth Program For Women. Englewood Cliffs: Prentice-Hall Inc., 1976. 232 pp.

Brief Summary - The authors, all sex professionals, explain "it became apparent that an easily understood self-help version of this program would be useful for those women who could benefit from such help, without the need for formal therapy" (p.xii). The first chapter outlines some guidelines for a woman who commits herself to the program. From here on, the text delineates the various essen- tial steps; developing an awareness of her own body and its sensual feelings, doing a personal sex history, getting used to self- pleasuring and using proper focusing in this regard, dealing with resistances, employing aids to orgasm such as a vibrator, and eventually expanding such pleasuring to an involved partner. The final chapter suggests continuing follow-up techniques and the possibility of seeing a qualified therapist.

Critique - Strengths

a.   Brief abstracts under Contents (p.v-ix), a Selected Annotated Bibliography under sub-headings, an Overview as to therapy steps (p.198-200), anatomical diagrams, sketches of exercises and the exercises (e.g. "Body Awareness" (p.49) are most helpful. Although the primary focus of the book is directed at clients, it also addresses itself to therapists as well. In a "Note to Professionals," it recommends source materials and the segmentation of the book depending if a client is involved in individual as opposed to group therapy.

b.   Innovative suggestions are offered (e.g. a list of erotic books and magazines (p.76-77); six " 'loosening' exercises" (p.71); ten "orgasm 'triggers' " (p.100-101)). Many thoughtful questions are posed in "Exercise I: A Personal Sex History" (p.21-24).

c. Pejorativity is absent.

d. Overemphasis on coital intercourse is avoided (e.g. Chapter 10 - "Intercourse - Another Form of Mutual Pleasure" (p.157)).

Deficiencies

a. While supportive suggestions for the male partner(s) are included (e.g. "delaying ejaculation" (p.186)), more information should have been added. Marital dynamics are complex and can lead to many secondary difficulties reinforcing an original female orgasmic dysfunction. These are minimally dealt with. Furthermore, sociosexual myths should have been examined. A brief overview on pertinent historical and cross-cultural material would have been most useful. Other researchers are not cited (e.g. the sexological exam of Hartman & Fithian (p.26-31)). Also no supportive statistics reinforce the text.

b. A mistake occurs on page 185 (i.e. "amyl nitrate" should read "amyl nitrite").

c. Concerning finding a sex therapist, the word "sexologist" is not mentioned while the statement "there is no such professional discipline to ensure adequate training of such people" (p.196) is no longer true.

122. Jehu, Derek. <u>Sexual Dysfunction: A Behavioural Approach to Causation, Assessment and Treatment</u>. New York: John Wiley & Sons, 1979. 313 pp.

<u>Brief Summary</u> - Chapter 1's Introduction concerns causation, assessment and treatment. Part I termed "An Overview of Causation" deals with some "Organic Factors," "Previous Learning Experiences" and certain stresses and "psychiatric syndromes" (p.61). Three chapters outline and delineate Part 2's "The Dysfunctions." Part 3 concerns itself with interviewing, "Sexual Assignments," and behavioristic rationales such as relaxation training, desensitization, flooding, vaginal dilation, classical conditioning, biofeedback, fantasy training, hypnosis, vaginal muscle exercises, drug therapy and prosthetic or mechanical aids. Part 4 analyzes "Assessment and Planning Treatment" in terms of resources, "behavioural formulation" (p.192), goal selection, planned treatment and "Methods of Data Collection." Part 5's "Outcome of Treatment" compares various research-study results. Jehu concludes "there can be no doubt about the necessity for further more rigorous and controlled investigation into the outcome of the behavioural treatment of sexual dysfunction..." (p.260).

Critique - Strengths

a. A 27÷page References section terminates the book. A useful and succinct Appendix summarizes client-assessment topics and variables. Apt topical cited references abound and thus historical subject-research is thoroughly provided. Some case-study examples are included (e.g. p.165).

b. Ten tables detail concepts, findings and immensely valuable research comparisons (e.g. physiology (p.13)). Dysfunctional research-treatment findings are well compared (e.g. "Programmes for Female Dysfunction" (five cited references)).

  c. Methodological differences are acknowledged (e.g. "All these arguments for and against the dual sex team are either _a priori_ or based upon unsystematic clinical experience and there is very little research evidence bearing upon questions such as..." (p.200)). Controversial aspects about certain modalities are admitted (e.g. concerning desensitization "the crucial ingredients and theoretical mechanisms responsible for the efficacy of the procedures are still far from clear, and they remain the topics of much experimental investigation and theoretical debate" (p.159, 19 cited references given)).

  d. Biased judgmentality is not present. Impartial and objective phraseology is utilized (e.g. "... unconventional sexual stimulation, such as that provided during homosexual, paedophiliac, or sado-masochistic activities" (p.78)).

  e. Parts 3 and 4 are particularly useful for the therapist-counselor while Parts 4 and 5 are necessary background-material for researchers interested in this area.

Deficiencies

  a. No visual aids, graphs or charts supplement the text. Only minimal cross-cultural input is provided as background material. More case studies would have been helpful.

  b. In the controversial behavioristic treatments such as desensitization or hypnosis, no long-term longitudinal-study research is documented. If such studies are not yet forthcoming, this fact should have been emphasized.

  c. Occasionally, a statement is left unreferenced (e.g. "The reliability and validity of the (Freund) instrument are satisfactory" (p.220)).

123. Jones, Clinton R. _Homosexuality and Counseling_. Philadelphia: Fortress Press, 1974. 144 pp.

  Brief Summary - The author, a clergyman and counselor, acknowledges in his Preface that "my specific field of counseling is in the area of homosexuality" (p.viii). Chapter 1 termed "A Counseling Position" provides some background on effecting a positive attitude. The following chapter emphasizes that young gays integrate self-worth with positive value-systems. Chapter 3 deals with "Love and Marriage," both from the gay bias and when a dyad undergoes pressure resulting from an awareness of an orientation mixture of homosexual and heterosexual. This is followed by how homosexuality can adversely affect gays at their "Vocation and Work." Chapter 5 explores problems that can lead to "The Law and Prison" as well as the further exploitive dangers if one is incarcerated. A final Chapter 6 deals with some allied topics of sex-role stereotypes, drag queens, transvestites, and transsexuals.

Critique - Strengths

  a. Many footnotes, referenced citations, quotations and anecdotal stories complement the text. Some background research is cited (e.g. Kinsey, p.2) as is cross-cultural (e.g. Ford and Beach, p.9) and historical (Eglinton, p.95) information. Many Biblical

references (e.g. p.12) are provocatively analyzed.
b. Myths are dispelled (e.g. "... most child molesters are not homosexual, but heterosexual... Few child molesters come from the field of the professional teacher or worker with youth..." (p.69-70)).
c. Useful insights are presented (e.g. "Homosexual feelings and responses are a part of one's total sexuality" (p.1). An innovative inclusion is the section "Questions To Be Discussed Before Making a Commitment" (p.62, citation included).
d. The text is non-judgmental in impact (e.g. "Since no definitive reasons have yet been established for the psychosexual development of any human being, it does not seem tenable to adopt the specific, rigid position that a symptomatology can be established for homosexual proclivity" (p.33).

Deficiencies

a. The lack of an index, visual aids, graphs, charts, tables and a generalized bibliography is serious.
b. Assumptive neofreudian concepts are of a most dubious validity and are not backed up by cited research references (e.g. "We spoke earlier about latent homosexuality; actually there are also persons who are latently heterosexual. Often they are the ones whom many therapists have been able to help move from an apparently strong homosexual orientation to an ability to enter into adequate relationships with persons of the opposite sex" (p.48)).
c. Certain sub-topics are not dealt with (e.g. consensual sadomasochistic practices in a gay context; also the expert knowledge required of a counselor for taking a gay client's sex history).

124. Kaplan, Helen Singer. <u>Disorders of Sexual Desire</u>. New York: Simon and Schuster, 1979. 255 pp.

Brief Summary - The author has modified her therapeutic approach to sex therapy by postulating "The Triphasic Concept of Human Sexuality" (p.xix) instead of the original biphasic model. A third component termed "desire" (p.6) has been added to the components of orgasm and excitement. Area I explores this triphasic concept dealing with its physiology as well as dysfunctional etiologies and their required "specific treatment strategies" (p.40). Area II is termed "Desire Phase Disorders of Males and Females" and diagnoses the variable causing these disorders, plus their etiology and treatment. Eclectic methods deal with resistances stemming from fear, anxiety, and anger affecting sex. Area III is called "Strategies of Psychosexual Therapy." It deals with the often "multiple causal levels" (p.145) of desire disorders, causes of couple-antagonism relating to desire disorders ("the fear of romantic success" (p.164) and "the fear of intimacy" (p.183)), and a final chapter which gives guidelines as to when treatment should cease.

Critique - Strengths

a. An abstract precedes each Area of the book. Twenty-two detailed case studies are most useful. An Appendix includes

four tables of immense value. A 6-page Bibliography refers to
"Physiology," "Treatment," and "Other References."

b. The triphasic model as described is innovative. Boundaries
are clearly given (e.g. "Desire phase problems occur when the
anxiety is aroused very early in the sequence of desire-
excitement-orgasm" (p.26)). Useful conclusions are given (e.g.
"Sex therapy is inappropriate for obsessive patients, regardless
of whether or not the content of their obsessive preoccupation
is sexual" (p.77)).

c. Objectivity is effectively maintained.

Deficiencies

a. A textual lack of charts, graphs, photographs and diagrams is
noted. A brief historical and cross-cultural overview might
have accorded a better initial perspective.

b. Kaplan's triphasic model seems based on limited observations,
intuitions and speculations, all of a qualitative nature (e.g.
"The outcome data cited in this book are preliminary and derive
from work that is still ongoing" (p.xvi)). Cited references of
sound previous research are lacking. No statistics are
proffered. Many unsubstantiated statements are given (e.g.
"There is evidence that sexual desire is highly sensitive to
experimental factors which determine and shape, in large
measure, the objects and activities which will and will not
evoke our desires" (p.12)). Kaplan's work must be treated as a
summing of hypothetical postulates (e.g. "The immediate causes
of inhibited sexual desire (ISD) are the most elusive, and have
not yet been clarified precisely" (p.36)).

c. The text at times overemphasizes the assumptive psychoanalytic
model (e.g. "... conflicts about intimacy are derivative of
preoedipal and oedipal problems" (p.185)). Unwarranted
conclusions are provided concerning homosexually-oriented
persons (e.g. "such patients, provided they are highly
motivated, have an excellent prognosis for rapidly acquiring a
heterosexual behavior pattern in response to psychosexual
therapy" (p.66)).

d. Belief-system bias occurs (e.g. "If a person is preoccupied
with sex and masturbates 10 times every day to orgasm, it is
safe to venture that there would be little professional dispute
that the patient's response is excessive" (p.59)).

125. Kaplan, Helen Singer. The New Sex Therapy. New York:
Brunner/Mazel, 1974. 560 pp.

Brief Summary - Area I entitled "Basic Concepts" deals with the
physical variables of sexual response in men and women. This
response, the author concludes, is biphasic in nature, with the two
interrelated phases being excitement and orgasm. Area II reviews
the literature in Section A on the effects of illness, drugs and
aging on sexuality. In Section B, the author explores "the
psychological determinants of the sexual dysfunctions" (p.117). She
espouses "a multicausal philosophy" (p.119), and intuitive treatment
based on symptom-treatment sex therapy coupled where applicable with
psychotherapy, systems therapy and behavioral models of learning.
Area III, "Treatment," and Area IV, "The Sexual Dysfunctions"

delineate the proper therapies for the various male and female
sexual dysfunctions. Area V sums the "Results" of her work as
compared to other researchers. Area VI connotes "Special Clinical
Problems" such as psychiatric disorders, marital discord, and sexual
maladaption. The marital discord chapter is written by Sager.

Critique - Strengths

a. Appropriate illustrations, tables, detailed case studies and
    abstracts preceding each Area are of immense benefit. Three
    graphs of the menstrual cycle (p.56) are seldom-seen textual
    supplements. Occasional footnotes aid the text. Cross
    References and Bibliography material close out each Area.
b. Kaplan's biphasic model (see Summary) is a useful construct.
    Interesting postulates provide a groundwork for future
    researchers (e.g. Concerning premature male ejaculation, Kaplan
    suggests "the absence of voluntary control over the reflex"
    (p.300) is due to patient failure to perceive preorgasmic erotic
    sensations). Distinctions are clearly portrayed (e.g. the
    contrast given between general sexual dysfunction in the female
    where "she is essentially devoid of sexual feelings" (p.361) and
    female orgasmic dysfunction (p.374)).
c. Client-concern and empathy are most evident from a perusal of
    the case studies.

Deficiencies

a. The addition of a brief introductory historical and cross-
    cultural overview would have been helpful.
b. Kaplan's biphasic model is based on some observations mixed
    with hypothetical speculations. Cited research references and
    statistical evidence are not forthcoming. The statement that
    "the concept ... provides a theoretical framework" (p.13) is
    premature.
c. Kaplan is overly influenced at times by assumptive psychoana-
    lytic theory (e.g. "Case 2: Oedipal Conflict Associated with a
    Sexual Dysfunction..." (p.142)).
d. Mistakes occur (e.g. androgen as this "hormone" (p.46. 93);
    also "estrogen" (p.53)). Some case studies purport to
    re-orientate homosexual behavior. This medical-model approach
    assumes an unproved and unwarranted premise (e.g. Case 20
    (p.333), and case 16 (p.284, which uses a dubiously ethical
    desensitization electric shock behavioral treatment)).
e. Occasionally, generalized judgmentality surfaces (e.g. "Some
    'therapists' seem to be exploiting the current interest in
    sexual therapy by initiating poorly conceived and sensational
    quasi-orgy 'therapeutic' procedures" (p.196)).

126. Kentsmith. David K. & Eaton, Merrill T. _Treating Sexual Problems_
in Medical Practice. New York: Arco Publishing Inc., 1979. 182 pp.

Brief Summary - The authors are both psychiatrists. The various
sub-topics are in the following sequence: "Identifying Sexual
Problems" and the taking of a sex history, the definitions of
"Normal Sexuality," "The Sexual Response (cycles) of Men and Women"
including the aging, "Sex in Everyday Life" from birth to old age

plus the issues of birth control, pregnancy, sexually transmitted diseases, normative sexual behavior and extramarital affairs, the "Major Sexual Dysfunction(s)," "Sex (activity) During Sickness," "Sex and the Psychiatric Patient," "Sex, Medication, Surgical Procedures, and Advice" as these factors apply in gynecologic and pediatric practice, "The Homosexual Patient" as well as transsexual and transvestite patients, "Deviant Sexual Behavior," "Sex and Marital Discord" including differentiation between and treatment of primary and secondary sexual problems, "Office Counseling of Patients with Sexual Problems," the whos, wheres and whys in patient "Referral for Sexual Therapy," and the final chapter entitled "Sex Education for Whom?"

Critique - Strengths

a. Colored and black-on-white sketches and anatomical diagrams immensely assist the textual content. Graphs, quotations, and Selected References after each chapter are further aids. Resources information on books, films and organizations is given (p.167). Historical (e.g. p.101) and cross-cultural (e.g. p.153) material is provided to some degree.
b. Myths are dispelled through emphasis (e.g. Twelve listed on p.133).
c. Various methods for the rapid-treatment of sexual dysfunctions are objectively contrasted (e.g. by Masters & Johnson, Hartman & Fithian, Kaplan, and Wolpe (p.153-156)).

Deficiencies

a. Some essential topics are insufficiently covered (e.g. "Sexually-Transmitted Disease" (p.50)). Certain definitions are too limiting (e.g. "A homosexual is someone who habitually and by choice obtains sexual satisfaction in relationship with a person of his or her own gender... This definition excludes persons ... who are concerned because they have erotic impulses toward persons of the same sex..." (p.101)). A few subjects (e.g. group sex) are not dealt with at all.
b. Homosexuality and other so-called deviant-behavior are examined exclusively through the medical-model approach that if a patient voluntarily seeks orientation change, a reasonable chance for treatment success is assured (e.g. "The person who desires to modify or change sexual behavior that is not egosyntonic is nearly always an appropriate candidate for psychotherapy" (p.114). Limited cited references do not offer longitudinal-study research to back up such claims.
c. Referrals to non-medical sexologists are not recommended (e.g. "An appropriate consultant may be a physician who specializes..." (p.151)). Since most physicians are poorly trained in sexological matters, such a recommendation may turn out to be counter-productive to the client.
d. Assumptive and pejorative phraseology occurs (e.g. "Promiscuity may be symptomatic in some cases of compulsive personality" (p.92)).

127. LoPiccolo, Joseph & LoPiccolo, Leslie, ed. Handbook of Sex Therapy. New York: Plenum Press, 1978. 551 pp.

Brief Summary - Part I, "An Overview of Sex Therapy," is a synopsis about current research and trends. Part II, "The Assessment of Sexual Function and Dysfunction," discusses sex-history procedures, the efficacy of certain questionnaire inventories, and advances in psychophysiology. Part III, "Female Orgasmic Dysfunction," has two sections, "Determinants of Female Orgasm" and "Treatment of Female Orgasmic Dysfunction." Part IV deals with "Dyspareunia and Vaginismus." Part V, termed "Male Orgasmic Dysfunction," and Part VI, "Male Erectile Dysfunction," cover this area. Part VII details "Sexual Dysfunction in Special Populations" such as the elderly, the pregnant, the postcoronary males, the spinal cord injured, those with renal failure, the diabetics and the ethnic Afro-Americans. "Group Procedures" make up Part VIII. Non-orgasmic women are especially amenable to this process. Part IX deals with two controversial issues, body work therapy utilizing sex surrogates and the traditional psychoanalytic approach versus behavioral therapy methods. Part X, titled "Professional Issues," describes the difficulty in quickly training dual-sex therapy teams and the contemporary difficulties of sex therapy as a discipline.

Critique - Strengths

a. Each chapter begins with an abstract and ends with a References section. Myriad charts, graphs, histograms and tables illustrate and clarify the reported research. Statistics are often employed and textual quotations abound. Occasional photographs are displayed.
b. Some papers are very well presented, either as descriptive overviews (e.g. "Impotence as a Practical Problem" (Reckless & Geiger)) or as serious statistical studies (e.g. "Sexual Behavior in Pregnancy" (Solberg, Butler & Wagner)). Part I is the book's best section. "Sexual Assessment and History Interview" (L. LoPiccolo & Heiman) furnishes an interesting sex-history questionnaire.

Deficiencies

a. In three instances, idiosyncratic information in the form of a single case study is presented (i.e. Razani, p.287; Newell, p.291; J. LoPiccolo, McMullen & Watkins, p.345). Anthropological-historical research background material is minimal.
b. Serious research methodological shortcomings are in many arti- cles. Conclusions based on no discernible measurements and low numbers of patient-samples are numerous (refer Chapters 22, 23 and 27). Conversely, other studies with excellent statistical analyses are limited by the small numbers of subjects studied (e.g. only six married couples in each group in "Secondary Orgasmic Dysfunction" (McGovern, McMullen & J. LoPiccolo)). "The Sexual Interaction Inventory" (J. LoPiccolo & Steger) has mixed scales and an inadequately structured first scale (i.e. "1. Never... 6. Always" (p.116) might be better phrased as "negligibly ... almost always").
c. Conclusions are often based on undocumented suppositions (e.g. "What Sherfey (1966) says about the inherent insatiability of

the female and her consequent multiorgasmic needs would seem to be applicable only to women who experience nothing but vulval orgasms (J. & I. Singer, p.183)). Chapters 33 and 34 display divergent views about the cause of male diabetic sexual dysfunction. The former study (Ellenberg, p.421) stresses organic neuropathy as the usual primary causal factor while the latter one (Renshaw, p.433) implicates psychogenic causes. A lack of presented definitive research data in both papers precludes knowing which viewpoint, or what ratio between the two, is correct for any given random sample of patients.

d. The senior editor displays subjective judgmentality (e.g. "California ... most psychotherapists consider to be the 'weirdness' capital of the profession" (p.519)).

128. Masters, William H. & Johnson, Virgina E. Human Sexual Inadequacy. Boston: Little, Brown & Co., 1970. 478 pp.

Brief Summary - The first two chapters deal with "Therapy Concepts" and "Therapy Format." The dual-sex therapy team approach is considered essential during the two-week treatment period. A sex history is first taken. By Day 3, a demythologizing educational roundtable discussion is implemented after a thorough medical examination. The so-termed sensate focus process is explained and homework begins to be assigned. Day 4 discusses progress to date. Then from Day 5 onward, the specific sexual dysfunction(s) is treated. Chapters 3 through 11 concern themselves with "Premature Ejaculation," "Ejaculatory Incompetence," "Primary Impotence," "Secondary Impotence," "The Treatment of Impotence," "Orgasmic Dysfunction" (in two Sections), "Vaginismus," "Dyspareunia," and "Treatment of Orgasmic Dysfunction." Chapters 12 and 13 elucidate the sexual problems of the aging (post-50) males and females. The final two chapters deal with program statistics of success-failure ratios and examples of failures.

Critique - Strengths

a. Apt sketches, diagrams, tables and relevant statistics are present. Useful case studies demonstrate treatment modalities. The "history-taking outline" (p.34-51) is given in detail. A 58-page Bibliography terminates the text. Medical-history forms are displayed (p.57-60).
b. Creative phrases are introduced which represent new concepts (e.g. "spectator roles" (p.11); also "sensate focus" (p.67)). Insightful comments occur (e.g. "... the sexual handicap of theological rigidity" (p.175)).
c. This rapid-treatment format which evolved from the authors' research, represents an important ideological breakthrough for sex therapy. Although now somewhat historically dated, it still merits close scrutiny.
d. Empirical observations useful in follow-up research are some-times evident (e.g. For those couples rejecting the use of moisturizing lotions, the "failure rate is more than 400 percent above the expected overall 20 percent failure rate" (p.81)).

Deficiencies

a. The absence of cited research references and footnotes is a serious detraction. A brief historical and cross-cultural overview would have been helpful. No graphs are offered.
b. The authors are often vague in procedural outline, thus making research replication difficult. This is compounded by rigid, arbitrary definitions which seem to betray a preoccupation with penile-vaginal sexuality (e.g. "When an individual male's rate of failure at successful coital connection approaches 25 percent of his opportunities, the clinical diagnosis of secondary impotence must be accepted" (p.157)). Research-design weaknesses are evident (e.g. "This clinical text has myriad shortcomings in concept and content - statistically limited and motivationally biased population, imperfect five-year patient follow-up, unproved alterations of basic concepts of psychotherapy, and inability to describe precisely subtleties so vital to effective treatment return are some examples" (p.v)). Some statistical reporting is confusing and is poorly identified (e.g. The comparison of Table 10 (p.363) with Tables 11A and 11B (p.366)).
c. Concerning homosexual orientation, men were accepted for treatment on the unproven premise that a patient wish for change can lead to a permanent sexual orientation restructuring (e.g. "these six men stated unequivocally their basic interest in and desire for facility of heterosexual functioning" (p.142)). This is a judgmental medical-model approach.
d. Pejorativity can be noted (e.g. Homosexuals are described as "patients handicapped" (p.213)).
e. "Little is known of the male climacteric..." (p.324) represents a subjective assumption of an entity both controversial and unestablished at present.

129. McCarthy, Barry, Ryan, Mary & Johnson, Fred. Sexual Awareness: A Practical Approach. San Francisco: Boyd & Fraser Publishing Co., 1975. 231 pp.

Brief Summary - Four premises are stressed: each person is a sexual being every day from birth until death, sexuality is an integral part of one's personality, sexual self-reponsibility is paramount, and sexuality should enhance one's life. Fourteen chapters progress from "self-exploration and enhancement" (p.33) programs to non-genital and genital pleasuring, increasing sexual response and understanding, oral-genital stimulation and non-demand pleasuring. In Chapter 12, advice for "Sexual Expression for the Aging Couple" is given. Chapter 13 discusses "Increasing Comfort with Sexual Intercourse." The concluding chapter deals with some examples of patients involved in sex therapy.

Critique - Strengths

a. A 3-page "Suggested Readings for Further Information" closes the book. The book emphasizes feelings while playing down the self-help therapy format. Supporting sketches assist the text. The many exercises for individuals and couples are well conceived.

b. Innovative appropriate sections are offered (e.g. "New Myths Replace Old Myths" (p.78)).
c. A sensible approach is offered to some controversial subjects (e.g. about premature ejaculation, "all these definitions are too arbitrary" (p.122); also "there is nothing abnormal or bizarre about anal intercourse" (p.200)).
d. This book can be recommended to lay clients.

Deficiencies

a. A brief historical and cross-cultural review is lacking.
b. Occasionally a mind-set does not represent the contemporary views of many sexologists (e.g. the definition of secondary impotence (p.218)).
c. One statement about male erection does not take into account psychic problems (i.e. "penile intromission is easiest ... in the male superior position" (p.192)).

130. Meyer, Jon K., ed. _Clinical Management of Sexual Disorders_. Baltimore: The Williams & Wilkins Co., 1976. 296 pp.

Brief Summary - Topical input concerns "Sexual Problems in Office Management...," "The Approach to the Patient," "Psychological Assessment of Sexual Disorders," "The Short-Term, Intermittent, Conjoint Patient," "Psychological Assessment of Sexual Disorders," "Behavior Therapy Techniques in the Treatment of Sexual Disorders," "Sexually Graphic Material in the Treatment of Sexual Disorders," "Effects of Drugs (both legal and illegal) on Sexual Arousal and Performance," "Treatment of Sexual Dysfunction in Patients with Physical Disorders" (such as the arthritic, the quadriplegic, "unresponsive organic impotence" (p.216), back disabilities, "Surgical Intervention in the Treatment of Sexual Disorders," "The External Male Genitalia - The Interplay of Surgery and Mechanical Prostheses," and "Psychodynamic Treatment of the Individual with a Sexual Disorder."

Critique - Strengths

a. Case-study photographs, tables, graphs and charts are aptly included. Summary and references are offerd. Occasionally, a tabulation summary is beneficially employed (e.g. (Bjorksten, p.191)). An abstract prefaces each chapter and case studies occur (e.g. O'Connor, p.91). Catchy acronyms are in evidence (e.g. BASIC ID (Lazarus & Rosen, p.158)).
b. Research data are presented (e.g. L. & S. Zussman, p.106). At times a thorough comparison of alternative options is given (e.g. Bjorksten, p.178). Constructive criticism is shown (e.g. "Further effort ... is required to document the therapeutic effectiveness, mechanisms of effect, limitations, parameters of patient selection, and other aspects of the dynamic therapies in relation to other treatment modalities" (Meyer, p.273)).
c. There are useful insights (e.g. "... It is imperative to be flexible, personalistic, and technically eclectic (Lazarus, 1971, 1972)" (Lazarus & Rosen, p.153)).

Deficiencies

a. Anthropological-historical precursors are not analyzed.
b. The editor supports neofreudian concepts (e.g. "Freud pointed out..." (p.266)). Meyer also tends to emphasize the medical-model approach and his definitions of dysfunctions have inbuilt limitations (e.g. p.11).
c. Unsubstantiated judgmentality occurs (e.g. "... "homosexuality may be the early signs of organic brain disease or perverse sexual activity the precursor of a schizophrenic decompensation" (Whitman, p.22); also " 'Swinging' ... operates in the service of denial, and provides narcissistic rewards..." (P. Keyer, p.273)).

131. Moses, A. Elfin & Hawkins, Robert O. Jr. Counseling Lesbian Women and Gay Men: A Life-Issues Approach. St. Louis: The C.V. Mosby Co., 1982. 280 pp.

Brief Summary - Moses and Hawkins collaborate as teaching professionals. Part I furnishes a historical overview, especially from religious, medical-model and scientific evolutionary perspectives. Current attitudes toward and legal rights (by Peters) of gays are also explored. In Part II, "The Gay Experience," information is supplied for nongay professionals on preference facts and hypotheses, what gayness means, and homoerotic dimensions of sexual activity and relationships. Part III investigates third-world and rural gay-identified persons, issues surrounding counselor confidentiality and relevant client-privilege (by Bernard), college-student gay legal rights (Bernard), the aging gay and the social and legal implications of gay parenting. A brief "Summation" (Part IV) warns counselors not to utilize "the heterosexual marriage model of intervention" (p.216).

Critique - Strengths

a. Voluminous references and appropriate quotations are provided. A 22-page Bibliography reinforces this input. The Appendix ("Toward a New Model of Treatment of Homosexuality" (Coleman)) is pertinent. Case histories (e.g. p.39) and anecdotal stories (e.g. p.47) personalize the text. Summaries are given. Good histroal input is provided (see Summary). The Chart for biosociopsychological model of psychosexual development (p.35) is an excellent tool.
b. Alternating views are offered (e.g. Marmor versus Jay and Young about "reasons for high number of contacts" (p.113)). Sensible arguments are presented (e.g. "... Two genetic males in sexual activity. If one of them is a preoperative transsexual ..., an outside observer would view the act as homosexual. However, to the transsexual, the act is heterosexual..." (p.32)). Expressed logic is thought-evoking (e.g. "The very concept of looking for causation ... suggests all too often that one needs to find the cause of homosexuality in order to effect a cure" (p.42)).
c. The authors are non-judgmental (e.g. "When golden showers are discussed ... it is advisable to drink liquids before engaging in the activity" (p.112). Non-pejorative terms are promoted (e.g. "nongay" instead of "straight" (p.xi)). Positive

counseling occurs (e.g. "Many nongays ... have sexual fantasies
about ... the same gender... When the person is content with
her or his sexual preference ... we see no need to infer
'repressed' or 'latent' homosexuality or lesbianism" (p.85)).

d.   There are analyses of existing research (e.g. "This is highly
     statistically significant ..., but is of questionable
     meaningfulness, since both percentages are so low..." (p.44)).

Deficiencies

a.   The lack of photographs, sketches, and graphs is noted.
     Cross-cultural data are basically ignored.
b.   The text is weighted more heavily into lesbian issues than to
     gay-male concerns (e.g. Chapter 9, 30 pages versus 13 pages).
     Gay-male information could have been expanded.

132. Pion, Ron with Hopkins, Jerry. The Last Sex Manual. New York:
Wyden Books, 1977. 250 pp.

Brief Summary - The first two chapters detail the professional
medical training of Pion. Chapter 3 describes "The Top Ten Sexual
Complaints." These are separated into "Problems of Desire,"
"Problems of Arousal," and "Problems of Orgasm." Chapter 4 divides
sociosexual interests into patterns of leftside (logical) and
rightside (artistic) brain behavior. The following five chapters
emphasize the fun of sex, the use of fantasy and tape-recording for
later analysis by a therapist or oneself. The book is
couple-oriented. Chapters 10 through 19 enlarge upon these common
sexual complaints. The final two chapters describe information one
should tape and the proper rationale "of looking at life" (p.237).

Critique - Strengths

a.   A few cited references, graphs and charts assist the text. The
     "Stuckness Scale" (p.40-41) is useful. A host of anecdotal
     stories and case examples is deftly told.
b.   It is a good background book for a therapist to recommend to
     new clients (e.g. "This chapter will assist you in describing
     the problem and then communicating it to someone else" (p.225)).
c.   Some historical material is furnished (e.g. Freud,
     Krafft-Ebing (p.17)). Constructive criticism is offered (e.g.
     "Many therapists - including Masters & Johnson - generally
     recommend what is called the 'squeeze technique'... This seems
     negative, even aversive to me. I prefer positive
     conditioning..." (p.209)).
d.   Myths are attacked (e.g. "Bigger (breasts/penis/etc.) is
     better" (p.80)). Vernacular labelling is denigrated (e.g. "
     'lousy lays' (and) 'quick trigger' " (p.23)). Perceptive
     insights are presented (e.g. "And so David learned to associate
     sexual intercourse - or sex of any sort ... with rapid
     ejaculation" (p.70).
e.   The text is essentially free from judgmentality.

Deficiencies

a.   Statistical data are not included. There is no bibliography or

index. Visual aids are not presented. Historical antecedents
are not mentioned nor are cross-cultural mores examined.
b. Certain conclusions are not backed up by references (e.g. "Only
5 percent of all erection problems are organic" (p.29)).

133. Pomeroy, Wardell B., Flax, Carol C. & Wheeler, Connie Christine.
Taking a Sex History. New York: The Free Press, 1982. 335 pp.

Brief Summary - Chapter 1's Introduction acknowledges that the
book's system is the one devised by Kinsey. The authors "recognize
that the method of eliciting information is more important than the
method of recording it" (p.1). In the following chapter, many
definitions are given of individual sexual normality. Two
subsequent chapters explore "Interviewing Techniques" which work and
the system's "Coding and Recording" sequential methodology. The
remaining twenty-sex chapters deal with "Background Information"
about respondent demographics, "Health" issues, "Recreation"
patterns, "Family Background," "Marriage" data, "Sex Education" of
the respondent, "Puberty," "Preadolescent Sex Play,"
"Self-Masturbation," sexual "Dreams," "Premarital Petting," "First
Coitus," "Premarital Intercourse," "Incidental Prostitution,"
"Premarital Coital Attitudes," "Marital Coitus," "Extramarital
Coitus," "Contraception," "Erotic Arousal," "Anatomy" particulars,
"Group Sex," "Incidental Homosexuality," "Animal Contacts," "Other
Sexual Behaviors," "Homosexual Inventory," and "Prostitution
Inventory."

Critique - Strengths

a. Many figure-drawings illustrate the correct sequential and
notational forms. Dialogue-examples are constantly given. The
first two chapters furnish historical, cross-cultural, and
cross-species information. Occasionally, statistics are cited
in a footnote (e.g. "Incidental Prostitution" (p.155)).
b. The system was designed as a research instrument and although
complex, is ideal for this purpose. Reasons for using the
interview technique in place of questionnaire methodology are
well covered (p.2). A non-research therapist can readily modify
it.
c. Background information is often provided (e.g. Nine reasons why
males seek out prostitutes (p.155-156)). Incisive suggestions
are prevalent (e.g. "... One such distancing technique is to
use a stilted and technical vocabulary" (p.9)).
d. The concept of multi-dimensional normality (refer to Summary)
is an essential tool in establishing a neutral attitude. This
is continually reinforced (e.g. "How often were you having sex
with your dog ten years ago?... (p.249)).

Deficiencies

a. No bibliography is included and cited references are few. This
leads to unsupported statistics (e.g. "We know that masturbation
occurs in ... and 65 to 80 percent of all females" (p.105)).
b. Certain assertions and sections require amplification (e.g.
"Persons who have deliberately tried to exaggerate have reported
that it is almost impossible to accomplish" (p.20); also "for

elaborate group sex experiences, a more extensive questionnaire
needs to be constructed" (p.231)).

134. Qualls, J. Wincze & Barlow, D. ed. The Prevention of Sexual
Disorders. New York: Plenum Press, 1978. 212 pp.

Brief Summary - Chapter 1 presents an overview by Qualls. The next
chapter by LoPiccolo and Heiman details a historical resume. Green
discusses "Intervention and Prevention: The Child with Cross-Sex
Identity." Green proposes that society moves toward "an androgynous
solution" (p.90). Bancroft summarizes "The Prevention of Sexual
Offenses." "The Role of Antiandrogens in the Treatment of Sex
Offenders" is given by Walker. Calderone elucidates on the role of
sex education as a preventative and this is followed by Wilson's
decision that pornography can be a preventative aid to sexual
disorders. Kolodny closes the book by discussing "Ethical Issues in
the Prevention of Sexual Problems" from various cultural
perspectives.

Critique - Strengths

a. Apt quotations, cited references, research studies, statistics
    and a few footnotes assist the text. An "Editors' Introduction"
    for Chapters 2 to 8 is useful. Chapter 2's historical overview
    is well critiqued (e.g. Freud, p.51; Kinsey, p.58). One
    cross-cultural reference is useful (Bancroft, p.104).
b. Proper conclusions (e.g. "An assumption ... is that prevention
    is possible with respect to the atypicalities of sexual
    identity. This assumption has not been proved at this time in
    the history of psychosexual research" (Green, p.79-80)) are
    given. Positive insights are offered (e.g. "... what we do
    about a problem depends to a major extent on how we define
    it..." (Qualls, p.19)).
c. Value-judgments and pejorative statements are absent.

Deficiencies

a. No visual aids, graphs, tables or charts are included. No
    generalized bibliography terminates the book.
b. The continuum concept of sexual disorders is not discussed.
c. The medical-model approach occurs in overly generalized
    analogies (e.g. "Concepts of Prevention" (Qualls)).
d. Questionable research is sometimes cited (e.g. Green's citing
    Gelder & Marks, 1969 (p.80) and Bancroft, 1974 (p.81)).

135. Silverstein, Charles. A Family Matter: A Parents' Guide to
Homosexuality. New York: McGraw-Hill Book Co., 1977. 227 pp.

Brief Summary - The first section concerns "Information for
Parents." The next section furnishes stories of several familes'
problems over having a homosexually oriented child. Part 3
discusses a case-study of a homophobic gay-oriented married father
having to deal with a gay son, the concept linking masculinity and
the male homosexual, the medical-model way of futilely attempting to
change an orientation, utilizing therapy as heterosexuals would, and
a final chapter instructing gays on the process of coming out to

parents.

Critique - Strengths

a. A 5-page "Additional Reading" is included. The many extended
    case studies are instructive. Support organizations are
    identified (e.g. "The Parents of Gays" (p.113)). Historically
    pertinent (e.g. ancient Greece (p.157)) material is included.
    Research references are included and footnoted (e.g. p.184,
    cited reference included).
b. Certain areas of the book are very instructive (e.g. "Some Dos
    and Don'ts for Parents of Gays" (p.130)).
c. The book can be recommended to appropriate lay clients. It
    attacks the medical-model approach (e.g. refer to Summary).

Deficiencies

a. No visual aids, charts, graphs or tables complement the text.
    Definitive research studies and concepts are largely ignored
    (e.g. the Kinsey studies, including the 0-6 Rating Scale). No
    index is included and cross-cultural input is minimal. The book
    is of limited value to the professional therapist or researcher.
    It has somewhat more value to the counselor or educator, but
    cannot be considered definitive here either. For example,
    parent sociosexual-background information-gathering techniques
    are not in evidence.
b. A few statements are judgmental (e.g. "Your parents ... don't
    care if gays are promiscuous, but they care if you are"
    (p.209)).

136. Woodman, Natalie Jane & Lenna, Harry R. Counseling with Gay Men
and Women. San Francisco: Jossey-Bass Inc., Publishers, 1980. 159 pp.

Brief Summary - The topics analyzed are: "Social and Clinical
Responses to Homosexuality," "Basic Concepts, Issues, and Counseling
Procedures," "Resolving Sexual Identity," "Promoting a Positive
Self-Image," "Exploring Dilemmas of Social Acceptance,"
"Understanding the Special Problems of Youth," "Enhancing
Interpersonal Relationships," and "Building Community-Based Support
Systems."

Critique - Strengths

a. A 10-page References and 7-page Annotated Bibliography are of
    assistance. Resource organizations are listed (p.119-122).
    Cited references including research studies (e.g. p.75),
    quotations and case studies (e.g. p.26) complement the text.
    Historical (e.g. p.3) and cross-cultural (e.g. p.6) references
    occur.
b. Societal myths are effectively analyzed (e.g. "... debunking
    the myth of the isolated, lonely, or youth-chasing aged gay
    person" (p.108)). Labels are noted (e.g. "Gays are increasingly
    using the term nongay rather than heterosexual,..." (p.11)).
c. Precise phraseology is employed (e.g. "pseudoscientific theolo-
    gical belief" (p.4)). Definitions are concise and accurate

cited reference given)). Points are itemized and emphasized
(e.g. p.79)). Proper conclusions are proffered (e.g. "There is
no scientific evidence that particular experiences produce
homosexuals, but homosexual experiences do confirm homoerotic
feelings..." (p.72)).
d. The text is non-judgmental (e.g. "... in describing the gay
lifestyle as alternative, no value judgments are implied"
(p.12)).

Deficiencies

a. No visual aids, tables, graphs or charts augment the text.
b. One reference may be counter-productive (e.g. "Masters &
Johnson (1979) have added to the knowledge about sexual
counseling with gays" (p.92)).
c. On one occasion, a pejorative phrase is given (i.e. "promiscuous heterosexual relationships" (p.91)).

Sexual Minorities

137. Abbott, Sidney & Love, Barbara. Sappho was a Right-On Woman.
Briarcliff Manor: Stein and Day, 1972. 251 pp.

Brief Summary - Part I termed "What It Was Like," details the
serious difficulties which have faced all lesbians in our western
culture. Lesbians have "A Stake in the System" and so often try to
stay unobtrusive. To establish rapport with other lesbians, they
tend to seek "Sanctuary" in lesbian bars. Role-playing is inevitable and tends to a feeling of "The Necessity for the Bizarre."
Part II is entitled "Living the Future." Topics discussed are the
lesbian organizational struggle, "Lesbianism and Feminism," the
issues of gay liberation, suggestions for "Curing Society" of its
homophobic bias, and the necessary process of proclaiming "I'm a
Lesbian and I'm Beautiful." The authors decide "it just may be that
the Lesbian ... is a catalyst to a new culture" (p.238).

Critique - Strengths

a. Many referenced and anecdotal quotations support the text.
   Footnotes, a 2-page Bibliography and a Suggested Reading section
   are further assets.
b. Part II is the better one in its historical analysis of the
   emerging feminist and lesbian political movements and in its
   futuristic postulations (e.g. refer to Summary).
c. Myths are expertly dissected (e.g. the role-reversal statement
   " 'Can heterosexuality be treated?' " (p.163)).
d. Incisive phraseology occurs (e.g. "Passing for straight can be
   thought of as a sort of sane schizophrenia" (p.64-65)).

Deficiencies

a. No visual aids, graphs, demographic statistics or other data
   are presented. The book is limited to being a descriptive
   overview. Both cross-cultural background material and
   historical information prior to the recent-past are lacking.
b. At times the authors are vague (e.g. "Freud's classical

'defense mechanisms' seem to provide the only explanation for
the perplexing and agonizing reality that a Lesbian can deny who
she is..." (p.31) and assumptively general (e.g. "The bar scene
puts a sordid tinge on relationships..." (p.76)).
 c. Limited pejorativity is in evidence (e.g. "an increasing number
of women in the movement ... whether as promiscuity..."
(p.155)).

138. Altman, Dennis. <u>Homosexual Oppression and Liberation</u>. New York:
Avon Books, 1973. 256 pp.

<u>Brief Summary</u> - In Chapter 1's "Coming Out: The Search for
Identity," Altman maintains "the very concept of homosexuality is a
social one" (p.14). In Chapter 2, Altman laments that "self-hatred
reveals itself ... through the hostility that many homosexuals have
for any kind of homosexual movement ... (and) in the way in which
homosexuals 'objectify' each other" (p.63). The balance of the book
in analyzing, quoting and paraphrasing various theoreticians (e.g.
Freud, Marcuse), gay-supportive writers (e.g. Baldwin, Vidal) and
gay movements (e.g. Mattachine, Daughters of Bilitis) builds a
theoretical framework for Altman in which he concludes society must
change from antagonism past mere tolerance to open acceptance of the
gay world. Altman's utopean theory constitutues everyone's having
"to recognize our bisexual potential" (p.229).

<u>Critique - Strengths</u>

 a. Apt quotations, cited references and footnotes plus a 12-page
Bibliography reinforce the text.
 b. Provocative insights occur (e.g. "Women's liberation is primarily concerned with sex roles, gay liberation with sexuality"
(p.216)). Dynamic phraseology gives continual impact (e.g. "We
all need to come out of our particular closets" (p.12)).
 c. Straight-gay interrelations are societally complex and Altman
is aware of these subtleties (e.g. "The language of the gay
liberation press ensures that it is likely to be more acceptable
to the straight underground than to the square gayworld"
(p.188)).

<u>Deficiencies</u>

 a. No visual aids, tables or charts are present. Cross-cultural
data are minimal and the historical information is much too
selective. At times controversial statements are unreferenced
(e.g. "Recent research does suggest there may be some
correlation between homosexual behavior and chemical balance in
certain hormones" (p.17)).
 b. Altman's final solution of universal innate bisexuality (refer
to Summary) is not only much too simplistic a cure for societal
intolerance, it is also based on a generalized philosophical
abstract concept devoid of experimental proof. On the contrary,
many Kinsey 0's and 6's do seem to exist and no research study
indicates a shifting to 1-5's.
 c. The author tends to accept Freud's hypotheses as facts (e.g.
"Inevitably any such theory will rely heavily on Freud" (p.70)).
 d. Unwarranted judgmentality is sometimes evident (e.g. "The

transvestite ... and even more the transsexual ... (are) so
conditioned ... that the only way they can accept their own
homosexuality is by denying their bodies" (p.146); also
"compulsively promiscuous homosexuals" (p.64)).

139. Amary, Issam B. Social Awareness, Hygiene, and Sex Education for
the Mentally Retarded - Developmentally Disabled. Springfield: Charles
C. Thomas, Pub., 1980.   206 pp.

Brief Summary - In his Introduction, Amary advises that "sex
education for the MRDD must be viewed by all concerned as a reality
and not simply a formality" (p.viii).   The author expands upon
"Human Development" and its evolution to adulthood, some "Principles
of Good Grooming," "Principles of Health and Hygiene," aspects of
"Social Awareness" as this concerns manners, language, the use of
privacy, and the skills required in handling social interrelationships, suggestions for "Sexual Behavior and Awareness," various
important concepts of "The Family" including marriage
responsibilities, parenthood planning, issues of "Conception" and
"Childbirth," and the topic of "Venereal Disease."

Critique - Strengths

a. Many apt sketches complement the text. Many true-false questions (and their answers) are added. An Appendix termed
   "Student Questions" lists and answers 105 questions most likely
   to be asked by MRDD persons.
b. The text is simplistically, yet appropriately written. With
   some informational adjustment, it is suitable for sex-educating
   MRDD people if utilized by a competent sexological professional
   who is trained in basic teaching methods.
c. Advice is straightforward (e.g. "Finding out about sex is not
   like looking for a secret treasure. All you have to do is to
   politely and privately ask the right people" (p.98)).

Deficiencies

a. No historical or cross-cultural background material is presented. No bibliography, film or quotational references augment
   the text as aids to professionals. Birth control information
   (p.110-115) should have been expanded to include more specific
   instructional use of the various devices. Chapter 7 on
   "Venereal Disease" leaves out important infections (e.g. herpes
   simplex, trichomoniasis).
b. Unwarranted assumptions not based on documented facts may
   foster guilt feelings in the MRDD individuals (e.g. "If a person
   becomes preoccupied with masturbation and performs it on himself
   constantly, he may be risking a variety of health problems..."
   (p.108)). Value-judgments produce generalized suggestions not
   necessarily valid (e.g. "Sexual interaction is not appropriate
   and should be saved until such a time that each of you find the
   right person to marry" (p.100)). Negative terminology connoting
   sex as dirty or sinful is in evidence (e.g. "good clean fun"
   (p.104); also "a few moments of false fun" (p.105)).

140. Atwater, Lynn. <u>The Extramarital Connection: Sex, Intimacy, and Identity</u>. New York: Irvington Publishers Inc., 1982. 263 pp.

<u>Brief Summary</u> - The author, a sociologist, maintains in her Preface that "I intensively interviewed a group of fifty change-oriented women" (p.ix). The first chapter provides background referenced material. The following chapter comments upon the stages of preinvolvement, the final commitment to getting involved, the extramarital sexuality itself, and the postinvolved rationales and justifications. Chapter 3 focuses on "Extramarital Intimacy." The subsequent chapter discourses about the small sub-sample who developed an "Open Marriage." Chapter 5 details the new sexual learning techniques the women developed, and the types of partners they sought. Certain problems such as pregnancy or venereal disease are exemplified. The next chapter discusses "After-Involvement: Identities and Attitudes." Chapter 7 describes the subset of nine women who had "Extramarital Relationships with Women." The final chapter sums conclusions and futuristic postulations.

<u>Critique - Strengths</u>

a. Many expert and anecdotal quotations reinforce the text. Footnoted references plus a 13+page general Bibliography are aids. An Author's Note offers a proper disclaimer of subjective bias. Two Appendices describe the research methodology, sampling techniques, and the interview-questions.
b. Research shortcomings in methodology are stated (e.g. "I did not ... statistically analyze the results" (p.ix); also "I decided it was vital that the women interviewed be feminist-oriented" (p.26)).
c. Some myths are challenged (e.g. p.18) and insights provided (e.g. the extramarital continuum-behavior-scale (p.197)).
d. The final chapter projects some futuristic possibilities (refer to Summary above). Other-expert bias is mentioned (e.g. "even professionals may be negatively biased toward extramarital activity as Masters & Johnson revealed themselves to be..." (p.202-203)).

<u>Deficiencies</u>

a. No visual aids or graphs and few tables assist the text. Except for brief mentions (e.g. p.16), insufficient historical and cross-cultural background material is presented.
b. The study is small, descriptive, and full of methodological problems and biases (e.g. refer to Summary and Strengths (b.) above). It is useful only as idiosyncratic research.
c. Dubious definitions, some with pejorative overtones, occur (e.g. "An open or flexible monogamy" (p.83); also "emotional promiscuity" (p.65)).

141. Bartell, Gilbert D. <u>Group Sex</u>. New York: Peter H. Wyden, Inc., 1971. 224 pp.

<u>Brief Summary</u> - The author, an anthropologist, investigates the so-called swinging phenomenon which is practiced by a small segment of North American bonded couples as well as by some singles. Modes

and mores of swinging, both private and institutionalized, are discussed. The latter type is seen as having "benefited enormously from wide-scale publicity" (p.41). Chapter 12 is devoted to actual case histories of selected couples and singles. The following chapter details some reasons and case studies of drop-outs from the lifestyle. The final chapter is termed "Positive and Negative Aspects of Swinging: An Evaluation."

Critique - Strengths

a. The case studies add a positive dimension. Other-expert references are often made. A 1-page "References Cited" closes the text.
b. As the book progresses, both philosophical sides of the picture are presented.

Deficiencies

a. No visual aids, graphs or charts assist the text. Cross-cultural information is ignored. Historical background material is minimal. The author relies too much on hearsay from selected respondents. Not enough actual observation was done (e.g. "while old-time swingers assured us that this account is substantially correct, it is also out of date for the young swingers" (p.139)). The lack of data, both observational and statistical, seriously limits the book's usefulness.
b. Subjective moralizing is shown (e.g. "we feel that the individuals we interviewed are not really benefiting from swinging because the ideals that led them into it are not realized... Their activities with other couples reflect mechanical interaction rather than an intimacy of relationships" (p.219)). No documented evidence is given to justify these assumptions.

142. Bell, Alan P. & Weinberg, Martin S. Homosexualities: A Study of Diversity Among Men & Women. New York: Simon and Schuster, Inc., 1978. 505 pp.

Brief Summary - The authors researched this lengthy study of gays in the San Francisco area. Part 1's "Introduction" sets out the "Rationale and Methods of Investigation." The book's title is defined as "the numerous ways in which one can be homosexual" (p.23), the continuum represented in each of these ways, and how such "homosexual subgroups are delineated" (p.24). The actual research findings comprise the next three Parts. Part II analyzes where respondents are on the Kinsey 0-6 Scale. Other topics reported are "Overtness," "Level of Sexual Activity," "Cruising," "Sexual Partnerships," "Sex Appeal," "Sexual Techniques," "Level of Sexual Interest," "Sexual Problems," "Acceptance of Homosexuality" and "A Typology of Sexual Experience." Five stratified sub-groups emerge. These are individuals who are "Close-Coupled," "Open-Coupled," "Functional," "Dysfunctional," and "Asexual." "Social Adjustment" (Part III) deals with the variables of "Work," "Religiousness," "Politics," "Marriage," "Friendships," "Social Activities," and "Social Difficulties." Part IV concerns itself with "Psychological Adjustment" in terms of physical and mental health. "Suicidal Feelings and Impulses" are also included. Part V details "A Concluding Overview." An Epilogue suggests legislators, and others rid themselves of stereotypes. An Appendix A describes some "Ethnography of the Bay Area Homosexual Scene."

Critique - Strengths

a. Appendix B termed "Elaboration of Typology Procedures" and Appendix C outling 208 pages of statistical Tables are essential tools and aids. These statistics are well conceived and furnish both behavioristic and demographic comparisons using probability figures for gay white and black males and females, their five subgroups (refer to Summary) and a heterosexual control sample. Sampling techniques are adequate and shortcomings admitted (e.g. "We cannot stress too much that ours is not a representative sample" (p.22)). A pilot-study helped establish interview-question validity and reliability tests (p.45). The 0-6 Scale is correctly used as to respondent feelings plus behaviors. Anecdotal quotations, footnotes and an 8-page Bibliography fortify the text. An Overview summarizes each section.
b. Other research is cited and compared (e.g. "While the present data do not confirm Churchill's impression that most homosexual men are not likely to engage in cruising..." (p.79)).
c. The book's thematic title and its explanation (refer to Summary) represent an innovative philosophical concept. Value-judgments and assumptive unwarranted conclusions are not in evidence.

Deficiencies

a. No photographs, diagrams or graphs are included. Except for a hint under "Religiousness," no historical background material of significance is provided. Cross-cultural information is missing.
b. Many interesting facts emerge (e.g. "About two-thirds of the males in each race had at some time contracted a venereal disease" (p.118)) but these are never intended to be extrapolated to American society in general. San Francisco is tolerant of gays, and possibly its gay sample is unique as regards to its behavior patterns and its reactions to social pressures. Thus the sample must be deemed as idiosyncratic until the emergence of other broader-based studies.

143. Benjamin, Harry. The Transsexual Phenomenon. New York: Warner Books, Inc., 1977. 331 pp.

Brief Summary - Benjamin, a physician, admits transsexualism is "a subject that is not yet covered in the medical literature" (p.7). In the first chapter the author points out the complexities of sex-labelling. The following chapter differentiates between transvestism, transsexualism and homosexuality. For many indivi-duals, there is a shading of these traits along a linear continuum. Chapter 3 details the transvestite phenomenon, almost always a male proclivity. The next six chapters elucidate the world of the male transsexual; the etiology (basically unknown), the non-surgical treatment, the surgical conversion procedures, and the legal aspects. European theorists favour a biological causation while

American experts lean to psychological and/or psychoanalytic
interpretations. In Chapter 10, the author describes the female
transsexual, in most ways the mirror image in problems and dilemmas
of the male transsexual.

Critique - Strengths

a. Excellent photographs are included. Cited references, quota-
    tions from transsexuals, limited statistics (e.g. demographic
    (p.148-150)), charts and tables augment the text. Four
    Appendixes (three by others) accord insights into the
    philosophical mind-sets of transsexuals. An 8-page Bibliography
    concludes the book. Some historical (e.g. p.24-25) and
    cross-cultural background material (e.g. Appendix C (Green,
    p.206-221) is usefully provided.
b. Benjamin's hypothetical construct of the Sex Orientation Scale
    is innovative, although not as definitive as the Kinsey 0-6
    Scale (refer to Table 1). Clear conceptualization devoid of
    irrationality is in evidence (e.g. "no genetic cause has yet
    been proved for any transsexual manifestation... The absence of
    findings does not negate their possible existence" (p.95)).
c. The author evinces a great sympathy for preoperative trans-
    sexuals and successfully imparts the urgency of their problems
    (e.g. his device to the reader to "Please Read ... Paragraph(s)
    Again" (p.91, 176)).

Deficiencies

a. Some statements require more explanation (e.g. "Some indivi-
    duals do 'get stuck' in their infantile sexuality" (p.17)).
    Definitive research information is minimal.
b. The author shows at times a biased medical-model approach to
    sexual issues (e.g. "homosexuality is a sex problem" (p.42)).
    Occasional judgmentality surfaces (e.g. "promiscuity ... appears
    tempting" (p.141)).
c. "Androgen" and "estrogen" are termed "hormone" (p.19, 116
    respectively) instead of as each being a class of hormones.

144. Bryant, Clifton D. ed. Sexual Deviancy in Social Context. New
York: New Viewpoints (Franklin Watts, Inc.), 1977. 302 pp.

Brief Summary - Bryant, a sociology professor, in Part I states
"sexual behavior labeled as deviant ... is relative in its violation
of social norm and proscription and in the reception and reaction it
engenders from the public" (p.2). All subsequent Parts describe
sexual deviancy in a particular context, one chapter with "Private
Patterns" and the other chapter with "Commercial Configurations."
Topics discussed are: "Spurious Context" (the American sexual
stigmatization of the bidet and sex-house consumer fraud),
"Vicarious Context" (construction worker voyeurism and the pornographic arcade), "Verbal Context" (institutionalized male children
and raunchy entertainment), "Symbolic Context" (male exhibitionism
and the stripper), "Imitative Context" (male masturbators via
telephone contacts and non-technically-trained masseuses),
"Counterfeit Context" (male-to-female transsexuals and young male
hustlers), "Superficial Context" (depersonalized sex in the singles

complex and female escorts), "Symbiotic Context" (swinging couples and the mutually accepting relationship of the prostitute to the vice officer), "Disparate Context" (the geriatric sex offender and the child prostitute), and "Violent Context" (rape and prison sexual assault).

Critique - Strengths

a. Most authors include citations using footnotes and general References. Parts II-XI separate private from commercial activities (refer to Summary) in a useful way. Tables, charts, sketches and probability statistics (e.g. p.154) appear. Anecdotal and expert quotations help to validate the text. The editor submits a short preamble before each of the last ten Parts. Some pertinent cross-cultural (e.g. McWhorter, p.102) and historical (e.g. Shoemaker, p.242) information is provided.
b. Seldom-discussed sexual topics are often explored (e.g. refer to Summary). Novel conceptualizations are presented (e.g. "Nudity is considered ... to suggest that the genitals are more symbolically accessible" (Bryant, p.5)).
c. Research-study conclusions are often effectively abstracted (e.g. "Statistically, the data lend significant support to the first hypothesis (Table 1) but not to the second (Table 2)" (Kando, p.153)). Future research is suggested (e.g. "it may be useful to make contrasts between the nonpathological voyeur, as discussed here, and the pathological case..." (Feigelman, p.42)). Research disclaimers are included by some authors (e.g. "A word of caution is appropriate concerning the generalized statements made in this paper" (Boles and Garbin, p.121)).

Deficiencies

a. Not enough sketches and charts are included. Some chapters are not referenced and reflect slanted, judgmental approaches (e.g. "Sex as Athletics in the Singles Complex" (Proulx)).
b. Unreferenced assumptive statements are in evidence (e.g. "Homosexuality would appear to be more prevalent ... among strippers and prostitutes" (Bryant, p.6)). Mitchell (p.68-69) labels two boys as having transvestitic dispositions instead of having components more common to transsexuals.
c. The book contains judgmental phraseology of a patronizing, moralizing and pejorative nature (e.g. "dirty language" (Palmer, p.83); also "These psychiatrists and others like them say that swingers are bored, jaded, sick people who need either psychotherapy or marriage counseling" (Harris, p.207)).

145. Bullard, David & Knight, Susan. ed. Sexuality & Physical Disability: Personal Perspectives. St. Louis: The C.V. Mosby Co., 1981, 333 pp.

Brief Summary - The editors have fashioned a 2-part book ("Personal Perspectives," "Professional Issues"). This is dealt with in Part I by utilizing the topics of spinal chord injury, cerebral palsy, genetic disability, visual impairment, ostomy, radical hysterectomy and vaginectomy. men with organic problems requiring a penile prosthesis, disabled parents or children, and females with atypical body images. Most contributors are professionals in the field and who have a personal disability or live with someone who has a disability. Part II commences with an overview of disability and sexuality progress. Various experts then discuss sexuality as it pertains to spinal chord injury, hearing impairment, and various surgical and medical conditions (such as mastectomy, an abdominal stoma, or a head injury). The final two Units deal with sex therapy and counseling in cases of end-stage renal disease or organogenic erectile dysfunction, plus issues in family planning as they revolve around persons with physical disability.

Critique - Strengths

a. Two excellent appendixes detail a "Resource List of Agencies involved in Sexuality and Disability," and a "Selective Bibliography on Sexuality and Disability." After each chapter, a specific further References section is offered and often a Summary as well. Appropriate tables, charts, sketches and photographs are also in evidence. Some contributors make good use of case studies. Historical and cross-cultural input is given (e.g. Chapters 17, 18 (Calderone, Chigier)).
b. Part I imparts a sensitive subjectivity which is of great bene-fit in educating the reader. The brief note after each chapter about the author(s) also keeps the chapter in a proper focus.
c. Occasionally a chapter containing expert knowledge covers specific frontiers of research (e.g. "Neurophysiology of Sexual Response in Spinal Chord Injury" (Geiger)).
d. Negligible judgmentality or pejorativity occurs.

Deficiencies

a. More photographs would have been useful. Not enough technical advances detailing research in this area are documented. Nevertheless, because such research is limited, the book serves a valuable purpose until such information is forthcoming.
b. Chapters 12 and 13 seem mostly irrelevant to the main topical focus of the book.

146. Craft, Michael & Ann. Sex and the Mentally Handicapped. London: Routledge & Kegan Paul, 1978. 122 pp.

Brief Summary - This British physician-social worker team has summarized its expertise and research in this field. In the first chapter, the literature is reviewed after which resource services are examined as to viability and usefulness. Childhood and adoles-cent behavior-structures of the handicapped are next discussed. Chapters 5 and 6 entail the concepts of love and marriage for the handicapped. Potential and real legal problems follow while the final chapter delves into the "setting up a health and sex-education programme" (p.71) for the handicapped.

Critique - Strengths

a. Textual aids include tables, footnotes and case studies (e.g. Sally (p.27)). The two appendixes termed "A Guide to Resources" and "Courses and Workshops" are useful. Limited historical background is offered (e.g. p.16-18).

b. Some research information and data are presented (e.g. the authors' study of twenty-five partnerships (p.50-54); also the Mattinson (1976) study of thirty-two "mentally handicapped married couples ... who had in their single days all been labelled subnormal" (p.56)).

Deficiencies

a. Reference material is not described in depth or exhaustively collated. Most references are of a cursory nature or are merely acknowledged in the Appendixes. Visual aids are not included. Cross-cultural input is lacking.

b. The authors display judgmental conditioning from others who have preceded them as so-called experts (e.g. "Aversive-conditioning techniques may be used when subjects have developed bizarre or perverted sexual behaviours" (p.24)). Pejorative language surfaces (e.g. "How does society cope with a promiscuous youngster...? (p.27); also in Table 6.1, the symbols "PD/md" are defined as "Personality Disordered/moral defective" (p.52)).

147. Ettorre, E.M. Lesbians, Women & Society. London: Routledge & Kegan Paul, 1980. 217 pp.

Brief Summary - The author is a sociologist and self-identified lesbian-feminist. The opening chapter gives an overview on the relationships between sexuality and both culture and power, homosexuality as opposed to the "dominant sexual ideology" (p.19), and the societal differentiation between the traditionalist "sick, but not sorry" (p.26) lesbians and the emerging group-awareness "sorry, but we're not sick" (p.26) social lesbians. The subsequent chapter discusses "The Social Reality of Lesbianism." In Chapter 3, a discourse on lesbianism's historical background is followed by an analysis of lesbian self-identities as seen from the traditionalist, social, and more recently, the ideological viewpoints. The author qualifies her reported research study by stating it concerns only the first two categories. The next chapter relates the emergence of the various components of lesbian consciousness. In Chapter 6, Ettorre analyzes "The Emergence of Political Consciousness: Lesbian Feminism as an Ideological Form." An Afterword becomes a philosophical exposition of "the dialectics of power: sex vs class or nature vs labour?" (p.161).

Critique - Strengths

a. A 4-page Bibliography, a 6-page Glossary of Terms and six Appendices detailing the research methodology and some demographics are essential inclusions. Cited references, footnotes, respondent quotations, tables and simple statistics also are of great assistance. Some historical background is included (e.g. refer to Summary).

b. Information is logically presented (e.g. "Figure 1. The stages of lesbianism" (p.160)). Philosophical insights challenge the reader (e.g. "Gay men are 'social females'. They tend to look to men for sexual and social support... Lesbians are 'social

males' " (p.20)). The Afterword is thought-evoking (e.g. refer
to Summary). Future research possibilities are implied (e.g. "a
major drawback of my thesis is the lack of any definite analysis
of lesbianism and its relationship to social class" (p.2)).

c. Non-judgmentality and demythologization are textual traits
(e.g. "I decided that I would eliminate most of the works which
perpetuated the idea that lesbianism was an abnormality, a
psychological sickness, a disease, etc." (p.206)). Subjectivity
is acknowledged but never detracts from the book's objectivity
(e.g. "... being a woman and a lesbian, which I am" (p.13)).
Some philosophical positions are constructively criticized (e.g.
"Analysts use terms like a 'arrested heterosexuality' ... all of
which either caused the 'disease' and 'problem' or at least
helped 'it' along" (p.72)).

Deficiencies

a. No visual aids or graphs assist textual comprehension. The
lack of cross-cultural material is another omission.
b. The occasional generalized assumption is unreferenced and
unproven (e.g. "Bisexuals, lacking consciousness, become static
in their quest for personal sexual liberation" (p.134)).
c. Research methodology drawbacks are admitted but still very real
(e.g. "this study is ... limited in geographical scope... I was
unable to reach those lesbians who were totally closeted or
isolated" (p.1). Some questions are ambiguous (e.g. "27...
Have you ever been attracted to a man?" (p.182)). Sampling is
biased in that only 201 questionnaires were received out of two
groups totalling 700 (refer to p.183).

148. Feinbloom, Deborah H. _Transvestites & Transsexuals_. New York:
Dell Publishing Co., Inc., 1977. 303 pp.

Brief Summary - In her overview on transvestites, the author defines
such individuals (all males) as "men who dress in women's clothing
for relief of 'gender discomfort' " (p.3). Chapter 2 defines and
describes the fundamental and distinct differences between
homosexuality, transvestism and transsexualism. The next three
chapters explore the heterosexual transvestite. The balance of the
book details "The World of the Transsexual." The concepts of Money
and Ehrhardt ("Man & Woman/Boy & Girl," 1972) are freely
incorporated. The brief conclusion emphasizes the contrast in the
thinking of the transsexual as compared to the transvestite. "The
definition of a 'woman' or a 'man', transsexual style, is far less
stereotyped than in the transvestite world" (p.247).

Critique - Strengths

a. One appendix analyzes "Ethical Implications of Fieldwork" and
stems from her transvestite investigations. The other offers
critical comments by transvestites who reviewed this book before
its publication. A specific and a general bibliography in two
sections close out the text. Anecdotal and experiential
quotations are included.
b. As a sociologist, the author is willing to admit her shortcomings and to acknowledge her inherent biases. Her ethics are

above reproach. Positive criticisms and interpretive
disagreements are faithfully reproduced (refer to Appendix 2).
c. Interesting insights occasionally surface (e.g. the descriptive
word "femmephile" (p.118)).

Deficiencies

a. A lack of visual material weakens the book. Historical and
cross-cultural information is minimal.
b. The research is only qualitative in scope. Many assumptions
are unproven and uninvestigated (e.g. Eroticism is vigorously
denied as a goal in that cross-dressing " 'activity is an end in
itself...' (Prince)" (p.63)). A lack of research utilizing
statistics, numbers or scales is noted. The transvestite
section is limited to one small male heterosexual sub-group
(Argus). The allied component of fetishism is only partially
dealt with (i.e. "were a member to wear bra and panties only, he
would be excluded from the meeting" (p.118)). Questions about
sexual fantasies while cross-dressing are ignored.
c. Pejorative bias occurs (e.g. "His dressing is directed toward
gender comfort, not perverted ends" (p.119)).
d. Feinbloom speaks of the Kinsey 1-6 Scale (p.11, 13). Actually
the scale is 0-6.

149. Gilmartin, Brian G. The Gilmartin Report. Secaucus: The Citadel
Press, 1978. 492 pp.

Brief Summary - One hundred California middle-class suburban married
couples who practice a co-marital (swinging) lifestyle are matched
up to one hundred control married couples on the basis of demographic, social and economic characteristics. In addition to
descriptive comparisons, key statistically significant findings are
as follows. The childhood of swingers tends to be less happy than
that of normatives. Swingers make childhood peer friends more
easily. Swingers' parents' marriages were less happy. Swingers are
currently less involved with parents and kin. More swingers rate
their marriages as very happy. Swingers have better health.
Swingers have a higher rate of weekly intercourse with their mates.
Swingers more easily say "I love you" to their mates. Swingers
enjoy sexual intercourse more. Swingers are more satisfied with
partner-time and interest extended by their mates. Swingers display
more non-sexual affection to their mates. Swingers (especially the
female ones) achieve a higher emotional satisfaction from sex play.

Critique - Strengths

a. A comprehensive literature survey entailing contemporary,
historical and cross-cultural perspectives is presented. A
7-page Bibliography terminates the text. Seven Tables
succinctly summarize the major research results.
b. The research is the first serious attempt at quantifying
differences and similarities between swingers and non-swingers
as married couples. As such, not only their childhood formative
backgrounds, but also their current attitudinal and
behavioristic components are examined.
c. The author is a social scientist and non-swinger who effects

an objective viewpoint originally free from preconceived
subjective bias.

Deficiencies

a. No photographs, sketches or graphs accompany the text.
b. The interview-questionnaire technique is employed. However the
   questionnaire segment requires 60-90 minutes to complete. This
   is too long a time period to be certain of retaining a
   respondent's interest in providing answer-veracity. The
   co-marital sample is derived solely from atypical sections of
   suburban Los Angeles and San Francisco. These people may or may
   not be representative of North America as a whole. Close to 80%
   of the co-marital population was obtained by referrals from
   swing club owners. Since these referred couples would tend to
   be the most highly committed co-marital couples that the club
   owners could recommend, they would necessarily reflect to the
   owners' credit in any ensuing publicity fall-out. Gilmartin
   admits as well that he used only such couples since he felt they
   alone would truly reflect the lifestyle. These concerns along
   with the usual problems of a volunteer sample throw in unknown
   biases. Such atypical liberality in sample choice induces a
   sense of caution to one's acceptance of the Gilmartin findings.

150. Gochros, Harvey L. & Gochros, Jean S. ed. *The Sexually Oppressed*.
Chicago: Association Press, 1977. 319 pp.

Brief Summary - The "Introduction: Who are the Sexually Oppressed?"
states they are almost all who are not "the sexual elite" (p.xx).
Part I termed "Social and Historical Perspectives" addresses the
"Historical Roots of Sexual Oppression" (Haeberle) and "Society and
Sexual Deviance" (Kirk). In Part II, "The Young and the Old,"
sociosexual difficulties of "Adolescents" (Lister) and "The Aged"
(Wasow and Loeb) are explored. "Women," the title of Part III,
delves into the problems of "Women - Minority in Transition" (Jean
Gochros), "Black Widows" (Gossett), "Asexual and Autoerotic Women -
Two Invisible Groups" (Johnson), and child plus female "Sexual
Victims" (Schultz). Part IV's "The Homosexually Oriented" discusses
"The Gay Male" (Huggins and Forrester), "the Lesbian Woman - Two
Points of View" (Goodman & Rita Mae Brown), and "The Aging Male
Homosexual" (Kelly). Part V speaks to "Racial and Economic
Minorities" as epitomized by "Blacks" (Johnson), "Asian Americans"
(Ogawa) and "The Poor" (Chilman). Next follows Part VI, "The
Institutionalized," in commenting upon "The Institutionalized
Mentally Disabled" (Ginsberg) and "Prisoners" (Rothenberg). The
final Part VII called "The Handicapped, Ill and Dying" relates to
"The Mentally Retarded Person" (Kempton), "The Physically
Handicapped" (Romano), "The Deaf" (Smith) and "The Terminally Ill"
(Jaffe).

Critique - Strengths

a. References and Recommended Readings follow each chapter. Most
   authors use citations and footnotes. Anecdotal and expert
   quotations are often utilized (e.g. Gossett, p.90). The editors
   offer a preamble to each Part. Historical (e.g. Haeberle) and

cross-cultural (e.g. Johnson, Ogawa) input adds needed
perspectives.
b. Well-developed arguments sometimes are offered (e.g. Haeberle's
sin-crime-sickness evolutionary path of atypical sexual behavior
(p.6-26)). Seldom-discussed topics are included (e.g. "The
Asexual Woman as Ascetic ... (and) The Asexual Woman as
Neurotic" (Johnson, p.98)). Some contributions offer
recommendations for societal implementation (e.g. concerning
sexual victims, Points 5-10 (Schultz, p.116-117)).
c. Cultural biases and judgments are often attacked (e.g. "this
definition ... seems to imply that masturbation is
psychologically abnormal" (Johnson, p.100)). Myths are
dissected (e.g. "Stereotyping, in fact, is not uncommon in
supposedly scientific literature. Allen (1961) writes in The
Third Sex: 'The aging homosexual tends to become distinctly odd'
" (Kelly, p.161)).

Deficiencies

a. No photography or sketches complement the text. Only one table
(Johnson, p.180), no charts or graphs and only minimal
elementary statistics are to be found. Researched topics are
descriptive, with no research backed up by appropriate and
innovative methodology.
b. Very controversial subcultures which are sociosexually
oppressed are ignored. There is nothing except a minimal
acknowledgement by Kirk (p.32-33) on sexual minorities involved
in consensual incest, consensual sadomasochism, group sex,
consensual pedophilic activity, non-exploitive fetishism, and so
on. While gay-male and lesbian minorities are discussed, the
doubly-oppressed (by gay and nongay persons alike) bisexual
subculture is not covered.
c. So many subjects are included that many sub-topics are inadequately covered. The text is useful mainly as a back-up
reference.

151. Green, Richard & Money, John. ed. Transsexualism and Sex
Reassignment. Baltimore: The Johns Hopkins Press, 1969. 528 pp.

Brief Summary - Part I is entitled "Social and Clinical Aspects of
Transsexualism." Green reviews the subject's mythological,
historical and cross-cultural background. Boundaries are next
explored. "Certainly we are dealing with a spectrum or continuum in
this process in which every individual occupies a particular place"
(Pauly, p.38). "Psychological Aspects of Transsexualism," Part II,
is heavily influenced by Money, and much of his work on
hermaphroditism and hormonal aberrations is summarized before the
text gets into the transsexual topic by way of comparison. Part
III, "Somatic Aspects of Transsexualism," summarizes findings in the
neuroendocrine area and in the area of physical characteristics and
accompanying demographics. An extensive 13-chapter Part IV explores
"Treatment Aspects of Transsexualism." The university programs are
detailed and the surgical operative procedures discussed that have
evolved in the U.S., Great Britain and Scandinavia. Part V,
"Medicolegal Aspects of Transsexualism," updates progress in the
U.S., the U.K., Denmark and Sweden. Green in the Conclusion

broaches possible new avenues for research.

Critique - Strengths

a. Excellent usage is made of diagrams, tables, charts, drawings
    and photographs. A 13-page Glossary and a 17+page Bibliography
    complement the text. Historical and cross-cultural perspectives
    (see Summary) are extensive.
b. The editors are both outstanding researchers and their profes-
    sionalism shows up in their objectivity and choice of content.
    In addition to their own valuable contributions, Pauly is
    excellent in material-presentation. Stoller in Part II is
    provocative (e.g. "transsexualism, starting in early childhood,
    may occur when a bisexual woman marries a passive man..."
    (p.155)) in his hypotheses. Pomeroy cuts through to the basics
    without attendant myriad theories and Hamburger explains the
    correct hormonal interactions on a somatic basis.
c. Insights are often proffered (e.g. "in order to understand the
    transsexuals, one must realize that theirs is a sense of being
    merely in transition into the female gender role; having opted
    to pass, they must complete this transition" (Randell, p.367)).
    Future research possibilities are outlined (refer to Summary).

Deficiencies

a. The book is now outdated in parts by ongoing research and
    experiential knowledge garnered since that time.
b. Some contributors offer conclusions based on small-sample
    studies and inferential assumptions (e.g. Blumer's 15-sample
    study concludes that "a lobectomy, which might restore normal
    sexual functions, would undoubtedly be preferable in such cases
    to sex-reassignment surgery" (p.218)). Chapter 27 :on aversion
    techniques emphasizes a medical-model approach. Furthermore,
    only five transsexuals were treated, one of whom was unaffected,
    two relapsed after one month, one was lost to follow-up and one
    had a "temporary relapse" (Gelder & Marks, p.403). The authors
    magnify and distort the value of their findings.
c. A few authors display pejorativity (e.g. "some of these
    patients have quite a promiscuous period following operation"
    (Doorbar, p.192)).
d. In the Glossary, estrogen is wrongly defined as a "female sex
    hormone" (p.478).

152. Greene, Gerald & Caroline. S-M The Last Taboo. New York:
Ballantine Books, 1978. 351 pp.

Brief Summary - The authors describe consensual scenario-enacting
sadism and masochism as their devotees practice an essentially
dualistic relationship connecting the two activities. In the first
five chapters, the Greenes trace the historical-philosophical
rationale for S-M as it emerged officially from de Sade and Masoch
through recognition by Krafft-Ebing, Freud, Havelock Ellis and
others. The balance of the book discusses the manifold characteristics of S-M (and such subgroups as bondage and discipline). It is
play-acting in a controlled, erotic, imaginitive fantasy-land with
pre-set limits and utilizes the mutuality of absolute trust in the

boundaries of expression sought by the actors. The authors caution
that one must distinguish between erotogenic and moral masochism.
They assert the former is healthy and fun and is found in persons of
high self-esteem whereas the latter is merely a destructive "form of
self-punishment" (p.120). But "any excess - the shedding of blood,
in particular - competes with S-M arousal to its exclusion" (p.180).
The authors conclude by claiming the S-M community is trying "to
calm violence by love" (p.218).

Critique - Strengths

a. Many appropriate quotations, footnotes and the various literary
    components of the Appendix are useful. The historical-
    philosophical overview (refer to Summary) is both necessary and
    helpful. Cross-societal information (e.g. England, Germany, the
    U.S.) is provided.
b. S-M truisms are often well-defined (e.g. "To the true S-M
    person, cruelty is anathema, he dislikes it more than anyone"
    (p.10)). In so doing, the authors effectively demythologize an
    ignorant reader.

Deficiencies

a. No bibliography, index, visual aids, tables, charts or graphs
    complement the text. Research studies and background material
    are limited and not properly cited. Errors occur (e.g. the
    Toronto paper Justice Weekly is stated to exist when in fact it
    folded a decade earlier (p.140)). For these reasons, the book
    is of limited peripheral value. Case histories are from the old
    classical literature. Recent ones should have been included.
b. Some S-M rituals are not mentioned or explained (e.g. the usage
    of safe-words, anal object-insertion such as fist-fucking, or
    golden showers (only briefly mentioned (p.195)).
c. The authors, coming from a monogamous bias, are judgmental
    toward others (e.g. "This (S-M) is far more moral and
    responsible to the human condition than all the promiscuous
    screwing, sucking and eating advocated as the nirvana of the
    liberated life in so much of our slightly panting press"
    (p.173)).
d. While criticizing modern sex-researchers for being "metronomi-
    cally arithmetical..." (p.136), the Greenes do not substantiate
    this allegation. They often generalize in a speculative
    undocumented manner (e.g. "with the increase of ...
    civilization, there is an increased tendency to masochism..."
    (p.48)).

153. Hirschfeld, Magnus (as compiled by his students). Sexual
Anomalies and Perversions. (2nd Ed.) London: Encyclopaedic Press Ltd.,
1952. 630 pp.

Brief Summary - A Publisher's Preface furnishes the reader with a
biographical review of the author. Book I briefly describes the
"Normal Development of Sexuality," both physically and psychologically. Book II details the "Quantitative Irregularities of Sexual
Development" which includes various types of infantilism as well as
such states as hypererotism and castration. The major content of

the book follows with three sections entitled "Deflections of the
Sexual Impulse," "Sexual Aberrations Arising from Fixations on
Component Impulses" and "Other Partial Impulses." These three
sub-books cover many atypical forms of sexual expression such as
transvestism, homosexuality, sadomasochism, fetishism and
exhibitionism as well as the normative outlet of masturbation.
Additionally, two chapters in Book III cover physical anomalies as
they arise in persons who have a form of hermaphroditism.

Critique - Strengths

a. The book provides a historical and limited cross-cultural perspective. Numerous references and case-examples are cited.
   Backing this up are occasional animal references (e.g. hormonal
   research on rats (p.174)). This edition updates references and
   even includes the Kinsey studies (p.122) on masturbation.
b. The author who himself was a homosexual, is not negatively
   biased about this subject (e.g. "homosexuals cannot be regarded
   as degenerates" (p.278)).

Deficiencies

a. No visual aids, graphs, tables or personal statistical research
   are offered. Certain terminology is no longer in vogue (e.g.
   "androgyny" is today's pseudo-hermaphroditism and "scopophilia"
   becomes voyeurism).
b. Fallacious unproven assumptions are stated (e.g. adults who
   masturbate "when opportunities for normal sexual intercourse are
   present, we speak of (as practicing) pathological masturbation
   ... and are mostly people with a sadistic or masochistic
   disposition or perverts of another kind" (p.127)).

154. Hopper, C. Edmund & Allen, William A. Sex Education for
Physically Handicapped Youth. Springfield: Charles C. Thomas, Pub.,
1980. 143 pp.

Brief Summary - The authors explain that "this book for physically
handicapped youth, developed by people who work with the disabled as
well as by people who are themselves handicapped, is intended to
assist parents and other family members..." (p.viii). The first two
chapters define sex education as to purpose and usefulness and link
this concept with the necessity for positive self-esteem. Chapter 3
imparts a condensed version of important aspects of sexuality and
this is countered by Chapter 4's dialogued feedback on these issues
by some handicapped youths of both sexes. Next follows information
about "Sexual and Other Fantasies" which precedes a discussion on
masturbation. Social ways of "Getting to Know Guys and Girls"
subsequently is presented after which comes "Getting the Most
Enjoyment Out of Sex." Chapter 9 includes a short anatomical
presentation about conception to childbirth as well as some
recognized methods of birth control. Following a chapter on
venereal diseases, one is offered about normative and alternative
lifestyles. Genetic information is followed by a short chapter on
homosexual issues. The final chapter describes "the numerous
resources ready to serve you" (p.102).

Critique - Strengths

a. Aids include various sketches, plus a 2-page Bibliography and
   3-page Glossary. Chapter 4's feedback dialogue (refer to
   Summary) helps to focus on relevant sexual topics. Other
   resources include "Where to Get More Information About Specific
   Genetic Diseases" (p.96) plus a listing of community and
   national agencies of relevance (p.112-115).
b. Myths are dissected (e.g. "... When penises are hard, most of
   them are about the same size..." (p.16)).
c. Chapter 11 explores conventional and alternative lifestyles in
   a reasonably objective manner listing each of them as
   representing potentially viable opportunities for some
   handicapped persons (e.g. "Marriages among three or more people
   are taking place..." (p.91)).
d. This book can be utilized and referred to appropriate others by
   sexological professionals as one resource amongst others.

Deficiencies

a. The resource lists should have been expanded to include further
   books plus suitable video and film titles available. Cited
   references are not forthcoming and no historical or
   cross-cultural material is included.
b. Errors of omission, and emphasis occur (e.g. Chapter 10 on
   venereal diseases fails to mention trichomoniasis; also the
   statement "Orgasms for a woman takes place when there are
   certain muscular movements in the walls of her vagina" (p.49)
   neglects to describe the function of the clitoris. Indeed the
   word "clitoris" does not appear once in the text or in the
   Glossary).
c. There are several negatively implied messages with fallacious
   overtones (e.g. "The possibility of your becoming a homosexual
   decreases when you get accurate information about sex..."
   (p.20)). A value-biased definition occurs in the Glossary (i.e.
   "Sexual perversion - Method other than the right or normal way
   of performing sexual act" (p.118)).

155. Klaich, Dolores. Woman Plus Woman: Attitudes Toward Lesbianism.
New York: Simon and Schuster, Inc., 1974. 287 pp.

Brief Summary - A Prelude states "historical attitudes toward
lesbianism (reveal) ... a cartload of contradictory theories... The
movement's challenge: lesbianism is not a sickness" (p.10-11).
Part I, "Sex and Psychology," consists of four chapters bracketed by
two interviews of closet lesbians. Reality and myth along with
various historical viewpoints are discussed from the biases of the
medical-model sickness approach of Krafft-Ebing and Caprio, through
the more tolerant views of Freud and Havelock Ellis up to the
non-judgmental research of Kinsey and Money. In Part II, "Historic
Witnesses," Klaich outlines the biographies, literary lesbian contributions and lifestyle impacts of such famous lesbians as Sappho,
Renee Vivien, N.C. Barney, Collette, Radclyffe Hall and Gertrude
Stein. "Contemporary Voices" as Part III reviews current developments. Findings on specific issues stem from "a questionnaire
(which) was constructed by three women who are lesbians" (p.221).

Critique - Strengths

a. Numerous quotations, interviews and feedback comments from parts of the Questionnaire are most insightful. Referenced notes on each chapter plus an 8-page Selected Bibliography are included. Historical (e.g. see Summary) and cross-species information (e.g. the Harlow monkey experiments (p.53)) impart useful background material.
b. Correct pespective is maintained (e.g. "Lesbianism is a way of loving, a natural possibility... Like the other possibilities, it can be a matter of mutual stagnation, even destruction" (p.14)). Logical thinking emphasizes correct priorities (e.g. "Sappho was a poet who loved women. She was not a lesbian who wrote poetry" (p.160)).
c. The author does not exhibit pejorative phraseology and judgmental bias.
d. Myths are exposed (e.g. "Lesbian Sex: Reality and Myth").

Deficiencies

a. The questionnaire is not provided in its entirety, nor can its data be statistically analyzed. The results given are idiosyncratic. No tables or charts and only one photograph assist the text. Cross-cultural input is minimal. Historical mythology is sometimes not referenced (e.g. "Between the spring rites, it is said, the Amazons' sex lives were lesbian" (p.159)). There is a shifting back and forth by the author from a subjective to an objective aproach to her subject. It would have helped if Klaich had stated her gender-preference.
b. The Kinsey 0-6 Rating Scale in the Questionnaire should have indicated that overtness plus fantasy-arousal are embodied in the scale. This is not done and many respondents may have erroneously assumed that only overtness applies (i.e. p.250).

156. Klein, Fred. _The Bisexual Option_. New York: Arbor House Pub. Co., 1978. 221 pp.

Brief Summary - Klein, a physician, stresses that a popular belief of society is that a bisexual person must be "closet gay" (p.2). In Part I "What is Bisexuality," Klein defines qualitatively and quantitatively the dimension of human bisexuality. The author sees the bisexual continuum in an individual manifesting itself through transitional or sequential (gender change of "sexual relationships ... with only one gender at any given time" (p.17)) modes. Self-identified bisexuality comes from a person's both-sex overt sexual behavior and/or erotic fantasy. Bisexuality as overtness may comprise episodic, temporary, experimental, or situational (as in prison) activity. To further complicate matters, "some people prefer sex with one gender and emotional involvement with the other" (p.18). Part II, "Bisexuality and Health" contrasts the neurotic bisexual to the healthy bisexual. Part III entitled "The Bisexual in Society" details the limited sociological findings available from other researchers who all agree "there are from five to ten times as many bisexuals as homosexuals" (p.117). Literary contributions are briefly analyzed. The final chapter extrapolates such present-day factors as sex roles and stereotypes, androgyny, friendships versus lovers, the family, gay liberation, feminism, erroneous myths and social dilemmas, into future considerations of how society may view the self-identified bisexual.

Critique - Strengths

a. The book is a positive, often anecdotal analysis of its subject. Famous bisexuals are chronicled (e.g. Alexander the Great, p.145) and literary contributions dissected (e.g. the novel and movie The Fox, p.160). Two Appendixes deal with media interpretations of notable bisexual personns plus a 144-person study. A 5-page Bibliography closes the book. The Appendix B survey-results provide hypotheses for future research.
b. Constructive critical evaluation of research theoreticians is given (e.g. Socarides (p.55)).
c. The book's two greatest specific contributions are the emphasis on the Kinsey 0-6 Scale (p.15) and the chart titled "Nonexistence Myth - Neurotic Myth" (p.176)).

Deficiencies

a. The book gives only two examples of cross-cultural data (p.25). Visual aids would have helped. In Part III, too much material is covered too briefly, and repeated in Appendix A. The research study is limited to being descriptive and idiosyncratic.
b. Klein promotes the idea that the Kinsey Scale might be better separated into two scales, one for overt behavior and one for fantasy (e.g. p.15-16; also p.116). This is a needless complication leading to perhaps differing instrument-measuring scales or definitions.
c. A major flaw is the classifying of all persons as bisexuals who have ever experienced both-sex overtness, whether self-defined or not. Pseudo-technical phrases confuse this issue (e.g. "nonerotic bisexual level" (p.35)). Assumptive, unproven conclusions occur (e.g. "repressing incestuous desires ... resolves the Oedipus Complex successfully... The person (can then) ... displace his or her love onto others..." (p.49); also "sexual orientation is ... established postnatally" (p.26)).
d. Some pejorative phraseology surfaces (e.g. "the spiritual desolation inherent in promiscuity" (p.33); also "the possessor of an abnormal sex drive" (p.147)).

157. Krafft-Ebing, Richard von. **Psychopathis Sexualis**. New York: G.P. Putnam's Sons, 1965. 640 pp.

Brief Summary - The author. a German psychiatrist (1840-1902) wrote the original book in the late 19th century. The book is a series of case studies of patients who displayed deviant sexual behavior as analyzed by the author. Krafft-Ebing uses these cases as a core nucleus in exemplifying and explaining the many deviations from the normative sexual impulse. A brief opening chapter furnishes some cross-cultural and historical perspectives. Chapter II entitled "Phsyiological Facts" interrelates physiology with the reasons for the human sexual impulse. After a short discourse on our

hormonal-genetic make-up, the author launches into the focus of the
book which is on the so-termed various sexual pathologies such as
sadism and masochism. Many rare deviations as well as the more
common ones such as fetishism and homosexuality are dissected.

Critique - Strengths

a. Referenced footnotes, anecdotal references, and case studies
    occur in abundance. Historical-anthropological data are amply
    supplied. As a major innovator and early researcher into
    atypical sexuality, the author offers an unparalleled view of
    this subject.
b. At times the author is objective in attitude (e.g. "the law-
    makers of the future may, for reasons of utility at least,
    abandon the prosecution of pederasty" (p.608)).
c. It appears that Cases 160-164 (p.435-444) of "viraginity"
    refer to transsexualism where each woman identified as a male.
    At the time of the book's being written, this phenomenon had not
    yet been defined and so these cases are of significant
    historical importance.

Deficiencies

a. No visual aids complement the text.
b. Krafft-Ebing is greatly influenced by his fellow professional
    colleagues into accepting their views without researching them.
    His judgmental biases are enormous (e.g. masturbation is
    attributed largely to a "hereditary taint" (p.85).
c. Myths are reinforced (e.g. in describing a certain lesbian, he
    adds the sequitur "but she had coarse features" (p.427)).
d. What we today term homosexuals, transvestites and transsexuals
    are often not distinguished from each other.

158. Libby, Roger & Whitehurst, Robert, ed. **Marriage and Alternatives:
Exploring Intimate Relationships.** Glenview: Scott, Foresman & Co.,
1977. 445 pp.

Brief Summary - Part 1 details "Traditional Monogamous Marriage" and
analyzes it from three perspectives. Part 2 is termed "Intimate
Alternatives to Marriage: Beyond Sexual Exclusivity." Nine
chapters evaluate singlehood, cohabitation, extramarital sex,
comarital (swinging) sex and group marriage. Part 3 entitled
"Alternatives for Whom?" critiques the influence of the women's
movement with regard to female sexuality, childhood sexuality, and
bisexuality. The final Part 4 is called "Exploring the Future of
Relationships" and covers the possible futuristic impacts of
intimacy, the media, our youth, personal growth, jealousy and self-
identity/esteem on interpersonal sex. Libby in an Epilogue defends
the new pluralistic trends while David and Vera Mace in a
Counter-Epilogue argue for new aproaches to support the traditional
monogamous marriage.

Critique - Strengths

a. An Abstract before each Part and Chapter is useful. Reference
    Notes usually follow each chapter. A 16-page Bibliography

terminates the book. Figures, tables and graphs are utilized
(e.g. Quotations and citations abound).

b. Many authors offer suggestions for future research (e.g. Libby, p.59). The closing Epilogue and Counter-Epilogue contrast controversial sociocultural directions.
c. Mythologies are often exposed (e.g. Whitehurst, p.14).
d. At times, an author achieves an insightful breakthrough (e.g. "Intensity Matrix for the Analysis of an Intimate Relationship" (Kieffer, p.273)).
e. Pejorativity is minimal.

Deficiencies

a. Visual aids are lacking. Comprehensive historical-anthropological material is missing. While most contributors are scientists professionally interested in contemporary lifestyles, a few are not. Rimmer is a writer whose hypotheses have little proven basis in fact. A more serious problem is the article by Duberman, a historian and playwright, entitled "The Bisexual Debate." Duberman does not write his paper from a lifestyle perspective. An addendum by Libby into research findings on bisexuality is also off the topic.
b. Few of the papers present any statistical research involving controls (an exception is Gilmartin's (p.161)). Too many conjectures and hypotheses cloud the many descriptive studies. Often an unreferenced conclusion is stated (e.g. "swinging has apparently seen a decline in the past few years" (p.36)). Hypotheses are sometimes passed off as theories (e.g. "sexual expressions should be proportional to the depth of a relationship ... (and) this conclusion is ... essential for our theory" (R. & D. Roy, p.31)).

159. Margolis, Herbert & Rubenstein, Paul. The Groupsex Tapes. New York: David McKay Co. Inc., 1971. 314 pp.

Brief Summary - The book utilizes the vehicle of the taped-interview technique between the interviewer(s) and respondent(s) to emphasize the many facets and ramifications of group sex. A cross-section of swinging couples and singles was selected for interviews with the total number reaching 628, of which ninety-eight granted in-depth interviews. This latter group comprised forty married persons, sixteen people living together, twenty-seven singles (fourteen women and thirteen men) and fifteen children of swingers. The final chapter relates the phenomena of group sex to comments of some of this era's prominent professionals in the social sciences.

Critique - Strengths

a. Chapters 2 and 28 provide some background and professional insight into this lifestyle. Various contemporary experts are quoted. The Glossary of swing terms is a needed inclusion.
b. Objectivity is established early in the book. This is maintained in reasonable balance throughout the book (e.g. If Michelle is groupsex-positive (p.83), then Gene is presented as macho, exploitive and cynical about the lifestyle (p.114)).
c. Two innovative chapters dealing with symposia of male and

female swingers (Ch. 24 & 25) are positive contributions from a different perspective than the main theme of the book.
d. Pejorative phraseology is not in evidence.

Deficiencies

a. No visual aids, graphs, charts or tables are included. Historical and cross-cultural material is basically not present.
b. The data and information are of the descriptive variety and limited primarily to the "upper middle class..." (p.2). The book uses an idiosyncratic population and provides minimal statistics. The authors are media personalities and not trained researchers.

160. Marmor. Judd, ed. Homosexual Behavior: A Modern Reappraisal. New York: Basic Books, Inc., 1980. 431 pp.

Brief Summary - After an "Overview: The Multiple Roots of Homosexual Behavior," Part I reviews "Ambisexuality in Animals" (Denniston), "Hormones and Homosexuality" (Tourney) and "Genetic and Chromosomal Aspects of Homosexual Etiology" (Money). Part II, "The View of the Social Sciences," deals with the historical background and cross-cultural perspectives of homosexuality, its social stigmatization, emerging cultural gay identities, the lesbian sub-culture, the variables of aging, some legal and religious aspects, and a final chapter by Voeller termed "Society and the Gay Movement." "The View of the Clinician" is the title of Part III. Subjects discussed are childhood sexual identity (Green), clinical aspects, a review of utilized psychological tests, latent homosexuality and pseudohomosexuality, various psychodynamic and psychotherapeutic approaches, and psychotherapy from a behavioral standpoint (Birk). Marmor, in his "Epilogue: Homosexuality and the Issue of Mental Illness," insists "the issue of homosexual object choice should be regarded as essentially irrelevant, therefore, to the issue of mental illness" (p.400).

Critique - Strengths

a. Many cited references, footnotes, and quotations along with tables, diagrams (p.44-45) and case studies (e.g. p.327) heighten the text. Most chapters end with a brief abstract. Key points are in italics. Marmor correctly describes the Kinsey Scale (p.6). Cross-cultural (e.g. Carrier) and cross-species (e.g. Denniston) information is portrayed.
b. Pervasive myths are often exposed (e.g. "... these latter myths..." (Marmor, p.19)).
c. Perceptive insights are presented (e.g. "there is in fact no such unitary thing as 'homosexuality' " (Birk, p.376)).
d. Conflicting study-results and methodological inadequacies are noted by many authors who suggest future research possibilities (e.g. Carrier, footnote 2, p.101; Money, p.69-70).
e. Part II constructively addresses many pertinent issues. Part I has some value in collating and analyzing research.

Deficiencies

a. No visual aids complement the text. Not enough statistics are
   furnished. Studies are almost entirely descriptive (e.g.
   "Clinical Aspects of Female Homosexuality" (Saghir and Robins)).
   Historical background material is insufficient.
b. At times studies are cited which are fallacious or poorly conceived (e.g. the Kallman study (p.7, 62); also "Dorner's own
   studies have not been replicated" (p.56)).
c. Part III supports the medical-model approach. Many authors
   opine that "heterosexual shifts" (e.g. Birk, p.387) are possible
   for gays voluntarily seeking orientation-change. No such proof
   is proffered in the form of methodologically sound research.
   These authors never use the Kinsey Scale in such a way as to
   clearly define whether such reported successes stem from
   diagnosed Kinsey 2's to 4's being changed, or Kinsey 5's and 6's
   being shifted. Thus the amount of shifting is never quantified.
d. Assumptive phraseology (e.g. "homosexuality of oedipal origin"
   (Ovesey & Woods, p.333)) and pejorative terminology (e.g. "They
   are much less promiscuous than their male counterparts" (Marmor,
   p.16)) are in evidence.

161. Martin, Del & Lyon, Phyllis. **Lesbian/Woman**. (Revised edition
pending publication, 1983). San Francisco: Glide Publications, 1972.
283 pp.

Brief Summary - These authors, as self-identified lesbians, speak
for their estimated 10% of the U.S. female population. In the first
chapter, myth as opposed to reality is compared. "Self Image" deals
with the necessity of developing positive self-esteem. Next comes
"Sexuality and Sex Roles." "Life Styles" as Chapter 4 delineate the
secretiveness and fears of lesbians. The following chapter admits
"Lesbians are Mothers Too." Teenage gayness is expanded upon in
"Growing up Gay." Chapter 7 delves into "Lesbian Paranoia - Real &
Imagined Fears." The following chapter describes the history of the
lesbian organization Daughters of Bilitis. Chapter 9 termed
"Lesbian/Woman" presents the polemics of lesbians supporting the
feminist organizations first as women, and only second, as lesbians.
The final chapter effects a philosophical summation of the necessity
for lesbian liberation.

Critique - Strengths

a. The authors write in a folksy style replete with stories and
   anecdotal expressions. Sharp metaphorical phraseology is noted
   (e.g. "irretrievably lost to the womb of the closet" (p.275)).
   Some cross-cultural material is included (e.g. p.82-83). As the
   pioneer book, it requires close scrutiny. The first chapter
   accords a limited historical overview.
b. Discerning observations can be noted (e.g. "the emphasis of
   research has been devoted almost exclusively to causation rather
   than to those facets of lesbian life itself" (p.24)). Proper
   perspective is maintained (e.g. "even having a Lesbian affair
   doesn't necessarily mean that you are a Lesbian" (p.172)).
c. Many cultural myths are dissected (e.g. refer to Summary).

Deficiencies

a. The book lacks cited references, a bibliography and an index.
   No visual aids, tables or graphs are included. Additional
   historical, literary and cross-cultural information would have
   been of value.
b. The text is sometimes assumptive (e.g. "those women undesirably
   discharged ... all became homosexuals. We believe, however,
   that a number of them probably would not have done so except
   for..." (p.202)). Some pejorativity surfaces (e.g. "... became
   sexually promiscuous with both sexes" (p.203)).
c. An erroneous reference occurs (e.g. the Kallman study of iden-
   tical twins where all "turned out to be homosexual" (p.148)).
   This study is invalid.

162. Martin, Mel. I'm for Group Sex. Toronto: Mystique Press, 1975.
223 pp.

Brief Summary - The author who runs a swingers' club in Toronto,
sets forth a largely autobiographical account of his involvement in
an open sociosexual marriage beginning in 1965. After tracing a
history of the Canadian swinging movement in general, he describes
the activities of typical married swingers, single swingers,
bisexual swingers, unusual swingers such as certain preachers,
policemen and judges, swingers who prefer group sex, and kinky
swingers. In Chapter 8, the reasons behind why certain swingers
exhibit mate-jealousy are examined. The final chapter details a
world-wide network of swing clubs and organizations.

Critique - Strengths

a. Some expert references are included and one is excellently
   critiqued (the O'Neills' book "Open Marriage" (p.33-34)). Many
   case examples authenticate the text. The Appendix listing
   useful resource organizations is an asset (see Summary).
b. Certain sections of the book reveal major insights (e.g. the
   chapter on jealousy (see Summary); also the author's "Ten
   Commandments of Swinging" (p.114)).
c. The author is not just tolerant, but accepting of other persons' sexual variations (e.g. "there is a bit of the kinky in
   everyone... I don't put down others for any superbent traits.
   If it's meaningful to them, that's enough" (p.149)).

Deficiencies

a. While it is a descriptive account of swinging, the book is not
   scientifically based. No cited references, bibliography, index,
   tables or charts are contained in the book and the only
   photographs are on the covers. Insufficient historical and a
   lack of cross-cultural or research background-material also is
   present.
b. The book is written from a distinct bias of the author-
   participant.

163. Masters, William H. & Johnson, Virginia E. Homosexuality in
Perspective. Boston: Little, Brown and Company, 1979. 464 pp.

Brief Summary - Divided into two Parts, the first embodies
"Preclinical Study, 1957-1970." The homosexual human sexual
response cycle is studied and reported on as to its physiology and
compared to its heterosexual counterpart. There is no discernible
difference. Section II entitled "Clinical Study, 1968-1977" deals
with the results from treating clients with male and female
homosexual dysfunction and dissatisfaction. This latter term
alludes to a homosexual who wishes to change gender preference to a
heterosexual orientation. Statistics are presented. Included is a
resume of recent hormonal research, much of it contradictory, by the
authors' colleague Kolodny.

Critique - Strengths

a. Statistical data, tables and case studies are included. A 24-
    page Bibliography and textual footnotes augment the presented
    material.
b. Some interesting findings appear in Part I (e.g. only "11 of
    the 42 committed male (homosexual) couples failed to include
    some form of nipple stimulation ... (and) was of far more
    significance ... than to married heterosexual men" (p.71)).

Deficiencies

a. No visual aids are in evidence. Insufficient historical and
    cross-cultural input is provided.
b. Some pejorativity occurs (e.g. "her unrestrained promiscuity"
    (p.319)).
c. Replication by other researchers is impossible. No appendixes
    are offered stating the complete methodology and research
    design. The selection-basis for choosing dissatisfied
    homosexuals is falsely grounded. Eliminating fantasy of
    sex-preference as one criterion for a Kinsey 0-6 number is both
    inaccurate and disastrous. Instead the sole judging factor is
    an individual's level of "overt homosexual experience" (p.8).
    How do we know which clients were 2's, or 3's or 4's, based on
    the properly-defined 0-6 Kinsey Scale? This built-in bias casts
    a genuine doubt on the so-called conversion and reversion
    statistics of the authors. As for treatment procedures, the
    authors are vague (e.g. "his confidence in heterosexual
    interchange was restored by the full cooperation of the older
    woman (partner) in the treatment program" (p.347)). The authors
    admit to a failure rate of 28.4% in dissatisfaction treatment of
    patients (Table 17-2, p.400). Follow-up statistics are
    inadequate (e.g. "the Institute's disaster area statistically"
    (p.398) was the loss in contact of 19 (of 47) homosexuals.)
d. In the ambisexual study, conclusions result from preformed
    speculations (e.g. "The research team is currently more
    comfortable with the speculation that ambisexuality represents
    more a prior point of departure than a societal end-point"
    (p.173)). The study sample of six men and six women is much too
    small for any meaningful conclusions to be made.

164. Mathis, James L. <u>Clear Thinking About Sexual Deviations</u>.
Chicago: Nelson-Hall Co., 1972. 229 pp.

Brief Summary - The author, a psychiatrist, notes in his
Introduction that sexual deviations today are "recognized as diag-
nostic entities by the medical profession (requiring) ... proper
treatment and ... a more humane legal attitude" (p.viii). An
opening chapter discusses "The Development of Sexual
Identification." Mathis then devotes one chapter each to homosexuality, exhibitionism, voyeurism, pedophilia, transvestism,
transsexualism, fetishism, sadomasochism, rape, incest, madonna-
prostitute syndrome, prostitution, group sex and finally
"Miscellaneous Deviations" such as urophilia. In his Epilogue, the
author points out treatment is often "indefensible in view of our
present state of knowledge" (p.213).

Critique - Strengths

a. The author writes in a clear, concise style using appropriate
    case histories. Definitions are competent and accurate.
b. The content comes across as emanating a sympathetic and mostly
    positive approach to the social difficulties of the sexual
    minorities who are discussed.

Deficiencies

a. Lack of a bibliography and reference system limits usefulness.
    Insufficient historical and cross-cultural references are
    mentioned. No visual aids are included in the book.
b. The book is oriented exclusively to the medical model of
    treatment-necessity. The author seems to have misgivings about
    such a universal philosophy (e.g. "perhaps it is most logical to
    view the activities of the participants in group sex simply as
    interesting variations of human behavior that should be of
    little concern to the nonparticipants" (p.187)). Thus Mathis is
    forced into a dichotomous philosophical position. The most
    incomplete chapter is the one on sadomasochism. Mathis
    describes these behaviours basically in non-consensual terms.
c. Claims of conversion to heterosexuality and statements of why
    "homosexual tendencies" (p.15) develop are unsubstantiated.

165. Mooney, Thomas O., Cole, Theodore M. & Chilgren, Richard A.
Sexual Options for Paraplegics and Quadriplegics. Boston: Little,
Brown and Co., 1975. 126 pp.

Brief Summary - Chapter 1 provides a rationale for disabled persons
to positively view their own sexuality. Chapter 2 describes the
necessary preliminaries and ongoing precautions required for these
disabled individuals to function sexually with a partner. The
subsequent chapter refers to the fantasies which can aid in this
process. Techniques culminating in reflex-style erections are
explored and examined. Positional alternatives for a couple are
included in Chapter 4. If erection is impossible, the disabled man
can utilize "the stuffing technique" (p.53). Facts are disseminated
about pregnancy possibilities. The final chapter deals with
"Oral-Genital and Manual Stimulation."

Critique - Strengths

a. Sixty-five excellent large-sized photographs with accompanying
    descriptions are of immense support. Instructions are
    simplistically presented. A 7-page Glossary defines terms.
    Demographic and sociohistorical information is included.
b. Although the book is directed at helping disabled persons, it
    is of value to health-care professionals and sexologists. It
    can be recommended to disabled clients.
c. Sexual concerns and potential resistances are positively
    handled (e.g. "at times a reflex erection may not last or stay
    hard enough for penetration... You also have hands, a mouth, a
    tongue and other body parts to use" (p.51)).
d. No value-judgmentality or patronization is evident.

Deficiencies

a. No quantified or even qualitative studies with tables, charts
    and statistics are included, nor is a Bibliography offered.
    Some simplified data should have been included as a
    reinforcement-mechanism. No case studies are given, even in
    anecdotal form. Other resource materials such as films
    available on the subject should have been included in an
    appendix. Where sources are listed under "Vibrators" (p.105) in
    the Glossary, some addresses are inaccurate (e.g. Multi Media
    Resource Center).
b. A brief chapter on human sexual physiology and the normative
    sexual response cycle should have been part of the early text.
    A short section on the possibility of multiple causes of
    dysfunctions might have been useful from a comparative
    viewpoint.

166. Morin, Jack. **Anal Pleasure & Health**. Burlingame: Down There
Press, 1981. 252 pp.

Brief Summary - The author, a psychotherapist, explores his subject
in two studies; a pilot study of twenty-nine men plus a more formal
one of 143 persons (114 men and 29 women). Sub-topics covered are:
the anal taboo from historical and cross-cultural perspectives and
as it currently applies to the helping professions, instructions for
self-help, an anal anatomical resume, emotional interactions,
learning voluntary anal muscle control, exploring the rectal shape
and sensations, confronting psychosocial blocks, enhancing verbal
communication, non-demand anal stimulation with a partner,
considerations of safety and comfort, the relevant particulars of
romantic fantasies, sex roles, gayperson considerations, confidence,
self-esteem, excitement as this especially pertains to
sadomasochistic practices, anal intercourse itself, and the
integration of new information with experience.

Critique - Strengths

a. A 5-page Bibliography, cited references, footnotes, graphs and
    tables assist the text. Many expert and anecdotal quotations
    abound. Anatomical and subject-related sketches are included.
    Extensive historical and cross-cultural material is presented

(e.g. p.5-10). Appendix A dealing with medical problems and
diseases specific to the anus and rectum is a useful addition.
b. Background research is examined (e.g. Kinsey, Hunt - p.4). The
author's research is extensively covered in Appendix B with
methodological parameters being included. Conclusions of
statistical and descriptive import are given (e.g. (p.226); also
concerning anal tension patterns and factors - 14 listed
(p.230-232)).
c. Perceptive insights occur (e.g. "The tendency of taboos to
function outside of consciousness assures that the perspective
on reality inherent in the taboo will be taken for granted"
(p.17)). The medical-model approach is constructively critiqued
(e.g. "The medical community, which could be a valuable source
of ... expertise about the anus, has little to say except 'Don't
touch it!' " (p.19)), and eclecticism promoted (e.g. "In
combining behavioral and evocative approaches..." (p.24)).
Positive cautions are emphasized (e.g. "... place the comfort of
your anus ahead of the desire of a sex partner" (p.33)).
d. The text is essentially non-pejorative (e.g. "Enjoyment of S &
M is not the result of psychopathology. It is found among
severely disturbed and exceptionally well-functioning
individuals" (p.177)).

Deficiencies

a. No index is included.
b. The selective research sample may or may not represent the continuum of anal-sex practitioners. It is highly weighted toward
men, and especially gay men (i.e. refer to p.210).
c. Concomitant anal-sex and recreational drug use are both recommended and denigrated subject to certain vague criteria. This
is confusing and complicates objectivity (e.g. "... heavy use of
any depressant with anal stimulation deprives the user of the
awareness he/she needs to guard against anal damage... Another
positive attribute of marijuana, from the standpoint of anal
health, is..." (p.98)).

167. Moses, Alice E. Identity Management in Lesbian Women. New York:
Praeger Publishers, 1978. 140 pp.

Brief Summary - In her Introduction, the author stresses that "the
primary framework to be utilized in this study is that of labeling
theory..." (p.xx). Chapter 1 gets into theoretical considerations
of labeling theory, deviance-models, and the management of passing
techniques necessary in the outside world. The following chapter
deals with the variables and concepts of "Lesbianism." Various
hypotheses used in the study are put forth. The study's
"Methodology" makes up Chapter 3. The next chapter details the
"Results" of the research. The final chapter is called "Discussion
and Conclusions."

Critique - Strengths

a. An 8-page Bibliography is an asset. Cited references, expert
quotations and anecdotal story-examples are aptly given. The
9-page questionnaire instrument is reproduced in an Appendix.

b. Tables and statistics including correlation and probability data cover the research (e.g. p.41; also Appendix B). Methodology and hypotheses are described (i.e. refer to Summary).

c. Moses is non-judgmental (e.g. "... the author does not believe that there is anything inherently deviant, pathological, immoral, destructive, or dysfunctional about lesbianism as a sexual preference" (p.xix)).

Deficiencies

a. The lack of an index, visual aids, charts and graphs makes interpretation more difficult. Some language labels could have been better phrased (e.g. "... when around straights" (p.41)).

b. The research instrument has a mixture of scales, thus putting into question the probability statistics generated through non-interval scales. There are serious methodological shortcomings (e.g. "this questionnaire was directed almost exclusively to lesbian women in partnerships. This was an oversight on the part of the researcher and one which also limits the generalizability of the results" (p.31)). Thus the author's conclusion that the results "are not highly idiosyncratic to the sample but are reflective of a broader reality" (p.37) is not justified. Furthermore, Hypothesis II A-D verification-results are invalid because Hypothesis II was incorrectly postulated (i.e. refer to p.27; Table 4.5, p.41; question 15, p.92). The Kinsey 0-6 Scale measures overtness plus fantasy-arousal stimuli. The statement "Hypothesis II: The more heterosexual experience a woman has..." (p.27) is thus not a reasonable postulation.

168. Ponse, Barbara. *Identities in the Lesbian World: The Social Construction of Self*. Westport: Greenwood Press, 1978. 239 pp.

Brief Summary - The author, a non-gay sociological researcher, in an Introduction discusses self-identification along with labeling theory. The first chapter portrays the author's problems in getting into this research project. After defining some "Sex-Related Identities," the second chapter relates historical-legal-psychiatric cultural models. Chapter 3 discusses "Secrecy: The context of Community and Identity Among Lesbians." Next follows "Supports for Lesbian Identity in the Lesbian Subculture." Chapter 6 comments upon the "Affiliation Between the Individual and the Gay Group." There are primary lesbians, elective lesbians, and those with "idiosyncratic identities" (p.163). The final chapter expresses "Theories and Experiences of Identities in the Lesbian World."

Critique - Strengths

a. Many anecdotal and expert quotations, cited references and footnotes highlight the text. A useful 4-page Glossary and a 7+page Bibliography are assets. Chapter 2's historical input is well referenced.

b. Ponse presents a philosophically adept sociological interpretation of today's lesbian community in both an individual and a collective way (refer to Summary).

c. Constructive criticisms of other researchers are useful (e.g.
    "Charlotte Wolff ... presents a sympathetic, yet ultimately
    damning, view of lesbians that employs the notion of 'the
    masculine lesbian' " (p.45)).
d. Ponse remains basically non-judgmental.

Deficiencies

a. No visual aids are included. Some cross-cultural material
    would have been helpful. The research is not quantified nor are
    the inherent methodological weaknesses examined. One acquires
    the impression that the study is solely derived from one lesbian
    community "housed in an ancient two-story building near the
    downtown area of a large southern city" (p.11). Graphs, tables,
    and statistical data, even of a demographic nature, are absent.
b. No direct attention is given to the concept that some persons
    tend to slide up or down the Kinsey Scale at certain times in
    their lives. Furthermore, the Kinsey Scale itself is
    erroneously described as behavioral only, and the correct ends
    of the scale are reversed (i.e. "The 0 end of the scale
    signified a completely homosexual behavioral history" (p.47)).

169. Raymond, Janice G. The Transsexual Empire. Boston: Beacon
Press, Inc., 1979. 231 pp.

Brief Summary - The study consists of "fifteen transsexuals,
thirteen of whom were male-to-constructed females" (p.15). The
first chapter relates historical background, the present medical
state of the art, and "the legal landscape" (p.38). Chapter 2 asks
"Are Transsexuals Born or Made - or Both?" and offers theories
focusing on "neuro-endocrine factors" (p.43). The subsequent
chapter is "devoted to psychological theories of transsexualism"
(p.43). Chapter 4 concerns itself with "The Transsexually
Constructed Lesbian-Feminist." The following chapter comments that
"the medical model is at the heart of the transexual empire" (p.120)
and is often a support-system for "fetishization" (p.127). The last
chapter discusses "Toward the Development of an Ethic of Integrity."
"It is my contention that, in a deep philosophical sense,
transsexual therapy and treatment have encouraged integration
solutions rather than helping individuals to realize an integrity of
be-ing" (p.154). For "transsexualism is merely one of the most
obvious forms of gender dissatisfaction and sex-role playing in a
patriarchal society" (p.184).

Critique - Strengths

a. Copious footnotes and cited references exist. Expert quota-
    tions abound. An Appendix called "Suggestions for Change"
    offers discerning arguments. The historical and cross-cultural
    background material is well documented (e.g. Chapter 1; also
    "Herodotus ... explained the origin of what he referred to as
    'the Scythian illness' " (p.43)).
b. The author presents contrasting views and constructs (e.g.
    Chapter 2 versus Chapter 3 (refer to Summary); also the various
    definitions of transsexualism (p.5-6)). Questions inviting
    future research are posed (e.g. seven on p.172-173).

c. The text is non-pejorative.

Deficiencies

a. No visual aids assist the text nor is a general bibliography included. The author's own research on the fifteen subjects is not directly given. Consequently, her methods of eliciting information cannot be examined nor her other methodological techniques critically evaluated. No charts, graphs, tables or statistics are forthcoming.
b. Belief-systems result in many hypotheses (refer to Summary) but these are speculative. Other theoretical works are reviewed but no new theory is developed. Lack of data from any research including her own makes it impossible to determine the merits of her hypotheses, some of which are very culturally broad in scope (e.g. refer to Summary). Furthermore, her sample of fifteen transsexuals is too small.

170. Rosen, Ismond, ed. Sexual Deviation (2nd Ed.). Oxford: Oxford Univ. Press, 1979. 568 pp.

Brief Summary - The second edition is revised from the 1967 edition. The editor is a contributor of Chapters 2 and 3 on "The General Psychoanalytic Theory of Perversion ..." and its regulation of self-esteem, and of Chapter 6 on "Exhibitionism, Scopophilia and Voyeurism." After Wakeling's reviewing "A General Psychiatric Approach to Sexual Deviation," specific topics are examined. Also, fetishism, the gender disorders, homosexuality, the role of aggression, psychotheray with sex-offenders, behavior therapy, the law's position, and biological facts from the rationale of "phylogenetic and ontogenetic terms" (p.441), are presented.

Critique - Strengths

a. The best chapters are on law (Freeman) and on biological factors (Michael & Zumpe). These are objective, and historically and cross-culturally informative about key issues (e.g. "Lesbianism has never been a crime in England, nor anywhere else, so far as is known" (Freeman, p.418)). Cited references, charts, and some selected case studies are of benefit. A 49-page Bibliography utilizes sub-headings.
b. Valid criticism of some studies is offered (e.g. "These studies await replication with larger groups and with proper attention to all the relevant control factors" (Wakeling, p.7)).
c. The book has some limited use as a historical vehicle on Freudian theory and on behavioral modalities.

Deficiencies

a. No visual aids are included. The book is committed to the medical-model approach (psychoanalytic and behavioral). Deviations must be cured or at least behaviorally neutralized.
b. Value-judgments and genitally-laden aims are prevalent (e.g. "Perverse sexuality denotes a sexual preference which departs from the accepted norm of heterosexual coitus with orgasm" (Rosen, p.30); also "Promiscuity ... is a disorder of object

relationships" (Rosen, p.35)).

c. Most contributors offer postulates and theories as unsubstantiated facts based on a few case studies or cited references.
These studies are unscientific, non-rigorous and bereft of
proper research controls (e.g. "Fetishism is clearly associated
with a very severe castration complex" (Greenacre, p.83)).

d. Often an activity is described by using medical nonentities
(e.g. "Perversion, then, is a sexual erotic neurosis" (Stoller,
p.110); also "Male homosexuality of the obligatory type ...
arises from unconscious conflicts" (Socarides, p.263)).

171. Seligson, Marcia. Options. New York: Random House, 1978. 290
pp.

Brief Summary - The title "Options" refers to lifestyle variations
which represent alternatives to the traditional, normative and
monogamous marriage. Part I talks about Seligson's first visit to
Sandstone, a California open-sexual encounter type of group. Using
such a vehicle as a futuristic example, she describes our cultural,
nuclear-family, patriarchal heritage. Part II deals with six
lifestyle case-examples: three of an open sexual marriage, two of a
triad and one of a group marriage. Part III recounts her flight
into a contemporary monogamous relationship after first
contemplating an open arrangement. Difficulties in accepting Dick's
children and insecurities toward sexual jealousy are detailed.

Critique - Strengths

a. References and case studies are essential inclusions. The pros
and cons of each situation are examined. Futuristic trends are
explored (see Summary).

b. The book is not scientific, but offers insights to professionals as well as laypersons (refer to Summary).

Deficiencies

a. No visual aids or research data of any type are offered.
Historical and cross-cultural background material is ignored.

b. The book is idiosyncratic and limited in scope. Communal and
swinging modes of lifestyle are not exemplified. The book is
flawed by prejudgment (e.g. "Swinging is essentially a hula
hoop, a phenomenon of impersonal sex largely passe, preposterous
and thoroughly irrelevant" (p.14)). No evidence justifies this
statement. The author, by subtly biased reporting, reinforces
her belief-systems (e.g. "Marty was acquiring a headful of
alternative-lifestyle dogma which he quickly learned to spout in
proper syntax" (p.149)).

c. One source reference is incorrectly cited. The O'Neills ("Open
Marriage") are vague about sexual (as opposed to social)
openness and do not express a "peppy so-you-wanna-have-sexual-
freedom approach" (p.248).

172. Shipes, Ellen A. & Lehr, Sally T. Sexual Counseling for
Ostomates. Springfield: Charles C. Thomas, Pub., 1980. 116 pp.

Brief Summary - The authors are both nursing professionals. After the first chapter's description of the human 4-phase sexual response cycle, the following chapter talks about the physical effects on sexual functioning of persons with colostomies, ileostomies, and urostomies. Many paraplegics and quadriplegics are also ostomates so these individuals are next covered. Chapter 4 delineates some "Psychological Effects on Sexual Functioning" which concern all ostomates. The following chapter expands upon "What is Sexuality?" Suggestions for the positive counseling of ostomates comprise Chapter 6. The final chapter deals with aged, homosexual, or teen-aged ostomates.

Critique - Strengths

a. Humorous yet apt cartoon-styled drawings accompany the text. Additional anatomical diagrams are also provided. The chart on self-esteem (p.57) is an asset as are the 2-page Glossary of unusual terms and the 3-page Bibliography which refers to the book's cited references. Some simple statistics are also given from referenced material (e.g. p.36-37).
b. The book is detailed enough for all sexological counselors to utilize, and to refer to their ostomatic patients and clients.
c. Myths are often listed and negated (e.g. p.38).
d. Differing therapy procedures are mentioned (e.g. Masters & Johnson, Annon (p.61)).
e. Belief-systems are challenged and pejorativity is scored as undesirable (e.g. "How do you react to the idea of homosexuality? Oral sex? Anal sex?... Group Sex?..." (p.57); also "the counselor should eliminate certain words from his vocabulary" (p.56)).

Deficiencies

a. Not enough research statistics and no such tables or graphs are included. Original research would have been useful. Instead, only positive generalities are given. A resource list of available video and film support-material is missing. No cross-cultural input but limited historical information is included (e.g. p.40-41) but not cited.
b. Sexual eroticization of the stoma has been reported by some researchers. This issue is not addressed except for the unreferenced statement "2. Sexual activity will not damage the stoma as long as the stoma is not used as an orifice" (p.66).
c. One alleged myth, according to recent reported research, may, for at least some women, not be a myth (i.e. "11. During orgasm, women also ejaculate" (p.17)).

173. Smith, James V. & Smith, Lynn G., ed.   Beyond Monogamy. Baltimore: The Johns Hopkins Press, 1974. 347 pp.

Brief Summary - In a 43-page Introduction, the Smiths define the scope and boundaries of their book. They note a decided societal "ongoing shift from traditional to companionate forms of marriage" (p.9). Part 1, "Preliminary Analysis: Orientation and Perspectives," furnishes background material about open marriage, intimate networks, communes, group marriage, and extramarital relationships including the mutually permissive variety of swinging.

Part 2 is entitled "Preliminary Research: Findings and
Interpretations." Articles such as "Group Sex Among the
Mid-Americans" (Bartell), "Communes, Group Marriage and the
Upper-Middle Class" (Ramey), "Sexual Aspects of Multilateral
Relations" (the Constantines), "Sexual Liberality and Personality:
A Pilot Study" (Twichell), and "Sexual Deviance and Social Networks:
A Study of Social, Family, and Marital Interaction Patterns Among
Co-Marital Sex Participants" (Gilmartin) compose the text.

Critique - Strengths

a. Most contributors furnish cited references, end-of-chapter
   References, and case examples (e.g. advertisements (p.187)).
   Part 2 authors are also more apt to include tables, charts and
   statistics. Quotations are often usefully employed (e.g. the
   editors quote Simmel, Lindsay, H. Ellis and Russell (p.5)).
   Also, the editors in their Introduction use footnotes.
b. Part 2 is far superior in its depth of presentation. Facts and
   their derived statistics are provided (e.g. Gilmartin (p.319)).
c. This book includes presentations on all the major alternative
   sexual lifestyles (refer to Summary).
d. Pejorative phraseology is basically avoided.

Deficiencies

a. No visual aids complement the text. No author accords more
   than minimal space to any relevant historical or cross-cultural
   material. The editors should have included one such chapter.
   Most articles are preliminary in their research coverage and
   methodological bias control is inadequate.
b. Many authors offer generalities unsubstantiated by references
   or statistics (e.g. "Infidelity tolerance..." (Bernard, p.157)).
   Denfeld ("Dropouts from Swinging: The Marriage Counselor as
   Informant") in Part 2 offers statistics using a questionnaire
   which generates answers from too much subjectivity and results
   in a dearth of demographic facts such as the length of time
   active in swinging, ages, and religious and ethnic backgrounds.

174. Spada, James. The Spada Report. New York: The New American
Library, Inc., 1979. 347 pp.

Brief Summary - An Introduction details "How the Questionnaire was
Designed, Analyzed, and Distributed," some demographics on "Who
Answered" it, plus the reasons for respondent-response. Part 1
discusses the "Coming Out" phenomenon. In Part 2, "Gay Male
Sexuality," the various sexual activities, their enhancers and their
locales are explored along with self-defined masculinity concepts.
"Relationships," Part 3, deals with lifestyle aspects of the
respondents who numbered 1,038 men from "all fifty states" (p.3).
Part 4 investigates the sample's interactional matrices with
"Women." Part 5 entitled "Problems" delves into the areas of
arrests, sexually transmitted diseases, and military experiences.
Part 6 checks out the rationales and difficulties of the gay
lifestyle.

Critique - Strengths

a. Some book references are given in an Afterword. All the ques-
    tions asked appear in the appropriate Parts. A "Statistical
    Breakdown of Replies" is provided (p.325). Demographics are
    included (p.12-17) and heavy type emphasizes key conclusions.
    There are some footnotes, especially in the statistical section.
    Many anecdotal quotations add impetus to an understanding of the
    conclusions reached.
b. Clear concepts are expressed as conclusions (e.g. "Thirty-five
    percent of the respondents report their first homosexual
    attraction before the age of ten..." (p.23)).
c. Outside of one dubiously worded statement (i.e. "some men see
    promiscuity as a threat to their relationship" (p.196)),
    judgmental phraseology is not employed.

Deficiencies

a. No bibliography, index, visual aids, graphs or charts assist
    the textual content. Outside of a few research references (e.g.
    p.273-274), minimal historical and cross-cultural input is
    generated. Myths are not sufficiently addressed.
b. Certain intriguing issues should have been expanded (e.g.
    "Would you rather be a woman?..." (p.242)). The author admits
    "injecting external material only when most necessary" (p.319).
c. The study's methodology has many serious flaws. No controls
    are used and the volunteer sample return is only 10% (i.e. 1,038
    responses from "ten thousand copies ... given out" (p.10)).
    Some questions lead the respondent into easily-biased answers
    (e.g. "Do you enjoy affection during sex?" (p.76)) with little
    statistical meaning. The statistics employed are rudimentary
    with no probability figures available.

175. Tanner, Donna M. The Lesbian Couple. Lexington: D.C. Heath and
Company, 1978. 154 pp.

Brief Summary - The author is a nongay sociologist interested in
women's issues. In her Introduction, she specifies that "this is a
study of self-identified urban lesbians who have lived in a dyadic
homosexual household arrangement for a period exceeding six months"
(p.1). Chapter 2 explores "Lesbianism: The Problem of Definition"
and this is followed by a chapter portraying historical research
from the biological, psychoanalytic and behavioral perspectives.
Chapter 4 details the research focus, methods, procedures, and data
treatment. The subsequent chapter describes "The Individual
Lesbian." The next two chapters detail the formation and mainten-
ance of lesbian couples as well as three "Types of Lesbian Dyads" as
exemplified by the traditional-complementary, flexible-
nurturing-caretaking, and the negotiated-egalitarian prototypes.
Chapter 8 accords some lesbian facets as a sub-group of the larger
gay community. A final Chapter 9 offers a "Summary and
Speculations."

Critique - Strengths

a. A 5-page Bibliography, a 4-page Appendix "Interview Schedule,"

copious cited references, footnotes and anecdotal quotations
fortify the text. Chapter 3's historical scientific review is
excellent (e.g. refer to Summary).
b. Myths and subject-stereotypes are exposed (e.g. "To demytholo-
    gize historical and popular stereotypes and misrepresentations,
    a closer look at the literature and research available ... is
    necessary" (p.15); also "Role Stereotypes..." (p.87)).
c. Research is constructively criticized (e.g. "These exponents of
    the biological perspective adhere to some or all of the
    following assumptions..." (p.16)). Good research parameters are
    presented (e.g. "the psychological (management of stigma and
    attendant guilt)..." (p.43)). The research methodology utilized
    is furnished (i.e. p.47-50), and future research possibilities
    are posed (i.e. four points, p.125)). Useful conclusions are
    advanced (e.g. "those who had come out in a 'physical way' first
    seemed to have more identity problems..." (p.55)).
d. Belief-system biases and pejorativity are not in evidence.

Deficiencies

a. No cross-cultural perspective is included. No visual aids,
    graphs, tables, statistics or charts are included.
b. The research study has many methodological limitations (e.g.
    "other females excluded ... are those who may be psychologically
    committed but do not exhibit or engage in overt homosexual
    behavior" (p.8)). The research focus is too narrow in scope for
    any generalized theory to be formed and utilized (e.g. "Detailed
    in-depth interviews were obtained from a small group of urban,
    middle-class, actively homosexual females, all of whom have
    educational training beyond high school" (p.43)).
c. Tanner betrays a lack of understanding toward the Kinsey 0-6
    Scale(e.g. "Kinsey's seven point scale ... does not specify
    overt sexual behavior and the identity-transformation
    process..." (p.7). A competent interviewer, however, can
    fine-tune the Kinsey Scale to pick up such information.

176. Tripp, C.A. The Homosexual Matrix. New York: The New American
Library, Inc., 1976. 315 pp.

Brief Summary - Tripp in his Preface outlines his aim which is "to
draw a picture not only of homosexuality but of its social matrix"
(p.ix) from the motivational influences stemming from biological,
psychological and sociological rationales. Tripp implies
homosexuality is an acquired state. Sexual patterns and response
become "keyed to specific cues" (p.17). In Chapter 3, Tripp
distinguishes between inversion and homosexuality. All persons, no
matter their orientation, require "a certain disparity, a
'resistance,' or distance" (p.44) in order to nurture any sexually
ongoing attraction. The author states a homosexual pattern is
seldom developed "through causal or 'accidental' experiences" (p.84)
nor from child seduction or at puberty. Dissonance toward the
opposite sex leads to aversion-reactions which are life-long. Tripp
enumerates the various traps into which self-denying homosexuals can
fall. Chapter 11, "The Politics of Homosexuality," details the
American historical and contemporary societal attack-modes of
homosexual repression. The final chapter decides "the establishment

of a sexual value system ... usually predates puberty" (p.254).
Women are "not as rigidly guarded by polar aversions" (p.255) so are
more potentially bisexual. Thus a societal reduction in sexual
prohibitions should not increase bisexuality in men but the future
is unclear as to women.

Critique - Strengths

a. Footnotes and 292 "Reference Notes" aid the scholar or student.
   An 8-page "Miscellanea" answers controversial questions by essay
   form. Excellent supportive data detailing cross-cultural (e.g.
   p.64, 70) and historical (e.g. p.199, 217) information is given.
b. Hypotheses and future possible trends based on reasonable
   axioms are prevalent (e.g. refer to Summary).
c. Tripp constructively discounts traditional interpretations of
   homosexuality as well as their psychotherapies for dealing with
   it (e.g. Chapter 5 (p.62-93); also Chapter 11 (p.229-252)).
d. The book is an excellent philosophical treatise and is required
   reading for all sexological professionals.

Deficiencies

a. References are not properly cited for so scholarly a work. No
   visual aids, charts, or tables are included. In-depth
   statistical research studies are not examined other than in a
   descriptive way (e.g. Kinsey, footnote, p.50).
b. Tripp's hypotheses are not always identified as such and seem
   to be stated definitive conclusions (e.g. refer to Summary) not
   supported by cited bias-free research. Some uncited statements
   may or may not be valid (e.g. "... Two males together does
   sometimes facilitate high-resistance sex practices ... which are
   rare in heterosexuality and are virtually nonexistent among
   lesbians" (p.117)).
c. Pejorativity sometimes occurs (e.g. "a wide variety of promiscuous contracts..." (p.141)).

177. Weinberg, George. _Society and the Healthy Homosexual_. New York:
Anchor Press/Doubleday, 1972. 148 pp.

   Brief Summary - The author is a psychotherapist. In "Homophobia,"
   he lists and embellishes upon biases and prejudices against
   homosexuality. Chapter 2 delineates "The Bias of Psychoanalysis."
   Next follows "The Case Against Trying to Convert" homosexuals. "The
   Healthy Homosexual" speaks to the issue of gay pride. The most
   difficult subject for most gays is "Communication with Parents." In
   Chapter 6, Weinberg details gay terminology, its origins and
   definitions. The final chapter discusses aloneness. Weinberg warns
   "one must not confuse existential aloneness (a universal experience)
   with aloneness produced by the quarantines of the day" (p.137).

Critique - Strengths

a. A 4-page Reference section terminates the book. Opinions and
   theories are expertly analyzed for their assumptive flaws (e.g.
   "The behavior therapists accept tenets of social convention as
   dictates on what will make people happy, and they show no signs

of re-examining them. Time and again, they give these tenets
scientific status alongside the most thoroughly verified of
their psychological principles" (p.47)). A questionnaire
(Chapter 6, Smith) on homophobia, is useful.
b. Myths are explored (e.g. Chapter 6, Smith).
c. The book is powerful in its positive message for sexologists
    and students. They should recommend it to confused and
    homophobic gays and their parents.
d. Insights are offered (e.g. "One need not conform to a national
    stereotype of preferred behavior to be happy in a culture as
    diverse as ours" (p.32)).
e. Pejorativity is not present.

Deficiencies

a. Visual aids are lacking. Inadequate cross-cultural and histor-
    ical material is included. Cited references, research-study
    statistical analyses and critiques, graphs and tables are
    essentially missing. Only male pronouns are used.
b. The book is now over a decade old. Important legal and
    sociocultural improvements have since taken hold.

178. Weinberg, Martin S. & Williams, Colin J. Male Homosexuals:
Their Problems and Adaptations. New York: Penguin Books Inc., 1975
(New York: Oxford University Press Inc., 1974). 476 pp.

Brief Summary - Part I outlines the study in sociological terms.
Part II, "The Homosexual's Situation in Three Societies," portrays
findings in the U.S. (New York City and San Francisco), The
Netherlands and Denmark and details cross-cultural comparisons,
conclusions and recent histories. "Questionnaire Study-Samples and
Procedure," Part III, deals with "Methods and Distributions" as well
as a breakdown on "Source-Respondent Variation." Part IV's
"Questionnaire Study-Results" provide collective research concerning
demographics, interrelationships and personal aspects. Part V
suggests some "Theoretical Implications" and "Practical
Considerations."

Critique - Strengths

a. Cited references with thirty-six pages of footnotes, anecdotal
    and expert quotations, maps, and photographs reinforce the text.
    The questionnaire is in an Appendix. The cross-cultural format
    (refer to Summary) is uniquely valuable. Historical information
    is provided (e.g. Freud, Kinsey (p.19-20)).
b. The research is well constructed with many tables utilizing
    probability and other statistics. This data-analysis matches
    general-population control samples against the localized
    homosexual samples. Proper qualifying statements admitting
    study biases are forthcoming (e.g. "Our procedures obviously
    precluded our having obtained 'representative' samples..."
    (p.125)). The methodology is well documented (e.g. refer to
    Summary). Innovative ideas are quantified and explored (e.g.
    "interpersonal awkwardness scale" (p.213)).
c. Myths are disclosed (e.g. "For example, homosexuals do not
    usually have sex with their homosexual friends" (p.283, cited

reference given)).
d. Insights occur (e.g. "Historically, the Scandinavian people
   never fully embraced Christianity... Consequently, the church,
   despite its efforts, has never achieved an effective regulation
   of sexual behavior in Denmark" (p.100-101)). Many conclusions
   are presented (e.g. "homosexuals who score higher in effeminacy
   are lower in psychological well-being on six of the eight
   measures (Table 10) (footnote 4)" (p.213)).
e. Judgmental and moralizing statements are not in evidence.

Deficiencies

a. No graphs or a generalized bibliography are given.
b. The questionnaire, in addition to at times encouraging biased
   answers (e.g. Q.9, 24, 40), and unduly mixing up its scales,
   omits certain key questions (e.g. "Have you ever thought of
   yourself as being female?").

179. Wolff, Charlotte. _Bisexuality: A Study_. London: Quartet Books,
1979. 272 pp.

Brief Summary - This is an expanded edition of the book first
published in 1977 by Dr. Wolff, a physician. The opening chapter
defines bisexuality as "the root of human sexuality, and the matrix
of all bio-physical reactions, be they passive or active" (p.1). It
reviews theoretical concepts. The next chapter describes
"chromosome abnormality (which) occurs in _physical_ bisexuality or
hermaphroditism" (p.41). This is followed by "Gender Identity and
Sexual Orientation." The author's research findings begin with
"Procedure of Study." The "Early Influences" of the respondents are
followed by statistical correlates, "Later Relationships" and
"Conflicts About Bisexuality" (p.93). Chapter 7 details three
in-depth interviews. The final chapter furnishes "autobiographical
reports of five women and four men" (p.123).

Critique - Strengths

a. Many case studies (as self-reports or interviews) complement
   the text. A 6-page Glossary and a 5-page Bibliography are
   useful aids. Thirty statistical tables including probability
   figures in Appendix II are given. Chapter 1 (refer to Summary)
   and Appendix I ("Bisexuality and Androgyny") give much
   historical and some cross-cultural background.
b. Other theoreticians are critically examined (e.g. "But Klein's
   view of bisexuality in women was flawed..." (p.5)).
c. Considering the methodological difficulties, the research is
   effectively conceived and executed from a non-clinical sample of
   75 women and 75 men. Some conclusions point to future research
   (e.g. Table 22, "Parents' Favourite Child" (p.231)).

Deficiencies

a. The book's style contrasts heavy, difficult-to-follow prose in
   the early chapters with extraneous respondent self-ramblings in
   the final chapter. Assumptive definitions occur (e.g. refer to
   Summary). Appendix I relating the concepts of androgyny and

bisexuality is cumbersome and neglects to define the former idea
in the accepted mode (e.g. "I disagree with the premise ... of
sex-bound attributes" (p.38)). The lack of graphs and visual
aids hinders textual comprehension.

b. Speculative, unproved statements are in evidence (e.g. XYY
chromosome combinations leave such males "with a tendency to
delinquency" (p.41)). Unproductive phraseology turns up (e.g.
"homosexual promiscuity" (p.91)).

c. Factual mistakes occur (e.g. "Paederasty" (p.248), "sexology"
(p.249) and "estrogen" (p.247) are wrongly defined). The Kinsey
0-6 Scale is not mentioned or utilized. Another definition of
ambisexuality is attacked in an unconvincing way (e.g. p.63)).

180. Ziskin, Jay & Mae. The Extra-Marital Arrangement. New York:
Nash Publishing Corp., 1973. 271 pp.

Brief Summary - The authors are doctors who explore alternative
sociosexual venues to the traditional monogamic marriage. Part I
elucidates the problems in today's marriages, the merits of extramarital sex as well as its logistical and emotional difficulties,
and the modes for extramarital sex in swinging, separate vacations,
partial living-apart, and separate dating. Part II describes some
examples of marital openness. In Part III, the Ziskins review
marital needs of our culture as they have traditionally evolved,
after which methods of opening up a marriage are examined. A sample
co-marital contract (p.251) is given.

Critique - Strengths

a. Interviews, quotations and a Bibliography complement the text.
b. The best section is Part III which imparts historical and
religious background into why our culture pays lip-service to
monogamous unions. The sub-part proffering advice as to the
implementation of an open-sexual marriage is challenging.

Deficiencies

a. No photographs, sketches, tables or charts occur. The lack of
cited references and cross-cultural material is a severe
limitation. Scientific data are lacking and selection of the
respondents seems biased in favour of what philosophical
position the authors wish to convey as valid.
b. The authors neglect to allow for the fact that most married
persons have high quotients of insecurity, pride and guilt that
they cannot easily overcome in ways that would make the Ziskins'
solutions effective and positive. To effect these changes, our
children and our children's children would have to be
re-imprinted and re-educated. The Ziskins do not propose the
methods necessary to accomplish this. The authors'
belief-system encompasses many alternatives, some of which are
possibly counter-productive for most persons (e.g. partial
living-apart). Moreover, no definitive research is presented to
substantiate any of their alternatives as being effective.

Index of Authors

The references below are to entry numbers, not page numbers.

Subject Index

The references below are to entry numbers, not page numbers.

Note: Headings in capitals indicate major-category chapter-titles. A book is listed in a specific category if a significant amount of, or a definitive section in its text pertains to that category. A book may be listed in several categories. An underlined number refers to a book primarily devoted to the category.

Title Index

The references below are to entry numbers, not page numbers.

About the Author

MERVYN L. MASON has edited the newsletter of the Association of Sexologists. He received his Ph.D. from the Institute for Advanced Study of Human Sexuality, where he serves as an assistant professor.